Human Rights and Social Justice: An International Overview

Human Rights and Social Justice: An International Overview

Ada Miller

MURPHY & MOORE
www.murphy-moorepublishing.com

Murphy & Moore Publishing,
1 Rockefeller Plaza,
New York City, NY 10020, USA

ISBN: 978-1-63987-314-2

Cataloging-in-Publication Data

Human rights and social justice : an international overview / Ada Miller.
p. cm.
Includes bibliographical references and index.
ISBN 978-1-63987-314-2
1. Human rights. 2. Justice. 3. Social justice. 4. International law and human rights.
I. Miller, Ada.
K3240 .H86 2022
341.48--dc23

For information on all Murphy & Moore Publications
visit our website at www.murphy-moorepublishing.com

MURPHY & MOORE

Contents

Preface

This book has been an outcome of determined endeavour from a group of educationists in the field. The primary objective was to involve a broad spectrum of professionals from diverse cultural background involved in the field for developing new researches. The book not only targets students but also scholars pursuing higher research for further enhancement of the theoretical and practical applications of the subject.

Human rights describe the standards of human behavior which are protected by different international and local laws. These are granted to individuals irrespective of their race, age, origin, ethnicity, religion or any other social status. They play a pivotal in protection against various forms of unfair and unjust treatment such as enslavement, genocide, etc. Certain rights such as the right to education, right to fair trial and freedom of speech promote a higher standard of living. The book studies, analyses and upholds the pillars of human rights and justice, and their utmost significance in modern times. It aims to shed light on some of the unexplored aspects and recent researches in this field. For all readers who are interested in this topic, the case studies included in this book on human rights and justice will serve as an excellent guide to develop a comprehensive understanding.

It was an honour to edit such a profound book and also a challenging task to compile and examine all the relevant data for accuracy and originality. I wish to acknowledge the efforts of the contributors for submitting such brilliant and diverse chapters in the field and for endlessly working for the completion of the book. Last, but not the least; I thank my family for being a constant source of support in all my research endeavours.

Ada Miller

1

WHAT IS TRANSITIONAL JUSTICE?

The Deputy Chairperson of the South African Truth and Reconciliation Commission provides an overview of issues of justice, human rights and nation-building in countries undergoing change from oppressive rule to democracy and the rule of law.

BORAINE, A 'TRANSITIONAL JUSTICE' (2004)

in Villa-Vicencio, C and Doxtader, E *Pieces of the puzzle*
Cape Town: Institute for Justice and Reconciliation

Transitional justice seeks to address challenges that confront societies as they move from an authoritarian state to a form of democracy. Frequently, these societies are emerging from serious conflict and violence that often includes widespread human rights violations and in some instances genocide and crimes against humanity. Such situations are often characterised by a breakdown in legal services; stark divisions and apportioning of blame; institutional collapse; and economic downturn. In this light transitional justice is not a contradiction of criminal justice but rather a deeper, richer and broader vision of justice which seeks to confront perpetrators, address the needs of victims and start a process of reconciliation and transformation toward a more just and humane society.

The Nuremberg Trials, the International Tribunal for Former Yugoslavia and the International Tribunal for Rwanda as well as the establishment of the Permanent International Criminal Court (ICC), are themselves major steps forward in the effort to confront impunity. They are also a stern reminder to those prepared to commit serious criminal acts that they will face grave sanctions if and when they are brought to book. However, realistically it is impossible to prosecute all offenders during times of transition. Who then should be prosecuted? This vexed question of selective prosecution is one that seems to undermine the very idea of individual criminal responsibility so fundamental to our understanding of the rule of law. Other problems also abound. In the wake of conflict national legal systems are often in disarray and trials are often both very lengthy and costly. Moreover, the almost exclusive focus by tribunals on the perpetrator(s) is often to the detriment of the victims. In short, the aim of transitional justice is wider than prosecuting perpetrators. Punishment cannot be the last word. Due to these shortcomings, it is impossible to deal with the true intent of justice by court procedures alone. A holistic approach to transitional justice seeks to complement retributive justice with restorative justice. There are at least five components of this holistic approach:

Accountability

The rule of law and the fair administration of justice deserve our greatest respect. No society can claim to be free or democratic without strict adherence to the rule of law. Dictators and authoritarian regimes abandon the rule of law at the first opportunity and resort to brazen power politics leading to all manner of excess. It is of central importance, therefore, that those who violate the law are punished. But there are limits to the law and we need to embrace a multi-faceted notion of justice that is wider, deeper and richer than retributive justice. It is not only impossible to prosecute all offenders, but an overzealous focus on punishment can make securing sustainable peace and stability more difficult. To achieve a just society, more than punishment is required. Documenting the truth about the past, restoring dignity to victims and embarking on the process of reconciliation are all vital elements of a just society. Equally important is the need to transform society so that it does not impede the consolidation of democracy and the creation of a human rights culture. It follows that approaches to societies in transition will be multi-faceted and will incorporate the need for consultation to realise the goal of a just society.

Truth recovery

One of the non-judicial mechanisms that has gained great prominence over the last ten years is the Truth and Reconciliation Commission (TRC). A TRC, as indicated by its title is concerned first and foremost with the recovery of truth. Through truth-telling, these commissions attempt to document and analyse the structures and methods used in carrying out illegal repression while taking into account the political, economic and social contexts in which violations have occurred. In some ways, it is unfortunate that the word 'truth' is used. Beyond its Orwellian overtones, many critics rightly point out that it is impossible for the truth ever to be fully known.

Reconciliation

A number of commissions have talked not only about truth but also about reconciliation. If the word truth conjures up problems for many people, so does the word reconciliation. It has religious connotations, especially in the Christian faith, and there are many who would prefer that the word and the concept of reconciliation not be used in TRCs that are seeking to recover the truth and promote the interests of victims.

At best, reconciliation involves commitment and sacrifice; at its worst, it is an excuse for passivity, for siding with the powerful against the weak and dispossessed. Religion, in many instances, has given a bad name to reconciliation, representatives often having joined forces with those who exploited and impoverished entire populations instead of being in solidarity with the oppressed. Reconciliation is unrealistic when it calls for mere forgetting or concealing. In Argentina, the concept of reconciliation is regarded with deep scepticism. In that country, the Roman Catholic Church, in large measure, supported the military junta, and the perpetrators of human rights violations were always the first to call for reconciliation. The same is true of Rwanda, where religious groups and officials participated in the massacre of the Tutsis. In this context, talk about reconciliation is highly suspect and can be viewed as a call for amnesia. Unless calls for reconciliation are accompanied by acknowledgment of the past and the acceptance of responsibility, they will be dismissed as cheap rhetoric. Perhaps one of the ways in which to achieve at least a measure of reconciliation in a deeply divided society is to create a common memory that can be acknowledged by those who created and implemented the unjust system, those who fought against it and the many more who, while in the middle, claimed not to know what was happening in their country.

Reconciliation, as a process for seeking an often elusive peace, must be understood through the lens of transitional justice. It is better understood if victims believe that their grievances are being heard and addressed, that the silence is being broken. Reconciliation can begin when perpetrators are held accountable, when truth is sought openly and fearlessly, when institutional reform commences and when the need for reparation is acknowledged and acted upon. The response by former victims to these initiatives can increase the potential for stability and increase the chances of a sustainable peace.

The process of reconciliation has often been hindered by the silence or denial of political leaders concerning their own responsibilities and the failures of the state. On the other hand, when leaders are prepared to speak honestly and generously about their own involvement or, at least, the involvement of their government or the previous government, then the door is open for the possibility of some reconciliation amongst the citizens.

Institutional reform

For truth and reconciliation to flourish, serious and focused attention must be given to both individuals and institutions. Institutional reform should be at the very heart of transformation. The TRC is an ideal model for holding together both retrospective truth and prospective needs. Unfortunately, most TRCs have chosen to focus almost entirely on individual hearings. This is important and critical, but if commissions were to hold institutional hearings, it would enable them to call to account those institutions directly responsible for the breakdown of the state and the repression of citizens.

In at least one commission, an opportunity was created for spokespersons from the military, the police and the security forces while also inviting politicians, faith communities, legal representatives, the media and labour officials to give an account of their role in the past and how they saw their role in the future. In other words, it is simply not enough to be merely concerned about the past. We must deal with it, but we must not dwell in it. We should deal with the past for the sake of the future.

On a recent visit to Serbia, it was obvious that one of the major problems preventing the country from moving on from its dark and ominous past was that its institutions had remained almost exactly the same: the same policemen were controlling the police forces; the same generals were controlling the army. This can be said to be true of most of Serbia's major institutions. As I moved from one group of leaders to another, it became clear that unless these institutions are radically restructured, there will be little opportunity for growth, development or peace in Serbia. This is not only true of Serbia but applies to the former Yugoslavia as a whole and to all states in transition.

In deeply divided societies where mistrust and fear still reign, there must be bridge-building and a commitment to both criminal and economic justice. For that to be a reality, institutions as well as individuals have to change.

Reparations

Reparations have a long history, but until now have not received sufficient systematic attention. The individual reparations issued by the Federal Republic of Germany were a watershed moment in the history of reparations. Until 1952, reparations were solely an inter-state affair, involving payments by the losing state to the victorious one, as in the Versailles Treaty. Reparations to the victims of the Holocaust were the first instance of a massive nationally sponsored reparations programme to individuals who had suffered gross human rights violations.

It is worth emphasising that from the standpoint of the victims, reparations programmes occupy a special place in a transition to democracy. Reparations are, for them, the most tangible manifestation of the efforts of the state to remedy the harms they have suffered. Criminal justice, even if it were completely successful, both in terms of the number of perpetrators brought to book (far from being the case in any transition) and of the results (which are always affected by the availability of evidence and by the persistent weaknesses of judicial systems), is in the end a struggle against perpetrators rather than an effort on behalf of victims.

From truth-telling, victims can obtain significant benefits that may include a sense of closure derived from knowing the fate of loved ones, and a sense of satisfaction from the official acknowledgment of that fate. But in the absence of other positive and tangible manifestations, truth by itself can easily be considered an empty gesture — as cheap and inconsequential talk. Finally, institutional reforms will always be a long-term project, which only indirectly affect the lives of the victims.

In many ways the dilemmas and challenges in reparations are a microcosm of the overall challenges of transitional justice. How does one balance competing legitimate interests in redressing the harms of victims and ensuring the democratic stability of the state? Similar to other areas of transitional justice, such as truth-telling or institutional reform, simple judicial decisions cannot provide the comprehensive solutions demanded by such interests. Rather, solutions must be found in the exercise of judgment and a creative combination of legal, political, social and economic approaches.

Conclusion

There are enormous difficulties in pursuing justice in a normal situation, but when one attempts to do this in countries undergoing transitions, the problems are intensified. There is a need to balance two imperatives: On the one hand, there is the need to return to the rule of law and the prosecution of offenders; on the other, there is a need for rebuilding societies and embarking on the process of reconciliation. In helping to make states work, it is important, therefore, to balance accountability with the shoring up of fragile emerging democracies. The overall aim should be to ensure a sustainable peace, which will encourage and make possible socio-economic development.

Goldstone, the first Chief Prosecutor of the International Tribunals for Rwanda and Yugoslavia, considers the relationship between peace and justice, focusing on the UN Security Council's establishment of the International Criminal Tribunal for the former Yugoslavia (ICTY). He identifies five contributions that justice makes to the peace process.

GOLDSTONE, R 'JUSTICE AS A TOOL FOR PEACE-MAKING: TRUTH COMMISSIONS AND INTERNATIONAL CRIMINAL TRIBUNALS' (1996)

28 *New York University Journal of International Law and Politics* 485

...

The link between peace and justice

Much has been written about the decision of the Security Council to establish an international criminal tribunal to investigate and prosecute war crimes in the former Yugoslavia [Yugoslav Tribunal], but what is not often stressed is that this decision was necessarily founded upon the recognition of a direct link between peace and justice. In establishing the Yugoslav Tribunal, the Security Council was acting under powers conferred upon it by Chapter VII of the UU Charter. In terms thereof, the Security Council is only authorised to pass resolutions binding on all states parties if it decides that enforcement measures are necessary to bring to an end a situation which constitutes a threat to international peace and security.

In September, 1991, the Security Council determined that the situation in the former Yugoslavia constituted such a threat that, acting under Chapter VII, it imposed a complete arms embargo on Yugoslavia. It was, however, Resolution 827, passed twenty months later, which explicitly acknowledged that the widespread violations of humanitarian law and human rights occurring in the region constituted a threat to international peace. This is made clear in the following paragraphs of the resolution:

> Expressing once again its grave alarm at continuing reports of widespread and flagrant violations of international humanitarian law occurring within the territory of the former Yugoslavia, and especially in the Republic of Bosnia and Herzegovina, including reports of mass killings, massive, organised and systematic detention and rape of women, and the continuance of the practice of 'ethnic cleansing', including for the acquisition and the holding of territory,
>
> Determining that this situation continues to constitute a threat to international peace and security,
>
> Determined to put an end to such crimes and to take effective measures to bring to justice the persons who are responsible for them,
>
> Convinced that in the particular circumstances of the former Yugoslavia the establishment as an *ad hoc* measure by the Council of an international tribunal and

> the prosecution of persons responsible for serious violations of international humanitarian law would enable this aim to be achieved and would contribute to the restoration and maintenance of peace,
>
> Believing that the establishment of an international tribunal and the prosecution of persons responsible for the above-mentioned violations of international humanitarian law will contribute to ensuring that such violations are halted and effectively redressed.

As we see, the Security Council resolved that the establishment of the Yugoslav Tribunal was the most appropriate way of dealing with such a threat.

In November, 1994, a similar decision was taken by the Security Council in respect of Rwanda, where an internal armed conflict had resulted in the commission of a genocide claiming the lives of up to one million people. It was thus anticipated by the Security Council that justice would help restore peace in both the former Yugoslavia and Rwanda and hasten the return of refugees to their former homes.

Particularly at the time of the negotiations at Dayton, Ohio, in September, 1995, there were many astute politicians and political commentators who suggested that, in fact, peace and justice were in opposition, and that the work of the Yugoslav Tribunal was retarding the peace process in the Balkans. Even at that late juncture in the history of the conflict, and in the context of that debate, people failed to see the link between peace and justice which had so deliberately (and in my view correctly) been made by a unanimous Security Council in May, 1993.

I have no doubt that in countries or regions where there have been egregious human rights violations, it is less likely that there will be an enduring peace without some attempt to bring justice to the victims. In particular, there are the following five positive contributions which justice can achieve.

First, exposure of the truth can help to individualise guilt and thus avoid the imposition of collective guilt on an ethnic, religious, or other group. During my visits to the former Yugoslavia, and particularly Belgrade, I was astounded at the manner in which Serbs I met were consumed by their historical hatred of Croats. Most meetings I attended began with a history lesson – if I was lucky the history began during the Second World War, but on less happy occasions it began with the Battle of Kosovo in the fourteenth century. It was no different in Zagreb or Sarajevo where collective guilt was ascribed to Serbs or Muslims, as the case may be. In the Balkans, violence has been erupting periodically over a span of six hundred years. Very seldom have the perpetrators of that violence been brought to account. Victims were denied justice.

The result is that blame has been ascribed not to the leaders who sponsored the violence, but to the communities or people represented by those leaders. In one respect, perhaps, the most important beneficiaries of the Nuremberg Trials were the German people. Credible evidence presented at those trials established the guilt of the Nazi leaders beyond a doubt. Through the criminal trial process, focus was placed upon the accused as individual criminals or leaders and not as Germans. So the group of men standing in the dock at Nuremberg were seen as the criminals they were, and not as representatives of the German people. I have no doubt that Germany would have had far more difficulty in coming to grips with its sordid World War II history but for the fact that those leaders were brought to trial.

Second, justice brings public and official acknowledgment to the victims. This usually is the first step in their healing process.

Third, public exposure of the truth is the only effective way of ensuring that history is recorded more accurately and more faithfully than otherwise would have been the case. The Nuremberg Trials have made the work of Holocaust deniers far more difficult. Without the exhumation of mass graves in Bosnia, the fabrications of some Bosnian Serb spokespersons would have had some credibility. The first Yugoslav war criminal to be sentenced, Drazan Erdemovic, confessed to having murdered over seventy innocent Muslim men outside Srebrenica in July, 1995. His evidence helped to verify the occurrence of mass murders at Srebrenica. This evidence was confirmed later by photographic material taken by the US government which showed bodies lying in the vicinity of a grave on the day of the shooting. Further photographs taken the following day showed the grave freshly covered with earth. According to a Bosnian Serb Army spokesperson, the grave contained the bodies of soldiers killed during battle.

The exhumations conducted by the Office of the Prosecutor in the summer of 1996, however, exposed the lie in such claims. The persons buried in the grave had been killed with a single bullet shot in the back of the head, most of them while their arms were bound behind their backs – certainly not the way in which people die in the course of battle. Through the establishment of the Yugoslav Tribunal, the massacre of thousands of innocent Muslims who sought safety in the UN 'safe haven' of Srebrenica has been established with a degree of certainty that otherwise would have been absent.

Fourth, in my experience, there is only one way to curb criminal conduct and that is through good policing and the implementation of efficient criminal justice. In any country there is a direct relationship between the effectiveness of policing and the crime rate. If would-be criminals believe that there is a good prospect of their being apprehended and punished, they will think twice before embarking upon criminal conduct. It is no different in the case of international crimes. If political and military leaders believe they are likely to be brought to account by the international community for committing war crimes, that belief in most cases will have a deterrent effect. Between the Nuremberg and Tokyo war crimes trials and the establishment of the Yugoslav Tribunal, there was not a single international attempt to enforce humanitarian law. Leaders of countries bent on fighting wars in blatant disregard of the laws of war could be confident that the international community would make no attempt to bring them to account. If they were safe in their own countries, they had nothing to fear from any external agency. An international deterrent can come only from the enforcement of international law.

Fifth, exposure of the nature and extent of human rights violations frequently will reveal a systematic and institutional pattern of gross human rights violations. It will assist in the identification and dismantling of institutions responsible therefore and deter future recurrences. That already has been the experience of the Yugoslav Tribunal in relation to the conduct of the Bosnian-Serb administration, and patterns may well emerge in the case of other parties to the Balkans conflict. It already is the experience of the South African Truth and Reconciliation Commission [TRC].

...

Mamdani deals here with the complex problem of the relationship between justice and reconciliation. He enquires as to the meaning of justice in countries coming out of colonial rule, while analysing (and problematising) notions of race and tribe in state institutions.

MAMDANI, M 'WHEN DOES RECONCILIATION TURN INTO A DENIAL OF JUSTICE?' (1998)

Sam Molutshungu Memorial Lectures
Pretoria: HSRC Publishers

I want to discuss the collapse of a paradigm, that of justice, which animated the post-war struggle for independence in equatorial Africa, and the ascendancy of another, that of rights, which goes by the name of 'reconciliation' in contemporary South Africa. I will argue that the pendulum has shifted from one to another, and that this swing is best illustrated by two paradigmatic cases: The 'social revolution' of 1959 in Rwanda and post-apartheid 'reconciliation' in South Africa. If post-1959 Rwanda represents a case of justice without reconciliation, then post-apartheid South Africa illustrates one of reconciliation without justice. Our dilemma, it seems to me, is how to transcend the polarity between justice and reconciliation: Are we condemned to choose between the two? Or, is a measure of justice, as I will argue, a necessary ingredient for a durable reconciliation? To manage the tension between reconciliation and justice creatively, do we not need to think of reconciliation as not just political but also social, and justice as not just criminal and individual, but also social and systemic?

The paradigm of justice and its pitfalls

The promise of state independence in equatorial Africa was summed up in a single demand: Justice. What did justice mean? What was the injustice of the colonial system? The answer lay both in the nature of power and that of production.

The nationalist political project was first and foremost a response to the nature of colonial power. The colonial state was a bifurcated power. It claimed a dual legitimacy, both modern and traditional. Modern power was urban-based and spoke the language of rights. In contrast, traditional power, rural-based, spoke the language of culture. These languages, of rights and of culture, signified two contrasting institutional set-ups, both of organising power and reproducing political identities.

Modern power claimed to be civilised. This claim should be understood in 18th century Hegelian terms, which identified the advent of civilisation with the modern state and its centralised monopoly over all legitimate means of violence – a development that was said to have rendered societal conflict free of violence. Thus, the modern state claimed to be the underpinning of a civil society, short hand for civilised society. Civil power and civil society were two sides of the same Hegelian coin. Civil power was the source of civil laws, which guaranteed civil rights to citizens. In the colonies, however, the power, the law and the bearers of rights were racialised. Racism was the original sin of civil society in colonial Africa.

The other face of colonial power was the Native Authority, the enforcer of 'customary' law. Before we accept its claim to being 'traditional', we need to recall that nowhere in pre-colonial Africa were there traditional chiefs with unchallenged powers over every domain of social life. Everywhere, traditional authorities were in the plural: There were clan-heads alongside chiefs, age-sets alongside gender groups, each with a legitimate say in a clearly defined and limited domain. The idea of an unchallenged and absolute executive authority holding sway over all domains of social life – as traditional – is foreign to pre-colonial Africa. Secondly, the existence of multiple sources of tradition also meant that tradition was never in the singular, always in the plural. Sources of tradition were not only several; they were often conflicting. This should not be surprising since tradition was always a lived reality, about which people had different memories, sources, convictions and hopes for the future. Lived and reproduced in tension, tradition was always changing. What was new and untraditional was the idea of a single tradition, officially sanctioned and officially enforced, as 'customary law'.

My interest is not really in challenging the universality of modernity and the authenticity of tradition. It is, rather, in underpinning the political significance of both. What should we make politically of the fact that while civil power was defined in racial terms, both the Native Authority and the custom it enforced as law were defined in ethnic terms? That while civil power and civil law were racialised, the Native Authority and 'customary' law were ethnicised?

My argument – made fully in a book I called *Citizen and Subject* – is that colonial power sought to reproduce two distinct identities through this legal and institutional apparatus: a racial identity amongst beneficiaries, and an ethnic particularism amongst victims. Race was the identity through which power united its beneficiaries as citizens, and ethnicity the identity through which the same power fragmented its victims as subjects. This attempt to build a Chinese Wall between racially united citizens and ethnically fragmented subjects was pioneered by the British who called it 'indirect rule'.

The French emulated it in the 1920s and called it 'association'. The Belgians followed in the 1930s, and the Portuguese in the 1950s. In spite of differences between them, it is significant that every colonial power in equatorial Africa reorganised its administration into one or another version of indirect rule. From this point of view, it is relevant to note that the re-organisation of the South African State by the National Party, called apartheid, removed the Native Affairs Department from rural to urban areas. The effect was to reorganise administration in rural areas in line with principles of indirect rule, by mediating racialised power through the ethnically defined authority of chiefs. In this sense, apartheid, I argued, should be understood as the generic form of the colonial state in Africa, not as an exception to it.

And yet, there was a crack in the proverbial Chinese Wall. In spite of political ideology and political practice, the civic and the ethnic could not be kept apart as two worlds: The imperative of colonial political economy was at cross-purposes with that of colonial power. While power was preoccupied with keeping everyone in their place, the logic of political economy compelled many to change places. This constant changing of places, this dynamic human flow, was a consequence of the system of migrant labour. Migrant labour created urbanised subjects. Race was no longer simply an identity of the beneficiaries of powers; it also turned into an insurgent urban identity, have urbanised subjects. Brought to town as migrants, urbanised 'natives' were beyond the lash of customary law but were still excluded from the regime of civilised rights. It is the urban subject nursing a racial grievance that formed the social base of nationalism. One need only think of Nkrumah's 'verandah boys' and Cabral's 'boatmen' or, closer to home, of the post-World War II ANC in South Africa.

Similarly, ethnicity too became a contradictory construct. It did not remain simply an identity of power, of chiefs organised as the Native Authority, but also turned into an insurgent peasant identity. In spite of the claim that tradition was singular and unchanging, there was never an unquestioned acceptance of the official version of custom. From the onset of colonial rule, peasants had their own version of custom against that of chiefs, as did women against that of men, and youth against that of the older generation. One need only think of the string of rural revolts that called for a 'genuine' custom to replace that, which had been officially crafted and enforced as customary law.

In the history of every nationalist movement, the key question was always how to link the revolt of the urban strata against racial exclusion with the revolt of rural subjects against an oppression justified as 'customary' in ethnic terms. In this context, justice meant, first and foremost, deracialisation, of urban society, civil society and the central state. For militant nationalism, which linked the revolt of the urban strata with that of insurgent peasants, justice also meant de-ethnicisation, the denial of that reified difference, that stigma which went by the name 'tribe'.The theorist who best captured the tenor and substance of nationalist resistance on this score was Frantz Fanon.

The demand for justice had also another side, particularly in colonies ruled from a metropolitan-based power. Here, the difference between settler and non-settler colonies was telling. For the nonsettler economy, the absence of state independence translated into unfavourable conditions for local capital accumulation. By and large confined to primary production under technologically backward conditions, the backwardness of this mainly agrarian economy was theorised by militant nationalism as a modern dependency.

Underdevelopment wrote dependency theorists, was a modern condition, reproduced through an international division of labour that was created through imperial domination and reproduced through a combination of the market and force. The leading dependency theorist on the African continent was Samir Amin, the author of Accumulation on a World Scale.

The core demand for justice was thus double: Deracialisation and de-ethnicisation within and breaking the chains of dependency without. Justice would require a reorganisation of both power and production. My argument is that it is the failure to reorganise power that was the key to the collapse of the nationalist project. Out of that collapse was born the paradigm of rights, so narrowly articulated that it has little room for a meaningful notion of justice. It is this revisionist, truncated, post-Cold War notion of rights that today goes by the name of reconciliation.

The failure to reorganise power was a double failure. Epistemologically, it was a failure to historicise and problematise notions of race and tribe as identities reproduced by a form of power, and embedded in a set of institutions. Militant nationalism either accepted these identities and definitions as the hallmarks of a positive science – as with race – or it dismissed them as ideological constructs, as with tribe. Politically, it was a failure to produce a practice that would change the paradigm. When revolutionaries succeeded, they managed to turn the world upside down; but they failed to change that world. More than anything else, that failure was political.

Rwanda: The pursuit of justice as revenge

The most spectacular instance of this double failure was Rwanda. To draw a few general lessons from the Rwandan experience, I will focus on one event, the 'social revolution' of 1959. This is the event that ushered in the volcanic landscape that we call postcolonial Rwanda. I will begin with the question of identity – who is a Muhutu and who a Mututsi – and the need to distinguish between cultural and political identities. If you go to contemporary Kigali and ask someone in the Rwandan Patriotic Front (RPF) as to the difference between a Muhutu and Mututsi, you will most likely be told: 'We live on the same hills, speak the same language and practice the same religion. We are the same people'. And so it is: Culturally, the difference between Bahutu and Batutsi is like a difference along a continuum. But not so politically. Bahutu and Batutsi have been produced as bipolar, often antagonistic, political identities: One as power, the other as subject. The cultural continuity, and the political discontinuity, is very much like that between Afrikaners and Coloureds in this country. As is well known, the Native Authority in colonial Rwanda, particularly after the late 1920s, were wholly Batutsi and the peasant masses predominantly Bahutu. Not surprisingly, peasant jacqueries against the Native Authority took on an anti-Tutsi character. Abetted by the Catholic Church and encouraged by Belgian colonial power, peasant resistance turned into an insurgent revolt against Tutsi power in the Native Authority.

The new power, the custodian of the 'social revolution' of 1959, was self-consciously a 'Hutu Power'. Institutions previously Tutsified were now Hutu-ised. A programme of redress, permanent and without limits, followed. Access to education, from primary to university, and to state employment was defined in terms of whether you were recognised by the state as a Muhutu or a Mututsi. 'Hutu' and 'Tutsi' became permanent identities, politically enforced, the former with a preferential access to power, the latter subject to that same power. The quest for justice had turned into revenge.

Post-1959 Rwanda raises a question: How did the pursuit of justice turn into revenge? Several lessons can be drawn from the historical tragedy that unfolded in the aftermath of the 'social revolution' of 1959.

First was a failure to historicise the nature of power and the identities it generated, one that turned into a failure to reform power and to transform the identities imposed by power. For the fact was that Tutsi was not simply the identity of chiefs in the Native Authority, it was also the identity of the native strata most directly affected by racial exclusion in the civic sphere. In other words, Tutsi was the identity both of power in the Native Authority and of an insurgent nationalism in the civic sphere. The irony is that both Bahutu and Batutsi had a victim consciousness, but in different realms of power: Bahutu resisted an ethnic dictatorship in the Native Authority, and Batutsi resisted a racial dictatorship in the civic authority. Whereas Bahutu resistance against a 'customary' Native Authority was called tribalism, Batutsi resistance against a racialised and modern civic power was called nationalism. Both tribalism and nationalism were insurgent ideologies, and yet both were limited in perspective and problematic in nature. Forged as movements of resistance in the womb of power, each was marked from birth by the contours of that power. So a racialised Tutsi identity came to be the birthmark of urban resistance and an ethnicised Hutu identity the birthmark of rural resistance. If the insurgency was to transcend the identities imposed by power as divisions inside the people – racial and ethnic – then it would have to reform the nature of that power. It would have to deracialise civic authority and detribalise Native Authority, as so many jumpstarts in an overall democratic process.

This, then, was a failure to differentiate political from cultural identity. It was not surprising in an age when politics was often considered to be a residual activity. If you were a rightist, you assumed that the contours of political identity were culturally given, and if you were a leftist you assumed they were economically determined. It was a failure to realise that political identity was not and did not have to be a simple and unproblematic translation of cultural or economic difference into the political sphere. Rather, political identity was reproduced through a set of historically defined institutions that underpinned a form of power. Only a reform of that power would reproduce a common political identity. In Rwanda, this was a failure to recognise that one could forge a common Rwandese political identity, without denying Bahutu and Batutsi as cultural identities along a cultural continuum, but at the same time without translating these into bipolar political oppositions.

Second, even if it led to a radical changing of places between Bahutu and Batutsi, the 'revolution' reinforced Hutu and Tutsi as political identities, rather than eroding them. The same process which turned the consciousness of being a Muhutu, previously a stamp of servitude, into a badge of pride and an identity of power, demonised the Batutsi. To make the revolutionary process 'permanent', it institutionalised the political opposition between Hutu and Tutsi. Rwanda raises the question of how identities consolidated in the course of a struggle can persist in a changed context, thereby subverting the very possibilities opened up by that struggle. It calls attention to the process by which past grievances is sanctified into a shield protecting a new power against future critiques. More specifically, it invites us to understand the process by which memories of a past tragedy – the Holocaust, the Genocide – become key ingredients in the forging of a new state ideology. Put in the language of revolutionaries, it underlines some of the ways in which demands for 'permanent revolution' as in Trotsky or 'uninterrupted revolution' as in Mao can turn into so many gravediggers of that same revolutionary process.

Third, as the programme of redress, heralded as revolutionary justice, became permanent – even turned into a prerogative of 'revolutionaries' – the failure to reorganise power turned into a failure to reorganise and create a political community inclusive of both Bahutu and Batutsi. Revolutionaries who vowed never to forget the past accented the past over the future, giving a longer leash to the identities which animated that past, and a shorter shrift to a process that might forge a common identity and a reorganised political community of survivors out of that past tragedy. It is the failure to frame justice within notions of an inclusive political community that turned justice into a permanent preoccupation, a vendetta that increasingly spelt revenge.

South Africa: The search for an alternative paradigm

The South African search for an alternative paradigm has been a conscious move. Beginning by distancing itself from the legacy of post-independence Africa, it has turned into a search for new and more appropriate analogies. The search for clothes that fit has also been a mixed experience, involving both discarding clothes that don't fit and appropriating those that do, even if they may not fit quite fully. I will argue that it is worth understanding the rationale behind this process of sifting, for it illuminates the logic behind the politics of reconciliation in contemporary South Africa.

The analogy that was discarded was that of Nuremberg. This conversion has recently been recounted by Kadar Asmal, a leading ANC activist, in a book he co-authored with two others. Asmal tells us that he 'campaigned for a South African equivalent of the Nuremberg trials', until faced with the reality of 'a negotiated revolution' which ruled out 'imposing victors' justice'. Any such attempt to identify and punish politically responsible individuals, he tells us, 'would result in what has been called "justice with ashes"'. In South Africa, he concludes, there should thus be 'no Nuremberg trials', 'no vindictive "lustration laws" on the recent Czech model disqualifying certain persons from the old order from holding office in the new', and 'no black-listing of collabourators as in post-war France and Belgium'. All these were rejected, says Kadar with a straight face, 'in favor of ideals of nation-building and reconciliation between the oppressors and the previously oppressed'.

I find Asmal's argument interesting on two counts. To begin with, he makes no distinction between justice and victor' s justice. He presumes that all justice is victor' s justice. From this point of view, all justice is the same as revenge. Is it then surprising that justice should appear as the price for reconciliation? Secondly, and perhaps for this very reason, Kadar's conversion is not really a change of political heart. It is more of a pragmatic political concession. The result is a breach in what the book considers politically possible and what it continues to uphold as politically desirable: While the demand for Nuremberg is dropped, the Holocaust continues to be the metaphor through which Asmal and associates seek to illuminate the injustice of apartheid. The Holocaust is, however, an inappropriate metaphor, for a variety of reasons. Key to these is that it abstracts from the real problem: Whites and blacks in South Africa are not akin to Germans and Jews, for Germans and Jews did not have to build a common society in the aftermath of the Holocaust. There was Israel. South African whites and blacks, however, do have to live together in the aftermath of apartheid. Here, as in Rwanda, yesterday's perpetrators and victims – today's survivors – do have to confront the problem of how to live together. Faced with identities inherited from the past, they must forge new and common identities. To paraphrase a friend, if the survivors of the Holocaust marched to the tune, 'Let My People Go' the survivors of apartheid would have to march to a different tune: 'Let My People Stay'.

It is this point of difference – that victims and perpetrators do have to continue to live together, and at that in a context in which past perpetrators would continue to wield considerable if not enormous power – that has become the basis for the South African leadership to embrace a different analogy. This is the analogy with the Latin American dictatorships, particularly those in Chile and Argentina. To this political insight, which I neither wish to dispute nor to diminish, can be added other points of resemblance between the South African and the Latin American contexts. Were there not in both instances gross human rights abuses in the confrontation between power and resistance? Did not both confrontations, in the absence of an outright victory on either side, lead to a mutual exhaustion and, born of it, a mutual recognition – political wisdom – that this waste of life and resources need not continue? Finally, did not the global situation, as the internal one, also underline the need for compromise and facilitate it?

While not wishing to detract from the insight that underlines the above observations, I do wish to point out its limited nature by raising a different question: How does one go beyond the compromise of 1994? 1994 has a double significance. While it shows that reconciliation is possible, it also raises a further question: How can reconciliation be made durable? I will argue that just as the possibility of reconciliation required putting aside the analogy of the Holocaust and Nuremberg, its durability requires acknowledging the extent to which the analogy with the Latin transition is inadequate.

Truth telling in South Africa has led to two unanticipated outcomes. Each raises doubts about the ease with which the process of reconciliation may be consolidated within its present framework. I will frame these outcomes as two sets of questions. First, is reconciliation an inevitable outcome of truth telling? Is it also not possible that the more truth comes to light – and the less justice is seen to be done – the more truth may breed outrage amongst the majority and fear in the minority? Could such a situation not lead a growing number in the majority to call for justice as criminal justice – a demand for a Nuremberg – and many in the minority to turn to flight, autonomy, and even separation as possible solutions to an increasingly fearful circumstance? The dilemma is this: While the argument to opt for truth-telling as opposed to criminal justice was underscored as a political necessity, the more truth is told the more it may fuel the very demand it is supposed to have displaced, that for justice!

Second, the analogy with Latin dictatorships has obscured the difference between perpetrator and beneficiary. As such, the more it unfolds, the more the process is subject to a critique: Whose truth? Which truth? The truth of the minority or the majority? Of the political activist or the population? Where the focus is on perpetrators, victims are necessarily defined as the minority of political activists; for the victimhood of the majority to be recognised, the focus has to shift from perpetrators to beneficiaries. The difference is this: Whereas the focus on perpetrators fuels the demand for justice as criminal justice, that on beneficiaries would shift focus to a notion of justice as social justice.

This shift, in turn, is likely to illuminate further the difference with the Latin transition. As a form of power, apartheid undergirded a particular system of privilege. A focus on power that obscures the relationship to privilege leads to accenting the relationship between perpetrator and victim as the minority. But a focus that links power to privilege links perpetrator to beneficiary, racialised power to racialised privilege, and puts at centre-stage the relationship between beneficiary and victim as the majority. To recognise this difference is, I think, key to thinking through how to make the reconciliation durable.

The distinction between perpetrator and beneficiary, and between victims as the minority and victims as the majority, allows us to distinguish between two forms of reconciliation: One narrow and political, the other broad and social. The reach of political reconciliation is limited to the political elite, to political activists on this side and to state agents on the other side; its embrace is limited to a minority, in a word, to perpetrators and their victims. Social reconciliation has a wider embrace. It reaches out to ordinary members of society, those who benefited or got victimised as part of the logic of an ongoing system, regardless of agency. The embrace of social reconciliation includes the vast majority, in a word, beneficiaries and victims.

I do not wish to oppose political to social reconciliation as alternatives, but to distinguish them so as to underline the relationship between them. My point is both to acknowledge the importance of political reconciliation as a pre-requisite to a social reconciliation and to argue that the political reconciliation may not prove durable without a social reconciliation. It is, thus, to raise questions like: What does it mean to reconcile beneficiary and victim as the majority? To deepen reconciliation from the political to the social? To broaden it from the political elite to society?

I suggest that, as a first step, we recognise that there are degrees of reconciliation that bear a relationship to forms of justice, even if the relationship is tension-ridden. Limiting justice to criminal justice, to punishment, is not necessarily to benefit victims. I have been arguing that the latter requires a shift of focus from the world of agents and activists to that of winners and losers, from those who were victimised individually and personally to those whose victimhood was more anonymous and circumstantial, from gross human rights abuses – murder, torture, rape – to gross systemic outcomes like those of pass laws and forced removals, abuses which racialised both poverty and affluence. It is a shift of focus that relocates agency in a historicised structure. But this shift in focus is also a shift in logic: Perpetrators are personally and individually guilty, beneficiaries may not be. They may be unconscious beneficiaries of systemic outcomes, where benefits cannot necessarily be linked to individual agency. Thus, many a white South African can have benefited from the system and yet be honestly surprised at the injustices perpetrated in the name of that same system. Isn't one objective of the TRC's televised hearings in fact to invite beneficiaries to be so outraged at the evil that was perpetrated in their name as to denounce perpetrators, and thereby isolate them? For beneficiaries to join victims in a common outrage at evil is a positive development, but for beneficiaries to shirk responsibility for the ongoing consequences of that evil is, I suggest, hardly positive.

Agency theory, whether in its rights or subaltern version, has a tendency to be blind to structural constraints. This is why I think it is not enough that we leave the responsibility for righting wrongs between beneficiaries and victims as the majority as a moral burden on the shoulders of beneficiaries. Rather, this needs to be understood as a legislative and executive burden of that agency which claims to be the upholder of the public good, the state. It is also why I would say that to make reconciliation durable requires moving from a narrow recognition of rights that individualises and dehistoricises it, accenting the rights of property holders above those of the rest, to a broad recognition that underlines the need to right historical wrongs, and thus to provide a measure of justice to previously excluded groups. To create the basis for a stable regime of rights, it may be necessary to address the tension between justice and rights as a tension between different kinds of rights, rather than to polarise it. The lesson we should draw from Rwanda is not that there should be no redress, because any justice would be victor's justice, but that redress should be limited in duration and be socially meaningful to the widest majority of victims. Without a measure of social justice, reconciliation cannot be durable.

Addressing the tension between social justice and individual rights may require moving away from an absolute emphasis on either, so as to contextualise and relativise the emphasis on both. If the first step in reconciliation was to guarantee security for the minority by temporarily breaching the rights of the majority – no Nuremberg, no regime of equal political rights in the short run so as to allow for minority vetoes in the interim, 'sunset' clauses that allow for a presence of the minority in the state apparatus, a presence out of all proportion to its numerical weight in society – then does not the second step call for a breach, also limited and temporary, but this time in the rights of the privileged minority, in order to ensure a measure of dignity for the majority, through a form of group redress that is equally dramatic if temporary, that gives the hitherto deprived majority a stake in reformed social institutions?

One may ask: What if there is no social justice, no durable reconciliation, but instead a sort of a pragmatic, day-to-day accommodation? What if racial privilege is entrenched as a constitutional right and comes to be defended in the language of rights in civil society and in the language of standards within institutions? Indeed, if we are to go by the experience of other privileged minorities on this continent – minorities like the Asians of Uganda or the Tutsi of Rwanda, those who were popularly seen, on the morrow of independence, as illegitimate beneficiaries of a colonial relationship – this alternative does give us pause to think. Does not their example illuminate what can happen when a privileged minority enters into a Hobbesian pact, trading political rights for security of privilege? Is the price not one of being branded permanently – and racially – as a minority, one whose wealth is considered an ill-gotten privilege, a fixed target against which any and every demagogue may organise in the name of social justice, while unleashing a tide of revenge? We need to consider whether a reconciliation that masks the continuation of privilege may not invite revenge as surely as does a demand for justice that knows no bounds.

Conclusion

One needs to resist the temptation to overlook the redeeming features of the new paradigm. Its contribution flows from the critique of the paradigm of justice, that it is not enough to change positions. Such a merry-go-round only triggers a cycle of revenge. Identities have to be transcended, not just displaced. To forge a common future for past perpetrators and beneficiaries, and their victims, it is necessary also to address them all as survivors.

If the paradigm of reconciliation has the virtue of pointing to a common future, its pitfall is that it does this on the basis of diminishing the nature of evil so grossly that accepting it requires nothing short of suppressing the agency of the majority. Telescoping the definition of victims to political activists may be justified as political necessity, as trimming the political agenda to fit the capacity of the moment; in short, as making the transition manageable. And yet, should we not resist the temptation to celebrate necessity as virtue, in the process turning that momentary necessity into a permanent condition? It is in this context that, I suggest we need to take a second look at the work of the Truth and Reconciliation Commission.

I suggest that while we accept the political imperative behind the compromise of 1994 that created the TRC as an amnesty commission, we nonetheless question its ideological claim to be a truth commission. I suggest we go beyond asking whether truth necessarily leads to reconciliation and recognise that the nature of truth is not an unproblematic given. Could there not be versions of the truth? If the relationship between perpetrators and victims highlights one truth, does not the relationship between beneficiaries and victims as the majority express a related but different truth? In as much as the commission highlights the former and obscures the latter, should we not ask: How much room does the truth, as tailored by this commission, have for the experience of the vast majority of South Africans? In tailoring the truth to fit the experience of agents and activists, and in obscuring the experience of the vast majority, is not the commission asking us to embrace the consequences of apartheid as ordinary people experienced it, to accept these as the price of reconciliation, even as part of normal life? Is reconciliation then turning into an embrace of evil? If so, how long can it hold?

I do not presume that the TRC should have been the agency to deliver a measure of justice to victims as the majority. But I do presume that the TRC could and should have prepared the ideological groundwork for practical initiatives to do so. In making a distinction between the two functions of the TRC, one political (granting amnesty) and the other ideological (defining the truth), my point is to focus attention on the ideological work of the commission. It is to make the argument that in highlighting the identity of perpetrators while obscuring that of beneficiaries, the TRC has given us a version of truth which obscures the link between perpetrators and beneficiaries, and thus between racialised power and racialised privilege.

If reconciliation is not to turn into an embrace of injustice, of evil – even if it is called truth – then the pursuit of social justice needs to be recognised as a political imperative. I recognise that what is politically desirable may not always be politically possible. And yet, that is reasoning enough to explore ways of making it possible politically. It is reason enough to explore how to resolve the tension between managing the reconciliation politically in the short run and making it durable socially in the long run, and to consider whether it is possible to manage the tension between reconciliation and justice by approaching reconciliation in degrees, as a step-by-step process that moves from the political leadership to the population, from perpetrators and victims as a minority to beneficiaries and victims as the majority. Just as the distinction between political and social reconciliation does not have to highlight the agency of the political leadership at the expense of denying popular agency, it does not have to overload the agenda of the moment at the risk of eroding a limited capacity. By recognising that degrees of reconciliation are linked to forms of justice, it can also allow us to explore ways of linking the two to make reconciliation durable.

Either we try and shape events by putting the question of social justice on the political agenda, or we let events compel us into that recognition, sooner or later. The difference, of course, is that whereas foresight will keep the initiative in the hands of political leaders, the lack of it will just as surely pass the initiative to demagogues.

2

CAUSES OF CONFLICT IN AFRICA

This celebrated report of the UN Secretary-General, Kofi Annan on the causes of conflict and the promotion of durable peace and sustainable development in Africa focuses attention to the need to deal with the underlying causes of conflict and to establish a comprehensive framework to prevent conflict and enhance human security. It also stresses the indivisibility of peace in Africa and global security.

ANNAN, K *THE CAUSES OF CONFLICT AND THE PROMOTION OF DURABLE PEACE AND SUSTAINABLE DEVELOPMENT IN AFRICA* (1998)

Full report available at http://www.un.org

...

(2) Africa as a whole has begun to make significant economic and political progress in recent years, but in many parts of the continent progress remains threatened or impeded by conflict. For the United Nations there is no higher goal, no deeper commitment and no greater ambition than preventing armed conflict. The prevention of conflict begins and ends with the promotion of human security and human development. Ensuring human security is, in the broadest sense, the cardinal mission of the United Nations. Genuine and lasting prevention is the means to achieve that mission.

(3) Conflict in Africa poses a major challenge to United Nations efforts designed to ensure global peace, prosperity and human rights for all. Although the United Nations was intended to deal with inter-state warfare, it is being required more and more often to respond to intra-State instability and conflict. In those conflicts the main aim, increasingly, is the destruction not just of armies but of civilians and entire ethnic groups. Preventing such wars is no longer a matter of defending States or protecting allies. It is a matter of defending humanity itself.

(4) Since 1970, more than 30 wars have been fought in Africa, the vast majority of them intra-state in origin. In 1996 alone, 14 of the 53 countries of Africa were afflicted by armed conflicts, accounting for more than half of all war-related deaths worldwide and resulting in more than 8 million refugees, returnees and displaced persons. The consequences of those conflicts have seriously undermined Africa's efforts to ensure long-term stability, prosperity and peace for its peoples.

(5) By not averting these colossal human tragedies, African leaders have failed the peoples of Africa; the international community has failed them; the United Nations has failed them. We have failed them by not adequately addressing the causes of conflict; by not doing enough to ensure peace; and by our repeated inability to create the conditions for sustainable development. This is the reality of Africa's recent past. It is a reality that must be confronted honestly and constructively by all concerned if the people of Africa are to enjoy the human security and economic opportunities they seek

and deserve. Today, in many parts of Africa, efforts to break with the patterns of the past are at last beginning to succeed.

(6) It is my aspiration, with this report, to add momentum to Africa's renewed quest for peace and greater prosperity. The report strives to do so by offering an analysis of conflicts in Africa that does justice to their reality and seeks answers in their sources. It strives to do so by proposing realistic and achievable recommendations which, in time, may reduce if not entirely end those conflicts. It aims to summon the political will of Africans and non-Africans alike to act when action is so evidently needed – the will without which no level of assistance and no degree of hope can make the difference between war and peace in Africa.

The sources of conflict

(7) Africa is a vast and varied continent. African countries have different histories and geographical conditions, different stages of economic development, different sets of public policies and different patterns of internal and international interaction. The sources of conflict in Africa reflect this diversity and complexity. Some sources are purely internal, some reflect the dynamics of a particular sub-region, and some have important international dimensions. Despite these differences the sources of conflict in Africa are linked by a number of common themes and experiences.

Historical legacies

(8) At the Congress of Berlin in 1885, the colonial powers partitioned Africa into territorial units. Kingdoms, States and communities in Africa were arbitrarily divided; unrelated areas and peoples were just as arbitrarily joined together. In the 1960s, the newly independent African States inherited those colonial boundaries, together with the challenge that legacy posed to their territorial integrity and to their attempts to achieve national unity. The challenge was compounded by the fact that the framework of colonial laws and institutions which some new States inherited had been designed to exploit local divisions, not overcome them. Understandably, therefore, the simultaneous tasks of State-building and nation-building preoccupied many of the newly independent States, and were given new momentum by the events that followed the outbreak of secessionist fighting in the Congo. Too often, however, the necessary building of national unity was pursued through the heavy centralisation of political and economic power and the suppression of political pluralism. Predictably, political monopolies often led to corruption, nepotism, complacency and the abuse of power. The era of serious conflict over State boundaries in Africa has largely passed, aided by the 1963 decision of the Organization of African Unity (OAU) to accept the boundaries which African States had inherited from colonial authorities. However, the challenge of forging a genuine national identity from among disparate and often competing communities has remained.

(9) The character of the commercial relations instituted by colonialism also created long-term distortions in the political economy of Africa. Transportation networks and related physical infrastructure were designed to satisfy the needs of trade with the metropolitan country, not to support the

balanced growth of an indigenous economy. In addition to frequently imposing unfavourable terms of trade, economic activities that were strongly skewed towards extractive industries and primary commodities for export stimulated little demand for steady and widespread improvements in the skills and educational levels of the workforce. The consequences of this pattern of production and exchange spilled over into the post-independence State. As political competition was not rooted in viable national economic systems, in many instances the prevailing structure of incentives favoured capturing the institutional remnants of the colonial economy for factional advantage.

(10) During the Cold War the ideological confrontation between East and West placed a premium on maintaining order and stability among friendly States and allies, though super-Power rivalries in Angola and elsewhere also fuelled some of Africa's longest and most deadly conflicts. Across Africa, undemocratic and oppressive regimes were supported and sustained by the competing super-powers in the name of their broader goals but, when the Cold War ended, Africa was suddenly left to fend for itself. Without external economic and political support, few African regimes could sustain the economic lifestyles to which they had become accustomed, or maintain the permanent hold on political power which they had come to expect. As a growing number of States found themselves internally beset by unrest and violent conflict, the world searched for a new global security framework.

(11) For a brief period following the end of the Cold War, the international community was eager to exercise its newly acquired capacity for collective decision-making. Beginning in the early 1990s, the Security Council launched a series of ambitious peacekeeping and peacemaking initiatives in Africa and elsewhere. Despite a number of important successes, the inability of the United Nations to restore peace to Somalia soured international support for conflict intervention and precipitated a rapid retreat by the international community from peacekeeping worldwide. An early and direct consequence of this retreat was the failure of the international community, including the United Nations, to intervene to prevent genocide in Rwanda. That failure has had especially profound consequences in Africa. Throughout the continent, the perception of near indifference on the part of the international community has left a poisonous legacy that continues to undermine confidence in the Organization.

Internal factors

(12) More than three decades after African countries gained their independence, there is a growing recognition among Africans themselves that the continent must look beyond its colonial past for the causes of current conflicts. Today more than ever, Africa must look at itself. The nature of political power in many African States, together with the real and perceived consequences of capturing and maintaining power, is a key source of conflict across the continent. It is frequently the case that political victory assumes a 'winner-takes-all' form with respect to wealth and resources, patronage, and the prestige and prerogatives of office. A communal sense of advantage or disadvantage is often closely linked to this phenomenon, which is heightened in many cases by reliance on centralised and highly personalised forms of

governance. Where there is insufficient accountability of leaders, lack of transparency in regimes, inadequate checks and balances, non-adherence to the rule of law, absence of peaceful means to change or replace leadership, or lack of respect for human rights, political control becomes excessively important, and the stakes become dangerously high. This situation is exacerbated when, as is often the case in Africa, the State is the major provider of employment and political parties are largely either regionally or ethnically based. In such circumstances, the multi-ethnic character of most African States makes conflict even more likely, leading to an often violent politicisation of ethnicity. In extreme cases, rival communities may perceive that their security, perhaps their very survival, can be ensured only through control of State power. Conflict in such cases becomes virtually inevitable.

External factors

(13) During the Cold War, external efforts to bolster or undermine African Governments were a familiar feature of super-Power competition. With the end of the Cold War, external intervention has diminished but has not disappeared. In the competition for oil and other precious resources in Africa, interests external to Africa continue to play a large and sometimes decisive role, both in suppressing conflict and in sustaining it. Foreign interventions are not limited, however, to sources beyond Africa. Neighbouring States, inevitably affected by conflicts taking place within other States, may also have other significant interests, not all of them necessarily benign. While African peacekeeping and mediation efforts have become more prominent in recent years, the role that African Governments play in supporting, sometimes even instigating, conflicts in neighbouring countries must be candidly acknowledged.

Economic motives

(14) Despite the devastation that armed conflicts bring, there are many who profit from chaos and lack of accountability, and who may have little or no interest in stopping a conflict and much interest in prolonging it. Very high on the list of those who profit from conflict in Africa are international arms merchants. Also high on the list, usually, are the protagonists themselves. In Liberia, the control and exploitation of diamonds, timber and other raw materials was one of the principal objectives of the warring factions. Control over those resources financed the various factions and gave them the means to sustain the conflict. Clearly, many of the protagonists had a strong financial interest in seeing the conflict prolonged. The same can be said of Angola, where protracted difficulties in the peace process owed much to the importance of control over the exploitation of the country's lucrative diamond fields. In Sierra Leone, the chance to plunder natural resources and loot Central Bank reserves was a key motivation of those who seized power from the elected Government in May 1997.

Particular situations

(15) In addition to the broader sources of conflict in Africa that have been identified, a number of other factors are especially important in particular situations and subregions. In Central Africa, they include the competition for

scarce land and water resources in densely populated areas. In Rwanda, for example, multiple waves of displacement have resulted in situations where several families often claim rights to the same piece of land. In African communities where oil is extracted, conflict has often arisen over local complaints that the community does not adequately reap the benefit of such resources, or suffers excessively from the degradation of the natural environment. In North Africa, the tensions between strongly opposing visions of society and the State are serious sources of actual and potential conflict in some States.

...

Against the backdrop of the complex causes and dynamics of conflicts, Cilliers examines the influence of the lack of capacity to manage conflict and insecurity in Africa. Specifically, he examines state incapacity to deal with conflicts.

CILLIERS, J *HUMAN SECURITY IN AFRICA: A CONCEPTUAL FRAMEWORK FOR REVIEW* (2004)

African Human Security Initiative
Full text available at www.africanreview.org

...

Africa and security today

Some characteristics

As Max Weber and others have repeatedly noted, the critical characteristic of a state is its monopoly on the legitimate use of physical force in the territory it claims to control. This is not the situation in most of Africa where it is generally recognised that conflicts are of a regional and unregulated character (more so because state capacity to regulate the amount of weapons in society is virtually non-existent and the existence of a myriad of sub-state groups that increasingly are able to challenge and threaten the authority of the state). In the absence of administration, and the application of any rule of law, the nexus between the legitimate and illegitimate activities of business, government, criminals and conflict triggers are often difficult to distinguish from one another. These flow across national borders and involve numerous national and international actors. Insecurity and instability in much of Africa has become a single, complex and interrelated problem that is an intrinsic part of the debate about the nature and capability of the African state. While there are only a few collapsed or failed states in Africa, most African states are weak, as governance has contracted rather than expanded in recent decades – parallel with the acute economic crises experienced by the continent.

Thus, in Liberia some 250 000 people are believed to have died in war related circumstances since 1989 – about ten per cent of the country's three million population. Liberia returned to war shortly after the carnage in neighbouring Sierra Leone was brought under control, after free and fair elections in 2002, and at a time when francophone West Africa saw its most prosperous country, Ivory Coast, divided between a rebel-held north and government-controlled south after conflict broke out in September 2003. That widening regional conflict has threatened Guinea and Liberia, and affected Mali, Niger and even Ghana.

In the DRC, an estimated three million people have died during the past three years as a result of conflict. In neighbouring Rwanda, 40 per cent of the population have been killed or displaced since 1994. In Burundi, some 300 000 people have been killed over the past decade and fighting between the government and Hutu militias force about 100 000 to flee their homes each month. In Uganda, the war with the Lord's Resistance Army (LRA) that started in 1986 has displaced an estimated one million people since 1986. To the north, the 20 years of civil war in Sudan have claimed the lives of two million people and caused the greatest displacement of people in Africa. Recently, 110 000 people have crossed the border into Chad to escape the conflict between rebel movements, militias and the Government of Sudan, while an estimated one million people have been displaced inside Darfur. Elsewhere in the Horn, the war between Ethiopia and Eritrea between 1998 and 2000 cost around 100 000 lives. Neighbouring Somalia, with the limited exception of Somaliland and the region of Puntland, has had no government since the abortive UN peacekeeping mission ended in failure in 1993.

Although most contemporary writing on the subject focuses on the international dimensions or manifestations of terrorism, sub-national terror, and even state terror, has been a longstanding feature of Africa. In fact, by any objective standard, Africa is the continent most afflicted by terrorism – albeit not yet by international terrorism. At the one extreme, those figures provided by the US State Department's 'Patterns of Global Terrorism' indicate that international terrorism is on the increase in Africa – although from a very low base with only six per cent of international terrorist incidents committed on African soil between 1990 and 2002. Evaluating the costs of international terrorism in terms of human casualties presents a different and more alarming picture. Africa recorded 6 177 casualties from 296 acts of international terrorism during the same period, second only to Asia in terms of continental casualties, with 1998 as the year with the highest number (5 379) due to the bombings in Kenya and Tanzania.

Terrorism in Africa is widespread. It is overwhelmingly of a domestic, sub-state nature that kills, maims and affects millions of people. Many latter-day insurgent movements and government forces have adopted practices that rely heavily on the use of fear and terror. These included União Nocional para a Independência Total de Angola (UNITO) and RENAMO in Angola and Mozambique, the Mai Mai, the LRA, the Liberians United for Democracy and Reconciliation (LURD), the Movement for Democracy in Liberia (MODEL), and so on. The list is almost endless and grows even longer if state-sponsored terror is added. While Algeria presents the country in Africa most closely intertwined with international terrorism, in much of Africa rebels and governments alike had been terrifying civilians in many civil wars for years. For decades, these had caused much more death and destruction than international terrorism. Databases on international terrorism reflect the reality that shootings – not explosives, assassinations, kidnappings or hijackings – are the dominant *modus operandi* for terror in Africa. It is a statement of the obvious that small arms and light weapons are not in short supply in Africa, with an estimated 100 million in present circulation.

In the aftermath of the Cold War, large sections of the state-run networks engaged in transport, training, provision of arms and equipment, money laundering and the like were privatised – not only in the hope of a more peaceful globe, but as part of the downsizing of the defence and security sectors that followed the collapse of the Berlin Wall. Not dissimilar to Afghanistan, failed or collapsed states such as the DRC, Liberia and Somalia have become free-trade zones for the underworld, where the black market in arms and in diamonds, and also trafficking in human beings, passports, gold and narcotics, connects local players to the global underworld economy.

The legal and illegal, the formal and informal, are blurred in conditions of neo-patrimonialism. The more informal the nature of local political and economic transactions, the easier they can be used for 'other' activities – with the result that the distinction between licit and illicit, between legal and criminal, between corruption, business and politics is opaque. Deeply embedded in these informal and hidden networks are the networks that supplied LURD, UNITO in Angola, the RUF in Sierra Leone, the Mai Mai, Interahamwe, and others in the DRC, the Sudan People's Liberation Movement/Army (SPLM/A), the Sudan People's Defence Force (SPDF), and others fighting in southern and central Sudan.

In Western Uganda, the armed rebellion by the Allied Democratic Forces (ADF) would not have been possible without sympathetic government support and the ability to access arms and supplies. Nor would the LRA have been able to execute its campaign in northern Uganda and southern Sudan without the commodities for war (including food, fuel, arms, ammunition, training, proviant, tyres, clothing, medical supplies and the like), operating with impunity across borders, which are in any case unregulated and uncontrolled. The same mechanisms provide the means to exacerbate and intensify communal violence, such as that between local farming communities and nomadic Fulani herders in Mambilla plateau, north-eastern Nigeria, as well as the clashes between Kenyan Turkana herdsmen and Toposa cattle rustlers near the border with Sudan in north-west Kenya.

In their controversial study 'The criminalisation of the state in Africa', Bayart, Ellis and Hibou argued that 'politics in Africa is becoming markedly interconnected with crime'. Their prognosis for Africa is not optimistic:

> The multiplication of conflicts, the main political logic of which is simply predation and which tend to be accompanied by a growing insertion in the international economy of illegality, as in the case of Chad, Liberia and Sierra Leone, the spread of a culture of institutional neglect, systematic plunder of the national economy and the uncontrolled privatisation of the state (for example in former Zaïre, Kenya, Cameroon, Congo, Guinea, Togo, Central African Republic, São Tomé, Madagascar and Zambia) all suggest that a slide towards criminalisation throughout the sub-continent is a strong probability.

These linkages represent a global security problem. In a country where flight plans, customs, and immigration and passport control can easily be avoided, crime is difficult to combat – and subversive activity hard to detect. Thus, the terrorists that bungled an effort to down a commercial airliner with a SAM 7 surface-to-air missile in Mombassa earlier this year could smuggle their arms into Kenya with impunity.

These are trends that have long been noted but largely ignored by the leaders of the rich nations – until the events of 11 September 2001 brought into stark focus the threat the global backyard could have on the affluent suburbs of New York, London and Paris.

Poverty, security and neo-patrimonialism

According to some, the political behaviour of people in the majority of African countries is distinctly derived from the continent's material poverty. Where resources are scarce, as is the case across much of the continent, the object of political contestation is to secure economic consumption – which in turn is best guaranteed by capturing state power or replacing the state in a particular region, such as in the Kivu's in eastern DRC. Thus, politics easily degenerates a life-and-death struggle over private access to limited public resources. The zero-sum nature of the struggle compels would-be political leaders to obtain material benefits in order to wield influence over followers and competitors. Accordingly:

> What all African states share is a generalised system of patrimonialism and an acute degree of apparent disorder, as evidenced by a high level of governmental and administrative inefficiency, a lack of institutionalisation, a general disregard for the rules of the formal political and economic sectors, and a universal resort to personal(ised) and vertical solutions to societal problems.

Other analysts point to the essential continuity in Africa, from pre-colonial to colonial and post-colonial eras, and the recent trend towards retraditionalisation. Both schools of thought agree that contemporary African politics is best understood as the exercise of neo-patrimonial power.

As a consequence of systematic clientelism, the reliance on the award of personal favour in return for political support, and the use of state resources for this purpose, neo-patrimonial regimes demonstrate very little developmental capacity, and do not provide security. Accordingly:

> The real institutions of politics in Africa are the formal relations of loyalty and patronage established between 'big men' and their personal followers. The unwritten rules of neopatrimonial politics shape the decisions of leaders, engender compliance from citizens, and pervade the performance of bureaucratic organisations. Formally, the domination of political patrons and the subordination of their clients is expressed in the monopolistic political organisations of military oligarchies and civilian one-party states. The constitutional and electoral rules decreed by personalistic leaders, as well as the systems of party and civic organisations that they permitted, embody and express the constrained expectations of the African political game.

At the extreme level, some state and sub-state actors may have a vested interest in continued war and disorder, since it allows them additional opportunities to extract and conceal rewards and thereby serve the various patrimonial networks that provide their legitimacy. In the absence of any other viable means to sustain neo-patrimonialism, there is inevitably a tendency to link politics to realms of greater disorder, be it war or crime under conditions of resource constraints. Violence is necessary to secure or maintain a slice of the pie. In this manner, disorder becomes a necessary resource and opportunity for reward while there is little incentive to work for a more institutionalised ordering of society. The use of violence and terror is a logic consequence and necessary requirement with the built-in escalation dynamic of basic survival politics. Since resources decline and competition is increasingly fierce and violent, few have any choice but to side with larger groups – and protect their interests through force of arms.

Unrecognised by many is the extent to which the provision of development aid inadvertently supports the development of patronage politics, and undermines state capacity and sustainable development in Africa. Where a country, such as Malawi, receives the vast majority of its funds from donors, not through taxation of its citizens, accountability moves offshore. Since there is no incentive to build a functioning accountable state, based on mutual accountability between rulers and the ruled, it comes as little surprise that it does not happen.

Underpinning Africa's security crisis is, of course, the continent's severe developmental failure. Undeniably the common denominator of civil war and conflict in Africa is poverty, and much of that poverty the result of bad policy and poor governance. As economic and social conditions have steadily worsened, so insecurity and instability have increased – thus affecting the general populace. A dramatic reduction in agricultural output, upon which much of Africa is dependent, is but one factor that illustrates the failure of economics and politics in much of the continent. Manufacturing output has fallen, and balance of payment difficulties followed shortly thereafter. Almost all sub-Saharan countries have been confronted with an endemic financial and debt crisis – leading to external indebtedness and high debt-service ratios. Physical infrastructure has been crumbling and public services have broken down. Unemployment has escalated, while skilled professionals emigrate to seek a better life abroad. Private capital has been disinvesting and substantial amounts of private wealth transferred overseas. Although GDP is no accurate indicator of human development, the severity of the African crisis is reflected in the static levels of GDP per capita in Africa, compared to that of other regions in the world.

Africa's share of global trade in 1950 was seven per cent and, in 2002, it was two per cent. Africa's share of global capitol in 1950 was six per cent and, in 2002, it was one per cent. Left behind in international investment and globalisation, Africa's share of global foreign direct investment in the 1980s was 30 per cent and in 2002, it was 7 per cent – in spite of its oil and gas output. One export that Africa can ill afford is people. According to the Geneva-based International Organisation for Migration, Africa has been losing 20 000 doctors, university teachers and other professionals each year, since 1990. The continent is producing expertise it badly needs, at considerable cost, without getting the benefits.

While African countries have generally failed to diversify and attract investors, their terms of trade have worsened. Average output per head was lower at the end of the 1990s than it was 30 years earlier, when Africa was widely thought to be on the way to new prosperity.

Sub-Saharan Africa's disappointing performance is even worse when compared to that of other regions of the world over time. The Middle East and North Africa, and East Asia and the Pacific – both of which were poorer than Africa in the early 1960s – have long since surpassed continental indicators. South Asia, a region that was significantly poorer than Africa in the early 1960s, has now almost caught up, and will probably surpass Africa in the near future.

Recent years have seen a limited turn-around in previous trends – largely through improvements in macro-economic policy. The picture in 2004 is, therefore, necessarily a mixed one. Recently Omar Kabbah, president of the African Development Bank, categorised Africa in three groups. About 20 countries were raising average income significantly and tackling poverty; a similar number growing more slowly and failing to reduce the number living below the poverty line; and the remainder stagnating or falling back through bad government or war. Thus, half of Africa's population now live on less than US$1 per day, and the absolute number of Africans in this category has increased from 241 million in 1990 to 314 million in 1999 – reflecting the decline in the average African per capita income over this period. Yet the average rate of economic growth has accelerated since 1995, and some 16 African countries grew at more than four per cent a year over the last decade. Amidst these harsh circumstances, primary school enrolments have improved from a low of 56 per cent in 1991 to 59 per cent a decade later – admittedly far short of the millennium development goals set in 1990.

Broad statistics obscure more complex realities, for example: Gambia, with almost 60 per cent of its citizens in absolute poverty, is one among five countries in the world to reduce child mortality; while Senegal and Uganda have dramatically reduced HIV infection rates through education and prevention programmes. While overall levels of international aid per head has almost halved in real terms in the last decade (and stabilised at about 1990 levels), about US$7 billion per annum is flowing into Africa, as direct foreign investment. Nigeria alone will stand to benefit from an estimated US$110 billion, and Angola from US$40 billion, in oil income over the next six years. African countries that have taken advantage of the provisions of the African Growth and Opportunity Act (Agoa), notably Lesotho and Swaziland, have enjoyed an enormous increase in formal employment. Perhaps most significantly, tenuous democracy continues to hold in Nigeria (124 million people), a peace agreement is in place in the DRC (50 million people), while resource-rich Angola is preparing for elections and Sudan is on the verge of an agreement that will end Africa's longest running war.

...

The fragility of the African state is epitomised by the sudden disintegration of Cote d'Ivoire, until recently viewed as politically stable. The following extract illustrates the inequalities in Cote d'Ivoire that the state failed to address over time.

UNDP HUMAN DEVELOPMENT REPORT (2005)

Full report available at www.undp.org

...

Cote d'Ivoire – horizontal inequalities unravel the 'African miracle'

Ten years ago few people would have considered Côte d'Ivoire a candidate for fragile state status. The country appeared to have institutions and political structures capable of accommodating the interests of different groups and regions. Today, after several bouts of violent conflict, Côte d'Ivoire's political stability remains uncertain. What went wrong?

Côte d'Ivoire has five main ethnolinguistic communities. The Akan (42.1% of the population) and Krou (11%), concentrated in the south and west, are Christian. The Northern Mandé (16.5%) and Voltaic (17.6%) groups live largely in the north and are predominantly Muslim. The fifth group is the Southern Mandé (10%). The country also has a large population of foreign origin who came during the 1940s from the current Burkina Faso to work on coffee and cocoa plantations. Many of these migrants settled permanently in Côte d'Ivoire. In 1998 one quarter of the population was of foreign origin, though they were born in Côte d'Ivoire.

After independence in 1958 President Felix Houphouet-Boigny instituted a one-party state. But he carefully nurtured a balance among regions and ethnic groups through a system of quotas for government positions. He also enfranchised immigrants and eventually introduced a multiparty system. During the first 20 years after independence Côte d'Ivoire experienced political stability and sustained high growth – a rare achievement in West Africa.

This relative success started to unravel in the 1980s. Falling coffee and cocoa prices increased economic vulnerability, inequalities between the north and the south widened and tensions between locals and economic migrants in the southern regions increased. The 1990s witnessed the rise of Ivorian nationalism. 'Foreigners' were no longer allowed to vote, a move that excluded political leaders from the north from contesting elections. The ethnic group of whichever regime was in power came to be increasingly overrepresented in state institutions, including the military.

Social and economic inequalities widened, partly through economic pressures and partly as a result of the use of state power to support favoured groups and regions. By the end of the 1990s five of the six regions with the lowest primary school enrolment rates were in northern areas. As measured by the Socio-Economic Prosperity Index, the period 1994-98 saw the southern groups (Akan and Krou) improve their positions relative to the national average, especially the Baoulé tribe, while the Northern Mandé and Voltaic remained far below the national average. The Northern Mandé's position worsened from 1.19 times the national average in 1994 to 0.93 times the national average in 1998.

The rising inequalities interacted with simmering grievances linked to political exclusion and the perceived use of state power to favour certain groups and regions. A coup in December 1999 led to the establishment of a military-dominated government. While this government agreed to hold new elections, it also introduced constitutional changes that barred those whose nationality was 'in doubt' from holding political office. Disagreements over election results in October 2000 led to widespread protests and another change of government. The new government continued to favour southern groups, prompting an uprising in 2001 led by the northern-based Patriotic Movement of Côte d'Ivoire, which extended its control over half the country's territory.

Under strong encouragement from France and the Economic Community of West African States, the rival groups signed a peace agreement in January 2003. But implementation lagged, with deadlock over disarmament of rebels, eligibility criteria for presidential candidates and nationality laws. Political fighting has started up again in recent months, together with growing resentment against French peacekeeping troops. The current president recently announced that the opposition leader could contest elections later in the year, but core issues remain unresolved.

Côte d'Ivoire's descent into state fragility is a product of complex social, economic and political forces. However, the failure of the state to redress rising inequalities based on region and on group membership has been an important contributory factor. So has the failure of the state to ensure that it was perceived as reflecting a fair balance among different groups. The conclusion: Horizontal economic and political inequalities can destabilise states.

...

Adejumobi focuses on the question of citizenship and rights as a cause of conflict and civil war in Africa. The post-independent state, inherited from colonialism, was based on the institutionalisation of ethnic entitlements, rights and privileges, creating differentiated and unequal status.

ADEJUMOBI, S 'CITIZENSHIP, RIGHTS, AND THE PROBLEM OF CONFLICTS AND CIVIL WARS IN AFRICA' (2001)

23 *Human Rights Quarterly* 148

This article undertakes a reinterpretation of the problem of internal conflicts and civil wars in Africa, from the perspective of citizenship and rights. The central argument is that although the genealogy and dimensions of conflicts and civil wars in Africa are quite complex and varied; underlying most of these conflicts, especially those that erupted within the last decade, is the issue of citizenship and rights. The construction and nature of the state in Africa, which is rooted in the colonial pedigree, tend toward the institutionalisation of ethnic entitlements, rights, and privileges, which create differentiated and unequal status of citizenship. This tendency de-individualises citizenship and makes it more of a group phenomenon. Rather than the state providing a common bond for the people through the tie of citizenship, with equal rights, privileges, and obligations, both in precepts and practice, people's loyalties are bifurcated. The result is usually tension and contradictions in the public sphere as claims of marginalisation, exclusion, and domination among individuals and groups are rife. The consequence is mostly conflicts and civil wars in Africa.

...

Struggles for social inclusion and citizenship rights have been waged in different ways in different African countries. In some countries, they have taken the form of armed expression in which ethnic groups take up arms against each other or against the state in the quest to claim their 'rights' as citizens, as occurred in Rwanda and Burundi. In other cases, the struggle has taken a more inclusive dimension with the clamour and popular agitation for democratisation. Democratisation in Africa is a struggle by the people for civil, political, and social rights, which are the substantive social values embodied in citizenship.

The Rwandan experience serves as an empirical illustration of this problem. There are two reasons why the case of Rwanda is quite intriguing and lends itself to a curious enquiry on the problem of citizenship. First, Rwanda is a relatively compact country in terms of social composition, which ordinarily should make the evolution of a nation-state less arduous and inter-group relations less conflictual. Second, the level of human tragedy that has occurred in Rwanda from its inception as an independent state in 1962, peaking with the genocide of 1994, has been alarming. The Rwanda narrative depicts how colonial construction of group identity was factored into the structures and processes of the state system, a phenomenon that thwarted the logic of a common national identity and equal citizenship for the people of Rwanda. This virus continues to plague Rwanda into the present.

In social composition and identity, Rwanda is a fairly homogenous country. Its three ethnic categories – the Tutsi, the Hutu, and the Twa – share the same language, type of social organisation, and often the same lifestyles, and have lived together peacefully for centuries while sharing the same collective commitment to monarchical symbols. Colonialism radically transformed the social structures and identity formation of this society. It created rigid identity differentiation and sharp social distinction among those groups. The background to this was the colonial cultural mythology and historiography of the Rwandan people, which sought to reconstruct social reality and identity in Rwanda. Colonial historians and anthropologists were the precursor of this historical reconstruction. Using differences in physical traits, they claimed that the groups in Rwanda were of different historical origins. The Tutsi were classified as being of Hamitic origin, the Hutu as Bantu, and the Twa as pygmies. A logic of racial superiority was therefore injected into these scholars' analysis with the claim that the Tutsi were superior *homo sapiens* than others. This dubious historical reconstruction, as Gerald Prunier noted, became a kind of 'unquestioned scientific canon' which actually governed the decisions made by the Germans and even more later by the Belgian colonial authorities.

For the colonial regimes (both the Germans and the Belgians), the Tutsi were considered to be 'the white man in black skin in Rwanda'. As such, they were formally designated as the 'first class natives' to whom decentralised local power and resources were to be devolved. The Hutu, though more numerous, were conferred with the identity of second-class natives, with the Twa completely relegated to the background. This identity reconstruction by the colonial state underwent the three processes of social influence which Herbert Kelman identifies as being central to identity formation and consolidation. These are compliance, identification, and internalisation. All the social groups complied with the new identities, acquiesced to them (with an initial threat of force) and internalised them through a socialisation and generational cycle. In addition, those identities were codified with the colonial policy of separate identity cards for the groups.

The colonial ideology of racial or group superiority among the native population had both normative and social consequences. In the former regard, the Tutsi identity became the standard or optimal identity by which other forms of social identities were to be measured. Its signs, symbols, and meanings assumed the cultural base for the society. In the latter regard, Tutsi identity came to be synonymous with power, wealth, and influence. The Tutsi controlled the native authorities, were in charge of land in the localities, and were the major recipient of colonial education policy. For example, by 1959, forty-three out of the forty-five local chiefs and 549 out of 559 sub-chiefs in Rwanda were Tutsi.

The colonial state transformed what were flexible and complementary social categories into rigid ethnicities, engineered group identity competition through an inverse process of the domination of one group by another, and gradually undermined the basis of a common national identity and equal citizenship among the Rwandese.

However, as the politics of decolonisation unfolded, contradictions began to set in, in the colonial state policy on ethnicities. The Tutsi elites, armed with the weapon of Western education, were at the vanguard of the clamour for self-rule. The Belgian colonial authorities were apparently dissatisfied with the position of their ethnic clientele, the Tutsi, and therefore decided to shift support to the Hutu in state policy. This is not a new politics of power control by the colonial authorities. The tendency by colonial powers is to give political support to groups that are least susceptible to nationalist agitation. The same thing happened in Nigeria. In Rwanda, this resulted in the gradual displacement of the Tutsi from the control of the state machinery. Hutus swiftly replaced most of the Tutsi chiefs, and overt support was given to the Hutu political party.

The decolonisation era saw the emergence of ethnic based political parties in Rwanda. The major parties were the PARMEHUTU (Rwandan Democratic Party for the Movement and of Hutu Emancipation) and the UNAR (Rwandese National Union), which represented the Tutsi. By 1960, when local elections were organised, the Hutu emerged as the new local power elite in Rwanda. They won about 80 per cent of the seats and took control of the local state; 210 communes came under Hutu control, while the Tutsi had only nineteen. As the transfer of power gradually proceeded, the sphere of political control by the Hutu also expanded progressively. In September 1961, the legislative elections were held, with the Hutu party winning about 78 per cent and having thirty-five seats out of a total of forty-four. The process of constructing Hutu hegemony in the political process was capped with the ascendance to power of Gregoire Kayibanda, a Hutu, as president in 1962. Rwanda became independent in July 1962.

While the Belgian colonial authorities considered their apostasy on ethnic clientele in Rwanda as a 'grand revolution', the process generated intense inter-group conflicts in Rwanda. The declining identity group in the political process fought back with a weak capacity, while the ascending power, the Hutu, unleashed their pent-up aggression and psychological demeaning of the colonial period on the Tutsis. Between 1959 and 1962, no less than 130,000 Tutsis were driven into exile in the neighbouring countries of Tanzania, Uganda, Zaïre, and Burundi. Right from independence, the stage appeared set for intergroup conflagration in Rwanda.

From 1962 to 1994, when the pogrom occurred, an ethnic republic in all ramifications except name was instituted in Rwanda. Hutu nationalism took the centre stage in which the Hutu sought to make up for the historical gap of inadequate social identity and recognition of the Hutu ethnic group. The process involved the ethnic appropriation of the state and the establishment of a regime of social exclusion on citizenship rights. During this period, to be Hutu was to be a recognised as a Rwandan citizen, *de facto* and *de jure*, by the state. This qualified one to have access to state employment, military service, right of association, participation in state affairs, and security. A uni-ethnic military formation was established in Rwanda, which was a Hutu preserve. Uni-ethnic military formation is a system of institutionalised inequality based on group domination and control of the military. It has a potential destabilising effect on the state, as the excluded groups often have real and psychological fear of insecurity that usually prompts them to recruit, train, and organise their own 'unofficial armies'. However, the idea of a uni-ethnic army in Rwanda was not because of what Cynthia Enloe regarded as the penchant of authoritarian regimes to construct an 'ethnic security map', but fundamentally because a logic of state enthnicisation had been set in motion and institutionalised in Rwanda from the colonial era. The structure of power in post-colonial Rwanda is a janus-face of its colonial background.

Also, in the post-colonial era, the Hutu elite turned colonial cultural mythology of the Rwandan society on its head, with the argument that if the Tutsi were of a superior race, then they could not have been part of the original local population or the natives, thus they are at best 'foreigners' and should not be regarded as *bona fide* citizens of Rwanda. This is the intellectual platform on which the institutional discrimination against the Tutsi was justified. Gerald Prunier puts it quite poignantly:

> Tutsi were still 'foreign invaders' who had come from afar, but now this meant that they could not really be considered as citizens. Their government had been grandiose and powerful: In the new version of the Rwandese ideology, it had been a cruel and homogenously oppressive tyranny. The Hutu had been the 'native peasants', enslaved by the aristocratic invaders: They were now the only legitimate inhabitants of the country. Hutu were the silent demographic majority, which meant that a Hutu controlled government was now not only automatically legitimate but also ontologically democratic.

The Rwandan state under both the Kayibanda (1962–1973) and Habyarimana (1973–1994) regimes mirrored its colonial ancestry. The state was the enforcer of exclusive group rights and privileges and provided the institutional context and legitimacy for the discrimination and domination of one group by another. Citizenship was not defined on an individual or common national basis, but from a group dimension. The ethnic identity card policy, which the colonial state instituted, was retained. (It was later to serve as the basis of easy identification of the target group during the human pogrom of 1994.) A perverse policy of 'quota democracy' or 'majoritarian rule' was enforced by the state, which reserved 80 per cent of all public goods to the Hutus. This policy was the flip side of the colonial one which emphasised the rule or governance by the 'superior specie' or 'qualitative rule'. Group identity and social stratification were fused into the state system.

The phenomenon of group exceptionalism or exclusivity became bizarre when Hutu extremists took control of the state or began to exercise overwhelming influence on it. The Hutu irredentists insisted that the Tutsi were not Rwandese and must be forced out of the country. In 1992, a journalist, Hassan Ngeze, published a political catechism known as the Ten Commandments, which was to serve as the Manifesto of the Hutu nationality. Those commandments include:

(i) Every Hutu should know that a Tutsi woman, wherever she is, works for the interest of her ethnic group. As a result, we shall consider a traitor any Hutu who: marries a Tutsi woman, befriends a Tutsi woman or employs a Tutsi woman as a secretary or concubine.

(ii) Every Hutu should know that our Hutu daughters are more suitable and conscientious in their race as women, wife and mother of the family.

(iii) Hutu women be vigilant and try to bring your husbands, brothers and sons back to reason.

(iv) Every Hutu should know that every Tutsi is dishonest in business. His only aim is the supremacy of his ethnic group. As such, any Hutu who does the following is a traitor: makes partnership with a Tutsi in business, invests his money or Government's money in Tutsi enterprise, lends or borrows money from a Tutsi or gives favours to a Tutsi in business.

(v) All strategic positions, political, administrative, economic, military, and security should be entrusted to Hutu.

(vi) The education sector (school, pupils, students, teachers) must be majority Hutu.

(vii) The Rwanda armed forces should be exclusively Hutu. No member of the military should marry a Tutsi.

(viii) The Hutu should stop having mercy on the Tutsi.

(ix) The Hutu, wherever they are must have unity and solidarity and be concerned with the fate of their Hutu brothers.

(x) The social revolution of 1959, the referendum of 1961, and the Hutu ideology must be taught to every Hutu. Every Hutu must spread this ideology widely. Any Hutu who persecutes his brother Hutu for having read, spread, or taught this ideology is a traitor.

Group exclusion from citizenship rights, as Anthony Marx rightly observed, tends to define subordinate identity and usually provokes a struggle for inclusion by the dominated groups. In other words, 'citizenship thus creates the "social construct" of relevant identities, with "oppositional consciousness" forged in reaction to the frame of domination'. The Tutsi who have largely become immigrants in neighbouring countries, persecuted at home and vilified abroad by their hosts, were compelled to countermobilise for political action. They realised that a 'stateless' individual or group has few rights or claims in a state-driven international system. Between 1980 and 1990, the Tutsi immigrants formed various movements and links abroad, with a view to sharpening their focus and organisation for effecting political change in Rwanda. The result of this was the birth of the Rwandan Peoples Front (RPF) in 1990, which waged a ceaseless war against the Habyarimana regime and seized political power in 1994. In the context of the war, no less than 800 000 hapless civilian Tutsis were murdered, in what is today referred to as the Rwandan genocide.

How is the Rwandan tragedy to be problematised? In my conception, what happened in Rwanda transcends the issue of elite manipulation of ethnicity. It is also not simply a case of shared material deprivation. It is a destructive phenomenon of social identity competition grounded in historical trappings of the construction of citizenship and rights in Rwanda. Rights and citizenship have been largely defined and institutionalised as a group affair, which are synthesised into the cultural and historical processes of the Rwandan society as reconstructed and legitimised by the colonial state. Citizenship in its normative and instrumentalist dimensions, both in the colonial and post-colonial era, as I have shown in the above narrative, was not a 'universal' and common public good in Rwanda. It was exclusionary and bifurcated. This is the basis of the intractable political conflicts and civil war which enveloped Rwanda.

Engendering peace, security, and stability in Africa are tasks which must be accomplished by Africans if the quest for development is ever to gain meaning and take firm roof on the continent. Clearly, war and debilitating conflicts are antithetical to development. Negotiating peace and stability will require reconceptualising citizenship from a group to a national or 'universal' perspective and re-individualising it. Citizenship is destructive of the social and political processes of a political community when conceived in group terms. It undermines national identity and attenuates the loyalty and commitment of the citizen to the state.

Putting things back together in Africa will require policy changes in two major areas. First is to begin to take liberal democracy very seriously. It is a means through which some of the values embodied in citizenship can be realised. Liberal democratic norms like elections, political participation, the rule of law, and the rights of association and expression, could provide the base for the expression of citizenship in its substantive form. However, this should be an all-inclusive process in which all state structures and institutions are to be democratised. This process should transcend the rural urban and the central-local state dichotomies. In other words, there should be the evolution of what Elizabeth Jelin described as a new 'culture of citizenship 'from below'', intertwined with formal institutional changes and the expansion of democratic practices and norms.

Second is to tackle the normative dimension of citizenship, which the liberal democratic project cannot guarantee. Who qualifies to be a citizen, and who does not, even in the juridical sense? How is national identity to be forged over and above sub-national or group identities? How is the state to be the primary and terminal point of citizens' loyalty and commitment? These are issues, which, though related to it, transcend the liberal democratic project. These questions have a bearing on how the state is constituted and how the direction of state policy ensures that the state affects the life-chances of the citizens in a just and equitable manner, such that subordinate identities do not contest the legitimacy or relevance of the state in the society.

Renner looks at the role of natural resources in causing and particularly sustaining conflicts, as evidenced in Liberia and Sierra Leone. This phenomenon has generated a huge literature captured by the notion of 'greed and grievance'.

RENNER, M *THE ANATOMY OF RESOURCE WARS* (2002)

Worldwatch Paper No 162

Full text available at http://www.worldwatch.org

...

Diamonds played a central role in the conflict that devastated Sierra Leone during the 1990s. Ibrahim Kamara, Sierra Leone's UN ambassador, said in July 2000, 'We have always maintained that the conflict is not about ideology, tribal, or regional difference ... The root of the conflict is and remains diamonds, diamonds, and diamonds'.

Even prior to the 1990s, corruption, cronyism, and illegal mining had squandered the country's diamond riches, to the point where few government services were functioning and educational and economic opportunities were scarce. Sierra Leone became a 'model' shadow state. Pressure from international lenders for financial austerity and cuts in the government workforce only worsened the situation. The International Rescue Committee has reported that one-third of all babies in the diamond-rich Kenema District die before age one. UNDP ranked Sierra Leone last on its Human Development Index in 2001.

Throughout the 1990s, Sierra Leone suffered from rebellion, banditry, coups and coup attempts, and seesawing battle fortunes. In March 1991, the Revolutionary United Front (RUF) invaded Sierra Leone from Liberia and seized control of the Kono diamond fields. The RUF had strong backing from

Liberian warlord Charles Taylor. The ranks of the RUF contained disaffected young men from slum areas, illicit diamond miners, Liberian and Burkinabe mercenaries, and others who welcomed the opportunity for pillage and violence. But many others (including a large number of children) were forcibly recruited. Though the RUF professed to act on unresolved grievances, its principal aim was to gain control over the country's mineral wealth. Characterised by banditry and brutality, the rebellion claimed more than 75 000 lives, turned a half-million Sierra Leoneans into refugees, and displaced half of the country's 4.5 million people.

Faced with the RUF rebellion, the government expanded its armed forces from 3 000 to 14 000. This undisciplined, ineffective, ragtag army brought together ill-trained soldiers, militiamen from neighbouring Liberia, urban toughs, and street children involved in petty theft. Mary Kaldor of the University of Sussex comments about the latter that 'they were given an AK47 and a chance to engage in theft on a larger scale'. Government soldiers often supplemented their meagre pay through looting and illegal mining.

Rebel forces and parts of the government army actually collabourated at times. Government soldiers by day sometimes became rebels by night. This co-operation between supposed adversaries culminated in May 1997 when disgruntled government soldiers staged a coup against a government that had been elected just a few months earlier, and invited the RUF to join the new junta.

Sierra Leone is a comparatively small diamond producer, but a large share of its gemstones are of very high quality and therefore sought after. The RUF purchased arms and sustained itself through its control of the diamond fields, but diamond wealth has also been a constant source of internal friction. At first, RUF fighters did the mining, but later the group relied more on forced labour, including that of children. The group's annual income has been estimated at $25 to $125 million. RUF diamonds have entered the world market disguised as Liberian, Guinean, and Gambian gemstones.

A UN investigative panel reported conclusive evidence in December 2000 that Burkina Faso is a key conduit in facilitating small arms shipments to Liberia and the RUF. In addition, arms have been transferred through Senegal, Gambia, and Guinea. And Côte d'Ivoire has directly assisted the RUF. Weapons originated primarily in Libya, Ukraine, Slovakia, and Bulgaria, and sometimes were shipped with the help of Western air cargo companies.

Charles Taylor's Liberia has played a pivotal role. The UN panel reported that it had found 'unequivocal and overwhelming evidence that Liberia has been actively supporting the RUF at all levels, in providing training, weapons and related material, logistical support, a staging ground for attacks and a safe haven for retreat and recuperation, and for public relations activities'. Under Taylor, Liberia became a major centre for diamond smuggling, arms and drug trafficking, and money laundering. The country exported diamonds to Belgium far in excess of the quantity and quality available in Liberia, with gems originating from illicit sources in Sierra Leone and elsewhere.

To the degree that international sanctions succeeded in clamping down on the trade in conflict diamonds, the importance of timber rose in Taylor's calculus. The warlord-turned president managed to claim Liberia's natural resources as his private domain. Close Taylor associates received the largest concessions in Liberia's forest-rich southeast, where 10 companies control more than 85 per cent of the country's total timber production. Liberian timber has been sold primarily in China, but also in France and Italy and to a lesser extent in Spain and the Netherlands. Global Witness estimated that the timber trade was worth at least $100 million in 2000. Only $7 million went to government coffers, even as civil servants went unpaid and the only university remained closed for lack of funds. Most of the money instead went directly to Taylor, into patronage payments, to Taylor-connected paramilitary units that terrorise the population, and to pay for arms purchases.

At least seven of the logging concessionaires have been involved in procuring arms for the RUF and importing weapons into Liberia in defiance of a UN embargo. One of the concessionaires is Exotic Tropical Timber Enterprise, run by Ukrainian arms and diamond dealer Leonid Minin, who was arrested in Italy in July 2001 for gun-running. But the key player appears to be the Oriental Timber Company (OTC). Controlling 40 to 50 per cent of Liberia's forests and its timber production, the company has been implicated in smuggling weapons to the RUF along its timber roads. OTC has not only engaged in rapacious clear-cutting methods, it has also bulldozed homes and entire villages with little warning and no compensation. Meanwhile, social and economic benefits from logging for local communities are close to non-existent. Unemployment is rampant, poverty widespread, and general living conditions desperate. The city of Buchanan, a provincial capital and OTC's base, has no electricity and its sole hospital lacks running water.

Liberia and Charles Taylor are now coming full circle. Having caused havoc in Sierra Leone, his regime is now falling victim to similar dynamics. In April 1999, anti-government rebels crossed into Liberia from Guinea. The insurgency grew, recruiting fighters from Liberia, Guinea, Sierra Leone, Côte d'Ivoire, and Ghana, and combined with other groups into Liberians United for Reconciliation and Democracy (LURD) in February 2000. Fighting flared up in late 2001, and as in Sierra Leone, the victims are mainly civilians. To weaken the Taylor regime, the rebels are not only destroying timber company equipment, but also attacking or occupying many diamond mining districts, and appear to have smuggled diamonds out via Guinea, Gambia, and Sierra Leone. The loss of revenue is making it more difficult for Taylor to pay his military and there is evidence that Liberian army units have been encouraged to plunder certain areas to supplement government payments.

In June 2002, a report by UN Secretary-General Kofi Annan warned of the risk that Liberia and Sierra Leone could be trapped in a vicious cycle, with civil war swinging back and forth between the two countries. With fighting in Liberia escalating, refugee movements and incursions by armed groups from Liberia into Sierra Leone could destabilise the latter country just as it struggles to emerge from a decade of devastation.

...

Building on the notion of 'greed and grievance', Menkhaus dismisses the idea of the 'new peace' in Africa and argues that the nature of conflict has been changed by protagonists using it as an extractive enterprise. Wars are no longer being fought to win; rather they are a means of sustaining pillaging, trade monopolies, labour extraction, land expropriation, and the diversion of relief aid.

MENKHAUS, K 'A "SUDDEN OUTBREAK OF TRANQUILITY": ASSESSING THE NEW PEACE IN AFRICA' (2004)

28 *Fletcher Forum of World Affairs* 73

...

Though each crisis is distinct, most of Africa's post-Cold War conflicts possess a bundle of common features that defy the logic and assumptions of those who mediate them and those who claim that the wars will only end when one side wins. Specifically, most of Africa's contemporary conflicts have had a political economy dimension that until recently was poorly understood. The political economy interpretation of the 'news wars' in Africa can be summed up as follows. Though these conflicts may have initially been fuelled by grievances and defined by conventional military objectives, over time they have mutated partially or principally into wars waged not to win, but rather to create conditions of 'durable disorder' from which key actors benefit economically or politically. Far from being senseless or irrational, these wars have been perpetuated by conflict constituencies with vested interests in maintaining certain levels of armed violence and in blocking efforts to promote reconciliation and effective government. These spoilers or veto coalitions may be relatively small in number and not at all representative of the wishes of the majority of the population, but are well-positioned to block efforts to end hostilities and re-establish rule of law. This explains the otherwise puzzling phenomenon of protracted conflicts in Africa, which, on the surface, appear 'ripe' for resolution either via victory or negotiated settlement, but which continue for years. Economic interests feature prominently in these conflicts and can transform war into 'an instrument of enterprise' via pillaging, protection money, trade monopolies, labour exploitation, land expropriation, and diversion of relief aid. Fortunes made by warlords – and in the case of the DRC, several neighbouring states – in this 'noxious cocktail of commerce and violence' are generated mainly by the leaders' capacity to monopolise both legal and illicit trade of valuable primary products into the global market, colluding with international firms. Because armed conflict produces profitable war economies for both government army officers and rebels, collusion between combatants is commonplace.

War in this context is virtually unrecognisable in the conventional (modern) sense. Parties to conflicts do not fight to win; direct armed clashes are avoided, minimised, or simulated; strategic towns are not taken; and armed violence is mainly directed at unarmed civilians, who constitute the vast majority of casualties. Looting of civilians is the primary form of payment for both soldiers and rebels, leading to what in Sierra Leone was called Operation Pay Yourself and producing the phenomenon of 'sobels' – soldiers by day and rebels or bandits by night. Militias often replenish their ranks by kidnapping young boys from villages and forcing them to commit atrocities, leading to an epidemic of child soldiering in Liberia, Sierra Leone, Angola, and northern

Uganda. Militias in both government and rebel forces operate virtually independent of a command structure, pursuing their own interests locally, frequently switching sides, and fighting against one another. This multiplies the number of non-state actors on the scene, few of which have knowledge of or interest in the Geneva Conventions and humanitarian law. Finally, humanitarian crises are in some cases transformed from being a tragic consequence of the fighting to an integral part of the war economy. Humanitarian crises are opportunities for enrichment by warlords and their supporters; famine can be provoked and/or exploited by parties to the conflict, as was seen in the 1991-1992 famine in Somalia and in the current crisis in Darfur, Sudan. Relief aid is a prized commodity over which warring parties and militias fight; camps of internally displaced persons are controlled and used as bait to attract international relief; and small fortunes are made via contracts for transportation, money changing, security, and other services provided to international aid organisations.

This interpretation of Africa's new wars has increasingly made its way into mainstream analysis. Its attractiveness lies in the fact that it has been able to provide a compelling explanation for the most puzzling aspects of Africa's civil wars – why they have been so protracted in nature, and why they are so impervious to external mediation and peacekeeping. A recent World Bank study on civil wars finds the political economy explanation persuasive:

> The expected duration of conflict is now double that of conflicts that started prior to 1980. One possible explanation is that sustaining a conflict is now easier than it used to be ... Another possibility is that rebellions have gradually changed their character, becoming less political and more commercial. Violence entrepreneurs, whether primarily political or primarily economic, may gain from war to such an extent that they cannot credibly be compensated sufficiently to accept peace ... Asking a rebel leader to accept peace may be a little like asking a champion swimmer to empty the pool.

The explanation is also attractive for its capacity to move us past the presumption of irrationality or 'Mad Max anarchy', which informs so many analyses of Africa's wars. Indeed, this rethink of the nature of contemporary civil wars turns the table on Western-centric notions of what constitutes rational behaviour in wartime. As David Keen observes:

> If contemporary civil wars have been widely labelled as mindless, mad, and senseless, in some ways nineteenth and twentieth century Western notions of war may be closer to madness. When war is seen as an occasion for risking death in the name of the nation-state and with little prospect of financial gain, it may take months of brainwashing and ritual humiliation to convince new recruits of the notion. A war where one avoids battle, picks on unarmed civilians, and makes money may make more sense.

Finally, this explanation has the added merit of focusing our attention on the interests of nonstate actors as key drivers of the conflicts. Interest-based analysis both goes some way toward explaining why the conflicts persist and provides clues as to when and under what conditions the wars are likely to end. By highlighting the interests perpetuating conflicts and by tracking changes in these interests over time, a political economy analysis of Africa's wars has the potential to identify opportunities for external strategies to shape those interests to promote peace.

The problem for analysts is that the very theory that appears best able to deliver a reasonably persuasive, parsimonious, and cross-national explanation for why Africa's wars persist is less well-equipped to provide a compelling explanation for why many of these wars suddenly appear to be ending. One possibility is that the wars are in fact not ending; what we are now witnessing could merely be a lull. The underlying interests driving these crises remain in place, according to this view, and will soon reignite the wars. A more hopeful political economy interpretation is that the interests of a number of key war entrepreneurs have changed over time. As they accumulate fortunes from war and plunder, they come to possess a greater appreciation of the benefits of rule of law and wish to protect their new wealth in a way that allows them to shift into quasi-legitimate business and political activities. This notion of warlords mutating into landlords is an intriguing possibility, and draws on an impressive body of historical research about state formation in Europe and elsewhere. A third interpretation is that the war entrepreneurs are simply adapting to new circumstances – mainly changes in the international environment – which are placing penalties on those who openly wage war. In this case, we could be witnessing a shift in tactics as warlords seek to create the appearance of peace, reconciliation, and governance, even to the point of accepting positions in a government of national unity, while quietly working to ensure that underlying conditions of lawlessness and violence continue to provide them with opportunities to engage in illicit war economies – what William Reno calls a 'shadow state'. Charles Taylor's behaviour, when he switched hats from warlord to president in Liberia but continued to foment violence and predation, is one piece of evidence to support this interpretation.

...

3

MECHANISMS FOR REALISING HUMAN RIGHTS AT THE DOMESTIC LEVEL

Human rights can be protected through law on the domestic (or 'national' or 'local') level, or on the international (which can be either 'global' or 'regional') level. In addition to the legal protection of human rights, the role of civil society in the protection of human rights has to be recognised. Here we look at the domestic mechanisms that law offers for human rights protection.

CONSTITUTIONAL PROTECTION

An-Na'im comments on the role of the state with regard to the realisation of human rights norms.

AN-NA'IM, A 'POSSIBILITIES AND CONSTRAINTS OF THE LEGAL PROTECTION OF HUMAN RIGHTS UNDER THE CONSTITUTIONS OF AFRICAN COUNTRIES' (1999)

in An-Na'im, A (ed) *Universal rights, local remedies: Implementing human rights in the legal systems of Africa* London: Interights; Afronet and GTZ

...

The basic concept of human rights as claims to which all people are entitled as of right by virtue of their humanity firmly locates these rights and their implementation in the social and political realm of human affairs. Whatever these rights are, their implementation will necessarily require collective and sustained efforts that require the allocation of resources over extended periods of time. The realisation of human rights also presupposes the existence of an authority that can mediate among rights in case of conflict and adjudicate the competing demands of claimants of rights. Therefore, the basic concept of human rights can only be realised through some form of wide-scale political organisation that is capable and willing to undertake these functions. The state is the form of political organisation that is universally established today, indeed assumed by the present system of international human rights. This reality not only involves the apparent paradox of expecting the state to vindicate human rights against its own organs and officials, but also to be able to act affirmatively in the implementation of these rights.

...

The following excerpts illustrate different approaches to human rights in national constitutions. In Ghana human rights are justiciable; that is, a person who alleges a violation of his or her constitutional rights can approach the courts to obtain a remedy for the violation. In Cameroon human rights are only included as guiding principles in the preamble of the Constitution.

CONSTITUTION OF THE REPUBLIC OF GHANA (1992)

Chapter five: Fundamental human rights and freedoms

12(1) The fundamental human rights and freedoms enshrined in this chapter shall be respected and upheld by the Executive, Legislature and Judiciary and all other organs of government and its agencies and, where applicable to them, by all natural and legal persons in Ghana, and shall be enforceable by the Courts as provided for in this Constitution ...
13(1) No person shall be deprived of his life intentionally except in the exercise of the execution of a sentence of a court in respect of a criminal offence under the laws of Ghana of which he has been convicted.
(2) A person shall not be held to have deprived another person of his life in contravention of clause (1) of this article if that other person dies as the result of a lawful act of war or if that other person dies as the result of the use of force to such an extent as is reasonably justifiable in the particular circumstances; (a) for the defence of any person from violence or for the defence of property; or (b) in order to effect a lawful arrest or to prevent the escape of a person lawfully detained; or (c) for the purposes of suppressing a riot, insurrection or mutiny; or (d) in order to prevent the commission of a crime by that person.
14(1) Every person shall be entitled to his personal liberty ...
15(1) The dignity of all persons shall be inviolable.
(2) No person shall, whether or not he is arrested, restricted or retained, be subjected to; (a) torture or other cruel, inhuman or degrading treatment or punishment; ...
16(1) No person shall be held in slavery or servitude.
(2) No person shall be required to perform forced labour ...
17(1) All persons shall be equal before the law.
(2) A person shall not be discriminated against on grounds of gender, race, colour, ethnic origin, religion, creed or social or economic status ...
18(1) Every person has the right to own property either alone or in association with others.
(2) No person shall be subjected to interference with the privacy of his home, property, correspondence or communication except in accordance with law and as may be necessary in a free and democratic society for public safety or the economic well-being of the country, for the protection of health or morals, for the prevention of disorder or crime or for the protection of the rights or freedoms of others.
19(1) A person charged with a criminal offence shall be given a fair hearing within a reasonable time by a court ...
21(1) All persons shall have the right to; (a) freedom of speech and expression, which shall include freedom of the press and other media; (b) freedom of thought, conscience and belief, which shall include academic

freedom; (c) freedom to practice any religion and to manifest such practice; (d) freedom of assembly including freedom to take part in processions and demonstrations; (e) freedom of association, which shall include freedom to form or join trade unions or other associations, national or international, for the protection of their interest; (f) information, subject to such qualifications and laws as are necessary in a democratic society; (g) freedom of movement which means the right to move freely in Ghana, the right to leave and to enter Ghana and immunity from expulsion from Ghana.

22(1) A spouse shall not be deprived of a reasonable provision out of the estate of a spouse whether or not the spouse died having made a will ...

24(1) Every person has the right to work under satisfactory, safe and healthy conditions, and shall receive equal pay for equal work without distinction of any kind ...

25(1) All persons shall have the right to equal educational opportunities and facilities and with a view to achieving the full realisation of that right; (a) basic education shall be free, compulsory and available to all; ...

26(1) Every person is entitled to enjoy, practice, profess, maintain and promote any culture, language, tradition or religion subject to the provisions of this Constitution.

(2) All customary practices which dehumanise or are injurious to the physical and mental well being of a person are prohibited.

27(1) Special care shall be accorded to mothers during a reasonable period before and after childbirth; and during those periods, working mothers shall be accorded paid leave.

(2) Facilities shall be provided for the care of children below school-going age to enable women, who have the traditional care for children, realise their full potential.

(3) Women shall be guaranteed equal rights to training and promotion without any impediments from any person ...

28(2) Every child has the right to be protected from engaging in work that constitutes a threat to his health, education or development ...

29(3) If the stay of a disabled person in a specialised establishment is indispensable, the environment and living conditions there shall be as close as possible to those of the normal life of a person of his age ...

33(1) Where a person alleges that a provision of this Constitution on the fundamental human rights and freedoms has been, or is being or is likely to be contravened in relation to him, then, without prejudice to any other action that is lawfully available, that person may apply to the High Court for redress.

CONSTITUTION OF THE REPUBLIC OF CAMEROON (1996)

Preamble

...

We, people of Cameroon,

Declare that the human person, without distinction as to race, religion, sex or belief, possesses inalienable and sacred rights;

Affirm our attachment to the fundamental freedoms enshrined in the Universal Declaration of Human Rights, the Charter of the United Nations and The African Charter on Human and Peoples' Rights, and all duly ratified international conventions relating thereto, in particular, to the following principles:

- all persons shall have equal rights and obligations. The State shall provide all its citizens with the conditions necessary for their development;
- the State shall ensure the protection of minorities and shall preserve the rights of indigenous populations in accordance with the law;
- freedom and security shall be guaranteed to each individual, subject to respect for the rights of others and the higher interests of the State;
- every person shall have the right to settle in any place and to move about freely, subject to the statutory provisions concerning public law and order, security and tranquillity;
- the home is inviolate. No search may be conducted except by virtue of the law;
- the privacy of all correspondence is inviolate. No interference may be allowed except by virtue of decisions emanating from the Judicial Power;
- no person may be compelled to do what the law does not prescribe;
- no person may be prosecuted, arrested or detained except in the cases and according to the manner determined by law;
- the law may not have retrospective effect. No person may be judged and punished, except by virtue of a law enacted and published before the offence committed;
- the law shall ensure the right of every person to a fair hearing before the courts;
- every accused person is presumed innocent until found guilty during a hearing conducted in strict compliance with the rights of defence;
- every person has a right to life, to physical and moral integrity and to humane treatment in all circumstances. Under no circumstances shall any person be subjected to torture, to cruel, inhumane or degrading treatment;
- no person shall be harassed on grounds of his origin, religious, philosophical or political opinions or beliefs, subject to respect for public policy;
- the State shall be secular. The neutrality and independence of the State in respect of all religions shall be guaranteed;
- freedom of religion and worship shall be guaranteed;
- the freedom of communication, of expression, of the press, of assembly, of association, and of trade unionism, as well as the right to strike shall be guaranteed under the conditions fixed by law;
- the Nation shall protect and promote the family which is the natural foundation of human society. It shall protect women, the young, the elderly and the disabled;
- the State shall guarantee the child's right to education. Primary education shall be compulsory. The organisation and supervision of education at all levels shall be the bounden duty of the State;
- ownership shall mean the right guaranteed to every person by law to use, enjoy and dispose of property. No person shall be deprived thereof,

save for public purposes and subject to the payment of compensation under conditions determined by law;

- the right of ownership may not be exercised in violation of the public interest or in such a way as to be prejudicial to the security, freedom, existence or property of other persons;
- every person shall have a right to a healthy environment. The protection of the environment shall be the duty of every citizen. The State shall ensure the protection and improvement of the environment;
- every person shall have the right and the obligation to work;
- every person shall share in the burden of public expenditure according to his financial resources;
- all citizens shall contribute to the defence of the Fatherland:
- the State shall guarantee all citizens of either sex the rights and freedoms set forth in the Preamble of the Constitution.

Udombana sets out the importance of the constitutional protection of human rights to ensure accountability of governments.

UDOMBANA, NJ 'INTERPRETING RIGHTS GLOBALLY: COURTS AND CONSTITUTIONAL RIGHTS IN EMERGING DEMOCRACIES' (2005)

5 *African Human Rights Law Journal* 47

...

Any approach to the protection of human rights in Africa must take the constitution as its point of departure because a constitution is the foundation of the legal system and a protocol of survival and continuity for any social group, ensuring that no one attains salvation or offers a programme of salvation to the populace by another route. It is a blueprint of intra-governmental relations, setting forth the general parameters of executive, legislative and judicial powers and embodying fundamental rights granted to individuals under the law. It provides both a framework of government for a society in a continual process of transition and a framework of fundamental principles of humanity and respect for human rights to control and guide the exercise of all governmental power. It provides a measure of rationality or consistency in decision-making, both in relation to the individual and society.

The constitutions of most emerging democracies in Africa begin by affirming faith in the universal values of justice, democracy, freedom, equality and the dignity of the human person. Of course, this does not mean that all constitutions share the same values, but each system shares most of them. Section 1 of the South African Constitution, for example, provides that the Republic of South Africa shall be founded, *inter alia*, on the values of human dignity, the achievement of equality, the advancement of human rights and freedoms, non-racialism and non-sexism, the supremacy of the Constitution and the rule of law. Similarly, the Preamble to the Constitution of Burundi affirms the country's:

> ... commitment to construct a political order and a system of government inspired by ... and founded on the values of justice, democracy, good governance, pluralism, respect of the freedoms and basic rights of the individual, unity, solidarity, mutual understanding, tolerance and co-operation between the different ethnic groups ...

Almost all of these constitutions contain lofty human rights provisions. While some constitutions guarantee primarily only civil and political rights, others guarantee economic, social and cultural rights as well. Civil and political rights underscore the fact that the nature and dignity of the human person have to be absolutely protected and indicate the inviolable, imprescriptible and inalienable rights to be promoted and protected by the state. Socio-economic rights have the aim of giving people the possibility of receiving help from the state, thus guaranteeing equality and social justice. Provisions guaranteeing civil and political rights typically begin with a solemn declaration concerning the principle of non-discrimination, that is, equality before the law and equal protection under the law.

...

Beyond equality and non-discrimination, most constitutions guarantee the right to life and personal integrity, the right to develop one's personality (physically, morally, socially and culturally), freedom from cruel and inhuman treatment and freedom from slavery or forced labour. These provisions usually precede a detailed or concise list of rights, such as the right to liberty and security of the person, freedom of domicile, the right to respect for a person's correspondence, freedom of movement and residence, freedom of expression and religion (except for Islamic countries where Islam is the state religion), freedom of assembly, demonstration and association, including the right to form or join a political party or a trade-union as well as political and citizens' rights.

However, certain rights that are often emphatically declared on the basis of universal principles only exist on paper, due to the legal constraints that they are dependent on, constraints which are either vague and indeterminate or, in contrast, extremely precise. Consequently, rights previously declared in such a solemn manner are deprived of any real meaning, a ready example being the fundamental right to life – often implicit in Western constitutions. Various constitutions in Africa – Equatorial Guinea, Ghana, Libya, Malawi, Nigeria, Seychelles and Uganda – contain provisions on the death penalty which directly or indirectly deny the right to life. The death penalty is permitted for numerous reasons: As a sanction or if the life of a person constitutes a danger to society or according to a law reasonably justified in a democratic society or to fulfil a death sentence imposed by a competent court of justice or confirmed by the highest court of appeal.

The second class of rights usually protected in national constitutions is social, economic and cultural rights. This is sometimes positioned under a special title in the part of the constitution concerning freedoms in general, as is the case in the Constitutions of Cape Verde, Madagascar, Mozambique and São Tomé and Principe. In others, they are arbitrarily placed with civil and political rights and sometimes they are positioned after them. Yet, in some African constitutions, such as that of Nigeria, these 'second generation' rights match the principles concerning policy or the fundamental directives of the state. Those social and economic rights that are protected in most constitutions include family and labour rights, the right to health and to a healthy environment, the right of ownership (individual or collective), economic freedom and cultural rights. Some systems provide for claims so as to eliminate sex discrimination deriving from historical customs and traditions and to guarantee equal political, social, economic and cultural rights, including labour rights and rights concerning personal matters. Such is the case with the Constitutions of Chad, Egypt, Ethiopia, The Gambia, Malawi, Namibia, South Africa and Uganda.

In the past, Africa's judiciary lacked institutional independence and financial autonomy, with judges holding their offices at the sufferance of the executive. Emerging constitutions contain formal commitments to the independence of courts. Almost all constitutions are cast in nearly the same mould, so that these guarantees are generally similar. But the difference in structure between federal and unitary states results in variations in procedures of judicial review and the organisation of the judiciary. These constitutions are characterised by the following main principles: Due process of law, legislative authority over the administrative structure of the judiciary, the obligation of the judiciary to uphold the constitution and the law and its immunity from dismissal and independence from the legislative and executive branches.

Some constitutions, such as those of Cape Verde and Ghana, contain specific clauses on the independence of the judiciary. Others, such as those of Benin, Central African Republic, Equatorial Guinea, Gabon, Mali and Togo, refer to judges and constitutional courts as 'the guardians of fundamental freedoms' and mandate them to enforce fundamental rights. Seventeen constitutions designate the judicial power as the 'guardian of human rights', including, randomly, Algeria, Burkina Faso, Burundi, Congo, Mali, Rwanda, Senegal and Togo. Other constitutions, such as those of South Africa and Uganda, confer a right of access to justice both on individuals and groups, thus mirroring the African Charter on Human and Peoples' Rights (African Charter). In some countries, like Benin, Central African Republic, Egypt and South Africa, the Constitutional Court is independent and autonomous; but in others, as in Burkina Faso and Nigeria, it is an appendage of the Supreme Court. The guarantees under the Bill of Rights are protected in some cases by enabling individuals to appeal to the Constitutional Court or the Supreme Court against laws or public acts or omissions believed to be detrimental to those rights. This is the case in Benin, Burundi, Cape Verde, Central African Republic, Congo, Djibouti, Liberia and Seychelles.

A number of countries, including Benin, Ghana, Mali, Namibia, Nigeria, South Africa and Uganda, have established other institutions to complement the judiciary, with the mandate to protect the public from abuses by government and quasi-government bureaucracies. These institutions, which are variously called Public Defender, Public Complaint Commission or simply Ombudsperson, are also given investigatory and prosecutorial powers and are expected to liaise with the judiciary and other appropriate national institutions. Other countries — like Ethiopia, Ghana, Nigeria, South Africa and Uganda — have established national human rights institutions with the mandate to promote and protect human rights and further the cause of social justice. Still others, such as South Africa, have gender commissions to promote, protect and uphold the fundamental tenets of gender equality.

It is not certain if the constitutionalisation of rights guarantees their respect in practice, but it provides, at least, an important mechanism for mainstreaming respect for the values that are associated with those rights, both in law and in policy making. It provides the basis for holding governments accountable and provides an instrument for political action and mass mobilisation. Meanwhile, the manner in which courts interpret these rights goes a long way to mainstreaming the values inherent in them.

An-Na'im discusses the limitations of human rights litigation before the courts as a strategy for improving the human rights situation in Africa.

AN-NA'IM, A 'THE LEGAL PROTECTION OF HUMAN RIGHTS IN AFRICA: HOW TO DO MORE WITH LESS' (2001)

in Sarat, A and Kearns, TR (eds) *Human rights: Concepts, contests, contingencies* Ann Arbor: University of Michigan Press

...

Recent studies of the legal protection of human rights in some fifteen African countries (representing a cross-section of cultures, colonial and postcolonial experiences, and legal systems) identified the following common problems:

Despite differences between the two systems, common law and continental civil law, followed in almost all African countries today, regimes suffer from similar problems of poor legitimacy and accessibility, as well as lack of human material resources. Neither common law nor civil law, both of which are foreign colonial legal systems, has gained public confidence as a means of protection.

Most current African constitutions provide for the protection of civil and political rights, including broad non-discrimination and equal protection clauses. Some constitutions, such as those of Ghana, Namibia, and Uganda, include economic, social and cultural rights as 'Directive Principles of State Policy'. There is also a good level of ratification of international treaties on human rights. But at this normative level, effective implementation is hampered by such factors as the lack of the incorporation of treaty obligations into domestic legislation, where it is required in common law jurisdiction; frequent and prolonged states of emergency; and claw back clauses permitting restriction on constitutional provisions by ordinary legislation.

At a practical level, the protection of human rights is seriously impeded by its reliance on judicial enforcement that is weak for civil and political rights and inappropriate for economic, social and cultural rights. Because of their conceptual complexity and procedural formality, both common and civil law are incomprehensible and financially inaccessible for the vast majority of African peoples. Moreover, state courts and law enforcement mechanisms are incapable of addressing massive violations of human rights that occur under customary and religious laws and practice at the local, rural level.

These difficulties are compounded by general structural and contextual factors, such as political instability, economic underdevelopment, and lack of independence for, and poor training of, the judiciary, as well as poor quality and unavailability of legal services. These features, in turn, lead to inadequacy of courtroom facilities, lack of essential material resources, and rampant corruption. In Nigeria, for example, litigants have to provide the stationery (writing materials and file folders) required for their cases and are routinely subjected to extortion by magistrates and court personnel. Since the vast majority of the two hundred legal practitioners in the whole of Mozambique are concentrated in the capital Maputo, the role of legal council in district courts is left to *ad hoc* 'public defenders' who have no legal training.

...

THE ROLE OF INTERNATIONAL HUMAN RIGHTS LAW IN DOMESTIC COURTS

Adjami discusses the role of international law in different legal orders in the context of a well-known human rights case from Botswana, Attorney-General v Dow.

ADJAMI, ME 'AFRICAN COURTS, INTERNATIONAL LAW AND COMPARATIVE CASE LAW: CHIMERA OR EMERGING HUMAN RIGHTS JURISPRUDENCE?' (2002)

24 *Michigan Journal of International Law* 103

...

Two alternative theories define the relationship between municipal law and international law. According to the monist theory, international law and municipal law comprise a single legal order within a national legal system, with international law superior to national law. In this system, national courts must give effect to principles of international law over superceding or conflicting rules of domestic law. Under the dualist theory, international law and municipal law form two separate and independent legal systems. International law prevails in regulating the relations between sovereign States in the international system, whereas municipal law takes precedence in governing national legal systems. According to the dualist theory, for a municipal legal system to give effect to international law, national legislatures must incorporate international law into domestic law, thereby creating justiciable rights suitable for enforcement by domestic courts.

...

Under article 1 of the [African] Charter [on Human and Peoples' Rights] parties must 'recognise the rights, duties and freedoms [of the] Charter and ... undertake to adopt legislative or other measures to give effect to them'. This creates a treaty obligation of domestic incorporation of the Charter for States Party. The failure to do so constitutes a breach of the Charter ... Of the dualist, African common law countries, only Nigeria has enacted implementing legislation to incorporate the African Charter of Human and Peoples' Rights into its municipal legal system.

Several African constitutions include specific provisions that define the role of international law in the municipal legal order. Although Namibia and Malawi have constitutions that have been described as 'international law friendly', South Africa is best known for its constitutional embrace of international law. The Interpretation Clauses of the South African Constitution mandate that courts take international law into consideration when interpreting the South African Bill of Rights, resulting in the emergence of a body of human rights jurisprudence that has gained international prominence.

...

It may seem as if African courts face insurmountable obstacles in developing a domestic human rights jurisprudence. Given the widespread non-incorporation of international human rights law into national legislation, the limitations on the status of international law in domestic courts, and the precarious cultural balance between indigenous African values and universal human rights norms, it is surprising that national courts in Africa have interpreted the fundamental rights enshrined in their postcolonial legal systems in light of international norms.

...

Judicial activism is not without its critics. The most common complaint is that the free license to stray from a national legal text leads to judicial arbitrariness. A particularly harsh critic of the new South African Constitutional Court's extensive use of international and comparative sources called this methodology 'rainbow jurisprudence', claiming that 'we have as much chance of finding genuine instruction about substantive reasoning in these wishy-washy pronouncements as we have of touching a rainbow'.

Proponents of judicial activism counter such criticism. First, as long as a judge's reasoning is transparent, that judge will be held accountable and will not act arbitrarily. Second, insofar as claims are raised under national constitutions, it is still within the judges' powers to look beyond the text to the values underlying the constitution ...

Not only do judges have an activist role in advancing human rights in Africa, so too do the lawyers in national legal systems. Lawyers determine when to raise claims under constitutional guarantees of fundamental rights and have the ability to draw international and comparative law parallels in their briefs and arguments before the courts. This encourages judges in the national court systems to take these sources into account in their adjudication ...

In [*Attorney-General v Dow*] the Attorney-General of Botswana appealed a decision of the High Court, which struck down provisions of the Citizenship Act challenged by petitioner Unity Dow as unconstitutionally discriminatory. Unity Dow, a citizen of Botswana had three children of an American father. Their first child, born out of wedlock, was entitled to Botswanan citizenship, yet the two born after their marriage, were denied citizenship under the Act, which confers citizenship in mixed marriages to children of Botswanan fathers only. Dow challenged the Act as violative of sections 3 and 14 of the Botswana Constitution.

The Court of Appeal, through Justice Amissah, framed its analysis of the case as a question of constitutional construction and nondiscrimination. First, Justice Amissah established that the court must adopt a liberal approach in construing the Constitution. He cited two Botswanan cases as precedent for this policy of constitutional interpretation, and stated that '[w]ith such pronouncements from our own court as a guide, we do not really need to seek outside support for the views we express. But just to show that we are not alone in the approach ... towards constitutional interpretation, I refer to ... dicta of judges from various jurisdictions'.

Next, Justice Amissah turned to an analysis of the substantive rights at issue, deciding to analyse the Citizenship Act in light of section 15, the Botswana Constitution's antidiscrimination provision. This provision does not explicitly guarantee freedom from discrimination based on sex. Nevertheless, Justice Amissah read section 15 in conjunction with section 3 to hold that the Constitution prohibits discrimination based on sex. In reaching this conclusion, he drew a parallel to the scope of the Fourteenth Amendment of the US Constitution, which has been read to cover discrimination despite the fact that the text refers to 'equal treatment' rather than discrimination.

...

As for the tension between custom and fundamental rights, Justice Amissah proclaimed: 'A constitutional guarantee cannot be overridden by custom. Of course, the custom will as far as possible be read so as to conform to the Constitution. But where this is impossible, it is custom, not the Constitution which must go'. In reaching this conclusion, Amissah also contended that the court's decision is bringing Botswanan law in compliance with his country's international obligations under the Universal Declaration and the African Charter.

...

INTERNATIONAL HUMAN RIGHTS LAW IN NIGERIA

While the French and, in general, the continental tradition is that international treaties, once ratified, become part of the law of the land (so-called 'monist' approach), in countries that follow the British or common law tradition they only become part of domestic law if they have been 'incorporated', that is, if the legislature has taken an explicit decision to that effect. Nigeria is the only common law country in Africa that has incorporated the African Charter into its national legislation.

SECTION 12(1) OF THE 1999 CONSTITUTION

No treaty between the Federation and any other country shall have the force of law except to the extent to which any such treaty has been enacted into law by the National Assembly.

SECTION 1 OF CAP 10

As from the commencement of this Act, the provisions of the African Charter on Human and Peoples' Rights which are set out in the Schedule to this Act shall, subject as thereunder provided, have force of law in Nigeria and shall be given full recognition and effect and be applied by all authorities and persons exercising legislative, executive or judicial powers in Nigeria.

In the following case the Supreme Court of Nigeria discusses the status of the African Charter in Nigerian law.

ABACHA AND OTHERS v FAWEHINMI

Supreme Court of Nigeria, 28 April 2000, per Ogundare JSC
(2001) African Human Rights Law Reports 172 (NgSC)

...

Where ... the treaty is enacted into law by the National Assembly, as was the case with the African Charter which is incorporated into our municipal (for example domestic) law by the African Charter on Human and Peoples' Rights (Ratification and Enforcement) Act Cap 10 Laws of the Federation of Nigeria 1990 (hereafter is referred to simply as Cap 10), it becomes binding and our courts must give effect to it like all other laws falling within the judicial powers of the courts. By Cap 10 the African Charter is now part of the laws of Nigeria and like all other laws the courts must uphold it. The Charter gives to citizens of member states of the Organisation of African Unity rights and obligations, which rights and obligations are to be enforced by our courts, if they must have any meaning. It is interesting to note that the rights and obligations contained in the Charter are not new to Nigeria as most of these rights and obligations are already enshrined in our Constitution. See Chapter IV of the 1979 and 1999 Constitutions.

No doubt Cap 10 is a statute with international flavour. Being so, therefore, I would think that if there is a conflict between it and another statute, its provision will prevail over those of that other statute for the reason that it is presumed that the legislature does not intend to breach an international obligation. To this extent I agree with their lordships of the Court below that the Charter possesses 'a greater vigour and strength' than any other domestic statute. But that is not to say that the Charter is superior to the Constitution. ...

THE ROLE OF THE JUDICIARY IN THE IMPLEMENTATION OF ECONOMIC AND SOCIAL RIGHTS

A small number of African constitutions provide that complaints over economic and social rights recognised in the Constitution can be adjudicated by the courts. The most prominent example is South Africa. After an introduction by An-Na'im, the provision in the South African Constitution dealing with the right to housing is set out, followed by an extract of a judgment of the South African Constitutional Court dealing with this right.

AN-NA'IM, A 'TO AFFIRM THE FULL HUMAN RIGHTS STANDING OF ECONOMIC, SOCIAL AND CULTURAL RIGHTS' (2004)

in Ghai, Y and Cottrell, J (eds) *Economic, social and cultural rights in practice: The role of judges in implementing economic, social and cultural rights* London: Interights

... [C]ertain fundamental entitlements are recognised as human rights precisely in order to protect them from the contingencies of the normal political and administrative processes of any country. While it is generally accepted that this function requires some degree or form of judicial enforcement for civil and political rights, there has so far been little effort to explore similar possibilities for Economic, Social and Cultural Rights (ESCR), except in India and South Africa. Moreover, it is sometimes claimed that judicial enforcement is neither appropriate nor feasible for ESCR, because their implementation requires allocation of resources among competing objectives of social policy, and other forms of affirmative action, that should be left to the discretion of politically accountable public officials. For example, it is said that the judges are unqualified by their training and requirements of political neutrality from, and within the judicial process render it inherently inappropriate for, evaluating and determining issues of social and economic policy raised by a right to housing or education. However, the fact that such objections are not raised against the judicial enforcement of civil and political rights which also involve vital questions of social policy, and risks of political controversy, indicates to me that the issue is more ideological or cultural than being inherent to ESCR as such.

...

CONSTITUTION OF SOUTH AFRICA, SECTION 26

(1) Everyone has the right to have access to adequate housing.

(2) The state must take reasonable legislative and other measures, within its available resources, to achieve the progressive realisation of this right.

(3) No one may be evicted from their home, or have their home demolished, without an order of court made after considering all the relevant circumstance. No legislation may permit arbitrary evictions.

THE GOVERNMENT OF THE REPUBLIC OF SOUTH AFRICA AND OTHERS v GROOTBOOM AND OTHERS (2000)

Constitutional Court of South Africa CCT 11/00

Full text available at http://www.constitutionalcourt.org.za/Archimages/2798.pdf

...

[42] The state is required to take reasonable legislative and other measures to achieve the progressive realization of the right of access to housing. Legislative measures by themselves are not likely to constitute constitutional compliance. Mere legislation is not enough. The state is obliged to act to achieve the intended result, and the legislative measures will invariably have to be supported by appropriate, well-directed policies and programmes implemented by the executive. These policies and programmes must be reasonable both in their conception and their implementation. The formulation of a programme is only the first stage in meeting the state's obligations. The programme must also be reasonably implemented. An otherwise reasonable programme that is not implemented reasonably will not constitute compliance with the state's obligations.

...

[45] ... The term 'progressive realisation' shows that it was contemplated that the right could not be realised immediately. But the goal of the Constitution is that the basic needs of all in our society be effectively met and the requirement of progressive realisation means that the state must take steps to achieve this goal. It means that accessibility should be progressively facilitated: Legal and administrative, operational and financial hurdles should be examined and, where possible, lowered over time. Housing must be made

more accessible not only to a larger number of people but also to a wider range of people as time progresses ...

The order:

[99] ... It is declared that:
Section 26(2) of the Constitution requires the state to devise and implement within its available resources a comprehensive and coordinated programme progressively to realise the right of access to adequate housing.
The programme must include reasonable measures, such as, but not necessarily limited to, those contemplated in the Accelerated Managed Land Settlement Programme, to provide relief for people who have no access to land, no roof over their heads, and who are living in intolerable conditions or crisis situations.

As at the date of the launch of this applications, the state housing programme in the area of the Cape Metropolitan Council fell short of compliance with the requirements in paragraph (b), in that it failed to make reasonable provision within its available resources for people in the Cape Metropolitan area with no access to land, no roof over their heads, and who were living in intolerable conditions or crisis situations.

Budlender here discusses the importance of socio-economic rights litigation, even if the situation for the complainant in a specific case might not always improve much as a result of the judgment.

BUDLENDER, G 'JUSTICIABILITY OF SOCIO-ECONOMIC RIGHTS: SOME SOUTH AFRICAN EXPERIENCES' (2004)

in Ghai, Y and Cottrell, J (eds) *Economic, social and cultural rights in practice: The role of judges in implementing economic, social and cultural rights* London: Interights

...

The impact of the *Grootboom* judgment has been varied. Government has started shifting its housing programme to have regard to the needs of people in intolerable conditions, or threatened with eviction – a process which has been accelerated by a highly publicised land invasion. When local councils seek to evict homeless people, they no longer obtain a court order for the asking – courts increasingly ask the councils what they are going to do to meet their *Grootboom* obligations in respect of the people concerned. But the *Grootboom* community, and many others are still living under highly unsatisfactory circumstances ... What *Grootboom* tells us is that the positive obligation to 'fulfil' the right to housing is justiciable even in resource constrained situations. A judgment may not always result in an order for provision of specific benefits to specific individuals, but even where this does

not happen, it can have results of a far-reaching and fundamentally important nature in the achievement of the right to housing.
...

THE ROLE OF NATIONAL HUMAN RIGHTS INSTITUTIONS

National human rights institutions – institutions created by the state with some independence to monitor the human rights situation in a particular country – have a role both in the promotion and the protection of human rights. In Africa there are more than 30 countries with such institutions. However, independence and effectiveness vary greatly among the national human rights institutions that have been established in Africa. Human Rights Watch has been very vocal about the role – and limitations – of these institutions.

HUMAN RIGHTS WATCH *PROTECTORS OR PRETENDERS? GOVERNMENT HUMAN RIGHTS COMMISSIONS IN AFRICA* (2001)

Full report available at http://www.hrw.org/reports/2001/africa/overview/conclusion.html

...
Throughout the 1990s, one African government after another set up its own national human rights commission. Increased UN and international donor support for the creation of human rights commissions by the mid-1990s served as a further impetus to African governments. In most countries it was part of some sort of political transition either to a new government or to promises of a more open political system following a history of repressive or authoritarian single party rule. While some of these transitions have brought real change, others have been incomplete. By the end of the 1990s, it was clear that many of these political transitions had stagnated and some governments were backsliding on their previously stated commitments.

In some countries, the creation of a human rights commission appears to be a genuine expression of the government's pledge to bring more transparency and government accountability, such as in Benin, Ghana, Malawi, Senegal, South Africa, and Uganda. Rwanda's human rights commission was established as part of the 1993 Arusha Peace Accord between the government of the time and the Rwandan Patriotic Front, which was then making war against it. In other countries, the creation of the commission seemed to be motivated more by a desire to deflect criticism of the government's recalcitrance to political liberalisation, that being the case in Cameroon, Chad, Kenya, Nigeria, Togo, and Zambia. This apparent hypocrisy was not restricted to governments being forced to concede to a multiparty system. Sudan's human rights body was set up in 1994 in the midst of severely repressive policies. Algeria and Tunisia formed commissions to offset criticism after crackdowns against Islamist-based political organisations. In the late 1990s, the post-war governments of

Liberia and Sierra Leone created human rights commissions after flawed peace accords that granted amnesty to their fighters, responsible for the killings and torture of thousands of civilians. The question which remains is: Can these institutions that are set up by governments with less than pure motives be transformed into independent and effective human rights bodies?
...
The development of state institutions to promote and protect human rights is a critical safeguard to ensure that people can obtain recourse and redress in the face of injustice. A dynamic and autonomous human rights commission can play a role in this process. For that reason, it is important that existing human rights commissions are encouraged to play an active and central role in the upholding of human rights. In some cases, where the political will is present, this task requires only training and funding opportunities. In other cases, greater pressure on a government is required for it to allow formal and actual independence of its human rights commission. Human rights commissioners also need to be supported and pushed by the international community to push the limit of their boundaries and to withstand the inevitable resistance from other government agencies. This is a process that can only be achieved with sustained national and international attention over a period of time.

The success by a human rights commission can only be measured through its actions. Some of the questions that need to be asked are:

Does it have the will and the means to perform the tasks given it by law?

Has it succeeded in gaining public as opposed to formal legitimacy?

What are the conditions for it to become an effective and trusted part of the human rights machinery?

How does it make itself accessible to the most vulnerable sections of society?

How far does its effectiveness derive from the bridges it is able to build with other institutions in society, governmental and non-governmental?

More importantly, are the individuals who serve within a human rights commission able to institutionalise their contribution in a lasting fashion or does a dynamic commission fade with the departure of the person heading it? Building an enduring human rights institution that will become an integral part of government is the greatest challenge for human rights commissioners and their proponents. That long-term contribution has yet to occur in Africa. In many cases it is still too soon. In other cases, it is clear that the human rights commission is falling short of achieving this goal. At this time, the independence and effectiveness of the human rights commissions within Africa depend heavily on the personality of the individuals heading the commission.

Another question that needs to be asked is whether the international community is playing as constructive a role as it can in contributing towards strong and sustainable national human rights institutions. It is a mistake to view the creation of a human rights commission, in and of itself, as a contribution towards human rights. The ability of a national human rights commission to function effectively is enhanced by independent judicial and legislative branches as well as a vocal civil society. A more nuanced approach by the international community is required. International support should be based on the records of the commissions, and weak or compliant institutions should be pushed to play a stronger role. A weak human rights commission that seeks to absolve or shield a government of its abuses through inaction may do more harm than its token or potential presence may justify. Additionally, international support for human rights commissions should be given as part of an integrated system of support for judicial independence and independent human rights NGOs.

Finally, it should be noted that a human rights commission is not a prerequisite for a government to uphold the human rights of its citizens. Other state institutions, such as an independent judiciary or a representative legislature, can equally provide oversight to ensure recourse and redress to human rights abuses. In fact, many countries with strong records of respect for human rights do not have such commissions. The creation of a national human rights commission can be an important mechanism for strengthening human rights protection, but it is not enough. It can never replace or diminish the safeguards inherent in an independent legal system and disciplined law enforcement forces.

The Ghanaian Commission on Human Rights and Administrative Justice (CHRAJ) is widely regarded as one of the more exemplary human rights institutions in Africa.

HUMAN RIGHTS WATCH *GHANA: WORKING WITH NGOs AND TRADITIONAL CHIEFS ON WOMEN'S RIGHTS* (2001)

Full report available at http://www.hrw.org/reports/2001/africa/overview/contributions.html

...

The Ghanaian Commission on Human Rights and Administrative Justice (CHRAJ) has proactively worked to address harmful traditional practices against women and girls. Not only is its work in this regard illustrative in its decision to address this frequently overlooked human rights abuse, but also because of its advocacy approach in working closely with both traditional authorities who wield a lot of power in local matters as well as local NGOs to seek solutions.

As elsewhere in Africa, some traditional practices still result in considerable discrimination against women and girls in Ghana. Although the Ghanaian Constitution and 1997 amendments to the 1960 Penal Code outlaw discrimination and slavery, harmful traditional practices continue largely because of deeply entrenched community beliefs that are unlikely to be eliminated by legislative prohibitions alone. This is precisely why attention to such an issue by a state body, which can conduct sustained education and advocacy work, is valuable.

In 1995, the commission undertook a joint project with a local NGO for the abolition of the practice of *Trokosi*. *Trokosi*, a traditional practice found among the Ewe ethnic group primarily in the Volta region, is a violation of children's and women's rights. It is a system in which a young girl, usually under the age of ten, is made a slave to a fetish shrine for offenses allegedly committed by a member of the girl's family. The belief is that if someone in that family has committed a crime, such as stealing, members of the family may begin to die in large numbers unless a young virgin girl is given to the local fetish shrine to atone for the offense. Most *Trokosi* girls and women are condemned to a lifetime of hard labour, sexual servitude, and perpetual childbearing at the service of the village priest. There are an estimated 3 500 girls and women bound to various shrines in the *Trokosi* system, a figure that does not include the slaves' children. Even if released, generally without skills or hope of marriage, a *Trokosi* woman often has continued obligations to the shrine for the duration of her life. In some cases when the fetish slave dies, the family is expected to replace her with another young girl for the fetish shrine. Some women in the shrines today represent the fifth successive generation to pay for a crime.

Over the past few years, the CHRAJ has conducted an awareness campaign with traditional leaders and practitioners in an effort to bring the practice to an end. Since 1997, a new law passed by Parliament bans the practice of 'customary servitude'. The CHRAJ's educational and advocacy efforts, taken in conjunction with International Needs Ghana, a local NGO, to approach village authorities and fetish priests have been effective. The work of the CHRAJ and other non-governmental organisations has resulted in the release of approximately 1 200 slaves by the end of 1998, many of whom were given counselling and retrained for new professions.

Another traditional abuse that occurs in Ghana is the practice of banishment and forced labour by traditional village authorities of predominantly rural elder women for suspected witchcraft. Hundreds of women accused of witchcraft were sent to penal villages in the northern region by traditional authorities. According to reports, two villages contained 400 elderly women and one village contained 2 000 women and family members, all sentenced by a village male or chief who claimed to have the power to divine witches. Although the women face no formal legal sanction if they leave, most fear that they would be beaten to death if caught. The CHRAJ issued a report on its investigations of a 'witches' camp in northern region. The report detailed the living conditions of the women in the camps and proposed ways to reintegrate them into society, through an educational campaign in conjunction with the Centre for National Culture and the House of Chiefs. The CHRAJ and human rights NGOs have mounted a campaign not only to persuade custodians of the 'witches'' homes to abolish the practice, but also to educate communities to allow the women to return safely to their homes.

The CHRAJ's willingness to work closely with the NGO community as an ally and its approach in fostering a constructive dialogue with traditional leaders, a constituency often overlooked by human rights activists, are both approaches that should be lauded. Through its efforts the CHRAJ has built awareness of human rights standards among chiefs and other traditional authorities, sent a message that a government body will not condone traditional practices that violate constitutional and international law, has legitimised and strengthened local NGO efforts on this issue, and has fostered a constructive working relationship with the NGO movement.

THE ROLE OF CIVIL SOCIETY

While acknowledging some of the limitations set out by other authors, Welch paints a more positive picture of the possible impact of NGOs on the realisation of human rights in Africa.

WELCH, CE 'THE NGO REVOLUTION' (1995)

in Welch, CE *Protecting human rights in Africa: Roles and strategies of non-governmental organisations* Pennsylvania: University of Pennsylvania Press

...

Millions of refugees and displaced persons eke out wretched lives in squalid camps. African women continue to labour longer and with far less reward than African men. Rural development of the Tostan sort remains confined to a few villages. Clogged court systems seem to apply one brand of justice for the few who can afford lawyers, another brand for the many with limited funds or knowledge. Despite veneers of democratisation, transparency and accountability in government operations remain limited. Almost everywhere, the unresolved problems far outnumber the successful solutions.

It would have been impossible for human rights NGOs to have corrected all these situations. That is not their responsibility. Their major tasks are to document and publicise problems and to press for an open political process through which the issues could be addressed. 'Solutions' should be sought by governments. But it is not easy. African governments themselves face major obstacles, given their limited resources, given the short period of time during which human rights has been prominent on their political agendas, and given the links between many issues and deep-rooted cultural norms (for example, early marriages and other harmful traditional practices leading to higher rates of maternal and infant mortality; limited employment opportunities interacting with family obligations that exacerbate corruption). I am not sanguine, however, that all governments in Africa can effectively and rapidly create rights-protective settings. But the attempt needs to be made. The crucial point is to see them launched in the directions pointed by NGOs, international treaties, and (increasingly) the desires of their citizens.

Human rights NGOs work at the margins, in gradual, cumulative ways. Small groups with handfuls of staff labouring mostly in the capital cities cannot transform popular attitudes and governmental practices in a short time. Let us be realistic. African human rights NGOs ameliorate rather than transform situations. They monitor and analyse, rather than achieve rapid, blanket changes. They take gradual steps rather than massive leaps. Their consciousness-raising and help for individual victims can have cumulative effects, however. Over time, the reforms they encourage may add up to a fundamental change in attitude and practices. The 'NGO revolution' – in the sense of their contribution to human rights – merits our attention.

Rather than point to weaknesses and problems, accordingly, I prefer to accentuate strengths and possibilities.

...

Effective implementation of international treaty obligations will assuredly diminish the number and severity of abuses over time. As already pointed out, ratification is but the first step, however. National laws and practices must be adjusted, adapted, brought into conformity – a continuous, on-going process. Long-standing customs must be consciously changed. Thus, while there is a finite period for negotiating and ratifying a convention, the period for implementing it stretches into the indefinite future. What the treaty sets as goals must be translated as rapidly as possible into realities.

Strengthening NGOs will rest, in this long-term perspective, on the concurrent development of civil society. Vigorous associational life should emerge, free of the confining cocoons of jealous governments or narrow ethnicity. More human rights NGOs would help. The most effective results seem likely to emerge from multiplicity. Many organisations to promote and protect human rights would both broaden and deepen the basis for the 'human rights consciousness' I have been advocating. Professional associations, women's groups, trade unions, cooperatives: The possibilities are endless. If human rights are seen as the exclusive province of self-defined organisations, they will suffer. Far better to have a profusion of NGOs with a broad basic consensus on human rights than a small number of highly focused organisations that risk being marginalised. Others may disagree; and certainly there will always be an important place for entities like the Constitutional Rights Project (Nigeria) or the Legal Assistance Centre (Namibia). But if the foundation of understanding is achieved, then a hundred diverse blooms (even including some weeds) will serve better than a few exotic, specialised plants.

...

Odinkalu argues that human rights NGOs often lack connection with the situation on the ground and are essentially being driven, not from below, but according to donor agendas.

ODINKALU, CA 'WHY MORE AFRICANS DON'T USE HUMAN RIGHTS LANGUAGE' (2001)

Carnegie Council on Ethics and International Affairs *Human Rights Dialogue: Human Rights in Times of Conflict: Humanitarian Intervention* Series 2, Number 5

The anti-apartheid and anti-colonial independence movements in Africa, along with the American civil rights movement, are examples of successful human rights initiatives that gained a popular following. They tell us that the realisation of human rights is an inclusive enterprise. Throughout history, the protection of human rights has been won by struggle, and struggle requires mobilisation. The process of mobilisation validates the movement, connecting it with the needs of the people and earning their commitment. To be successful, such struggles must be biased without being unfair and political without being wedded to a particular party. However, it is the practice of today's human rights organisations to claim to be 'impartial', 'unbiased', 'neutral', and 'non-political'. Fashionable though they may be, and donor-friendly though they certainly are, such expressions do not describe the complex realities of the struggle for human rights in Africa.

Africa is living through a human rights crisis and a crisis for human rights. It is impossible to locate any African country in which the hope held out by the Universal Declaration of Human Rights (UDHR), or any of the standards that have mushroomed under it, is not habitually assaulted by a combination of abuse of public power, private privilege, and resulting popular destitution.

While Africa's human rights problems are immense, even ubiquitous, most of our people do not describe their problems in human rights terms. Many communities and groups involved in social justice movements and initiatives in Africa are reluctant to make the Universal Declaration, or language inspired by it, their mascot or medium. To seek to explain this by reference to the high illiteracy level in Africa – itself a denial of several human rights – is to avoid the problem. Nor is it enough to wish this alienation away by inveighing against the unfortunate historical fact, true though it is, that Africa was hardly represented when the Universal Declaration was negotiated or adopted. After all, the struggle for independence in Africa predated the UDHR and remains, with the anti-apartheid campaign, the most popular and successful human rights movement known to African peoples. Although in some African languages there is no direct equivalent to the phrase 'human rights', neither the notion of justice that underlies human rights nor the experience of struggle to realise these rights is unknown to Africa.

What then explains the current crisis of human rights and the retreat from the human rights paradigm as an engine of struggle? The search for an understanding of this crisis begins with an examination of the evolution and practices of the organisations and institutions that espouse the protection of human rights around Africa.

In Africa, the realisation of human rights is a very serious business indeed. In many cases it is a life and death matter. From the child soldier, the rural dweller deprived of basic health care, the mother unaware that the next pregnancy is not an inexorable fate, the city dweller living in fear of the burglar, the worker owed several months arrears of wages, and the activist organising against bad government, to the group of rural women seeking access to land so that they may send their children to school with its proceeds, people are acutely aware of the injustices inflicted upon them. Knowledge of the contents of the Universal Declaration will hardly advance their condition. What they need is a movement that channels these frustrations into articulate demands that evoke responses from the political process. This the human rights movement is unwilling or unable to provide. In consequence, the real life struggles for social justice are waged despite human rights groups — not by or because of them — by people who feel that their realities and aspirations are not adequately captured by human rights organisations or their language.

The current human rights movement in Africa — with the possible exception of the women's rights movement and faith-based social justice initiatives — appears almost by design to exclude the participation of the people whose welfare it purports to advance. Most human rights organisations are modelled after Northern watchdog organisations, located in an urban area, run by a core management without a membership base (unlike Amnesty International), and dependent solely on overseas funding. The most successful of these organisations only manage to achieve the equivalent status of a public policy think-tank, a research institute, or a specialised publishing house. With media-driven visibility and a lifestyle to match, the leaders of these initiatives enjoy privilege and comfort, and progressively grow distant from a life of struggle.

In the absence of a membership base, there is no constituency-driven obligation or framework for popularising the language or objectives of the group beyond the community of inward-looking professionals or careerists who run it. Instead of being the currency of a social justice or conscience-driven movement, 'human rights' has increasingly become the specialised language of a select professional cadre with its own rites of passage and methods of certification. Far from being a badge of honour, human rights activism is, in some of the places I have observed it, increasingly a certificate of privilege.

Part of the responsibility for this sad state of affairs lies with the overseas sponsors of our human rights organisations. Unlike the groups they support, donor agencies and philanthropies that fund human rights work are accountable to their trust deeds and the laws of the countries (in the North) where they are incorporated. While exhorting national human rights groups in Africa to think globally and act locally, these agencies think locally and act globally. With overseas donors as sources of reference and accountability, the only obligations local human rights groups have are reporting requirements arising under grant contracts where these exist. The *raison d'être* of the African human rights movement is primarily to fulfil such contracts rather than to service a social obligation or constituency. Local human rights groups exist to please the international agencies that fund or support them. Local problems are only defined as potential pots of project cash, not as human experiences to be resolved in just terms, thereby delegitimising human rights language and robbing its ideas of popular appeal.

All this is not to say that we should do away with the norms of human rights or with groups that purport to promote or defend them. Human rights norms articulate values that are truly universal and essential. There is a distinction, however, between human rights norms and human rights institutions, which, as organisations of human beings, are necessarily imperfect. In an ideal world, we can envisage human rights norms without taking account of the deficiencies of the groups that promote them. But no such world exists.

Human rights organisations are probably here to stay with their imperfections. But they can do well to adopt the strategies and values of the successful social justice movements of the past, such as popular mobilisation and inclusivity. People will struggle for their rights whether or not the language of human rights is accessible to them. But they will not build their struggle around the notion of human rights unless that language and those who wish to popularise it speak directly to their aspirations and survival.

In this declaration African human rights NGOs set out a strategy for strengthening the human rights movement in Africa.

THE KAMPALA DECLARATION ON STRENGTHENING THE HUMAN RIGHTS MOVEMENT IN AFRICA (2003)

Also available at www.wmd.org/documents/demnews-nov2003/ kampala_declaration_on_human_rights.doc

We the delegates to the Africa Human Rights NGO Summit on 'Strengthening the Human Rights Movement in Africa; Prospects and challenges', representing human rights organisations from Africa and International human rights organisations; having met at the Grand Imperial Hotel in Kampala, Uganda from 22 to 26 September 2003;

HAVING examined the human rights movement in Africa including:

Civil society priority needs and agendas in democratising Africa;

The critical question of NGO leadership development and management for the human rights movement in Africa;

The global campaign against terrorism and its implications on the respect for human rights in Africa;

The relationship between international NGOs and their African NGO counterparts in the promotion of human rights and democracy;

NOTING that a strong human rights movement is a precondition for the promotion of democracy, human rights, the rule of law, peace and stability in Africa;

ENCOURAGED by the continuing growth and strength of African Human Rights NGOs in:

Networking with local and international NGOs in the promotion of human rights, democracy and the rule of law;

Mobilising and managing human and material resources in creating awareness about human rights on the continent;

Building expertise and professionalism in the struggle for human rights;

The evolving International human rights institutions, norms and standards;

CONCERNED that in spite of these strengths there are still perceivable weaknesses in:

Over reliance on the global north for financial and material support;

Developing closer linkages between human rights NGOs and their target constituencies, particularly the rural poor;

Accountability systems both to the target population and the donor community;

AWARE of the challenges that lie ahead for the human rights movement in Africa in terms of:

Sustainability of the Advocacy campaign;

Enforcement and observance of human rights and Constitutional reforms;

Ensuring full implementation of treaties signed by our respective governments and making these work in our domestic environment;

Threats to human rights posed by recent attempts of nations to counter terrorism;

Protecting human rights defenders on the continent;

(Re)-defining our platform of engagement with the state;

The ineffectiveness of regional human rights institutions and the absence of an African Court on Human Rights;

FURTHER AWARE of the challenges faced by human rights organisations in terms of:

Improving transparency and accountability in the work of human rights NGOs

Capacity building of human rights organisations including improvement in the management and leadership skills of human rights activists;

Restrictive legislation regarding the registration and operations of human rights NGOs in some countries;

Enhancing effective partnerships between African NGO's and their northern counterparts.

DO HEREBY recommend as follows:

African human rights NGOs and their international counterparts should strengthen their relations based on the principles of;

Co-operation in the exchange of information and expertise.

Joint ownership of projects and recognition of the same.

Avoidance of duplication, including substitution of local capacity, in projects of local NGOs by International NGOs.

Human rights NGOs should define a platform of constructive engagement with the state based on:

Principled co-operation and non-patronage.

Strong networking among the key stakeholders in the promotion of democracy - the judiciary, legislature, the executive and wider civil society.

Human rights NGOs should create and seek opportunities for organisational capacity building and leadership training for activists.
Human rights NGOs should take stock of best practices with the view to replicating them across the continent.
Human rights NGOs should co-operate more towards developing strategies for the protection of human rights defenders, especially those working in conflict situations.
Human Rights NGOs should advocate for Democratic Reforms to strengthen pluralism and the respect for the separation of power and the rule of law.
Both African NGOs and their international counterparts should explore ways of reducing donor dependence.
An Africa Human Rights Day should be declared to highlight the state of human rights and the work of human rights NGOs on the continent.
Human Rights NGOs should urge African states to speedily ratify both the Optional Protocol establishing an African Court on Human Rights and the Optional Protocol of Women's Rights in Africa.

4

APPROACHES TO TRANSITIONAL JUSTICE

In the following extract, the Gacaca *(or traditional court) process adopted by the Rwandan government to deal with those alleged to have been involved in the 2004 genocide in that country is assessed. Attention is given to local participation as a means of conflict management.*

WIERZYNSKA, AO 'CONSOLIDATING DEMOCRACY THROUGH TRANSITIONAL JUSTICE: RWANDA'S *GACACA* COURTS' (2004)

79 *New York University Law Review* 1934

...

Gacaca as a democracy-promoting mechanism

Although the Rwandese government has progressively tightened its grip over the Rwandese people, at the same time it has, almost paradoxically, created a forum that mandates popular expression: The *Gacaca* courts. Established to unburden the national court system while simultaneously promoting truth and reconciliation, *Gacaca* remains a bold transitional justice experiment. It has provoked deep apprehension from the international community, with prognoses of failure and inadequacy buzzing.

However, neither the international community nor the Rwandese government fully or accurately grasps the democracy-engendering potential of *Gacaca*. *Gacaca* may serve as a crucial steam valve for the expression of opposing views because it: (1) functions as the only forum where citizens are required to communicate both with each other and with the State, (2) has the discussion of taboo topics in its very mandate, and (3) has emerged from a community-based, restorative past. Thus, it has the potential to: (1) engender a culture of discourse in a society whose political culture is primarily characterised by its silence and compliance, (2) develop a practice of peaceful dispute resolution, and (3) ultimately provide fertile ground for the development of democracy in Rwanda.

The *Gacaca* courts experiment

When the RPF took power in Rwanda in July 1994, thereby ending the genocide, it faced the daunting task of dealing with the past. Rather than opting for a TRC-like mechanism to cope with the society-wide crimes committed in 1994, the new government ambitiously embarked on a mission to bring every genocidaire to justice. As President Paul Kagame has explained, 'There can be no durable reconciliation as long as those who are responsible for the massacres are not properly tried'. Rwanda initiated this plan through the use of a judicial system composed of the mere five judges and fifty lawyers that remained in the country. Nevertheless, the government incarcerated 125 000 genocide suspects – about ten percent of the adult male Hutu population – and placed them in jails meant to hold only 15 000 people.

To manage the overwhelming nature of its task, the government passed a genocide law in which it divided the crimes committed during the genocide into four categories: Category I for leaders of genocide or crimes against humanity, Category II for homicides and accomplices, Category III for serious assaults, and Category IV for offenses against property. Although the government managed to try 5 000 individuals by mid-2001, the number of detainees languishing in prisons, along with international abhorrence of the conditions of confinement and concerns over possible due process violations, forced Rwanda to reconsider its strategy.

In 2001, the government passed the *Gacaca* Law, which transferred crimes in Categories II-IV to an institution the government had co-opted from Rwandan customary law – *Gacaca*. Before the genocide, *Gacaca* was a traditional, community-based mechanism for resolving local civil disputes. In their traditional form, *Gacaca* proceedings were conducted by community members, with respected community figures serving as judges. The principles applied in *Gacaca* emerged from local customary values. The proceedings aimed to emphasise to the wrongdoer the gravity of the wrong committed so that he or she could reconcile with the community and thus be reintegrated into society.

When the Rwandese government adopted the *Gacaca* system, it retained certain traditional characteristics of the original model. These characteristics include requiring members of society to provide testimony and evidence against suspects, as well as to participate in hearings. However, it departed from the restorative nature of traditional *Gacaca* by granting the elders who serve as judges the power to sentence defendants to punishments ranging up to lifetime imprisonment, thus substituting retributive characteristics for some of *Gacaca's* rehabilitative ones.

The *Gacaca* courts established by the government were put in place to serve two official purposes: Justice and reconciliation. Most pressingly, the *Gacaca* courts supplement the national courts in their mission to try genocide crimes retributively. Second, the community involvement element the existence of a forum for community members to voice their concerns and make known their suffering – endeavours to imbue this retributive mechanism with the spirit of social rehabilitation and reconciliation.

Therefore, the single institution of *Gacaca* aims to do the work for which two distinct transitional justice mechanisms – criminal tribunals and TRCs – are typically utilised. In light of *Gacaca's* goals, the international community has raised concerns about its efficacy. Whether *Gacaca* will prove to be a success in light of these official goals remains to be seen. *Gacaca* has only recently begun its operations. As of 2003, only ten percent of *Gacaca* courts had held pretrial hearings, and none had actually begun to try suspects. Thus, any discussion of *Gacaca's* success or failure remains speculative.

Gacaca courts – The birthplace of civic culture

Even if *Gacaca* fails to attain its stated goals of justice and reconciliation that does not necessarily discredit *Gacaca* as an effective transitional justice mechanism. Because it can contribute to the consolidation of democracy, in order to truly pass judgment on *Gacaca* it is important to re-examine it in light of the link between transitional justice and democracy. Assessing *Gacaca* through the lens of Dahl's democracy criteria of participation and contestation – critical processes for Rwanda – it becomes apparent that *Gacaca* can serve as the birthplace of civic culture in Rwanda. This can happen in two ways. First, *Gacaca's* structural characteristics can promote civic culture, thus facilitating their replication in future transitional justice mechanisms. Second, civic culture can be promoted incidentally, as a by-product of the power struggles between the government and the people currently taking place through *Gacaca*.

Gacaca's structural characteristics and the multiple dimensions of developing civic culture

In its contemporary form, *Gacaca* draws its unique strength from its combination of indigenousness and state involvement. Although *Gacaca* has been co-opted and altered by the government, it nevertheless retains its traditional origin and communal style. As such, it allows the Rwandese people to retain a sense of ownership and comfort within the forum. This innate familiarity may encourage the people to approach *Gacaca* with a participatory attitude. Furthermore, the very fact that this community-based mechanism is now utilised by the government creates a critical communication bridge between the people and the State that did not exist before. Consequently, any effects that *Gacaca's* structure may have will impact not just local communities, but also the relationship between the people and the government. Such linkage plants civic culture directly where it should reside: In the space between society and the State.

Gacaca's procedural dependence on public participation has made it a forum in which speech is relatively free and protected. Thus, the democracy-engendering consequences of free speech can begin to emerge within this forum. To start, freedom of speech in *Gacaca* can serve as a crucial safety valve for the ethnic opposition and discontent that is currently building up in Rwanda. As Thomas Emerson writes:

> [F]reedom of expression is a method of achieving ... a more stable community ... [T]he process of open discussion promotes greater cohesion in a society because people are more ready to accept decisions that go against them if they have a part in the decision-making process ... Freedom of expression thus provides a framework in which the conflict necessary to the progress of a society can take place without destroying the society.

Freedom of speech allows the Rwandese people and government to confront their conflicts openly. Furthermore, open discussion of differences is apt to promote public autonomy and public inquisitiveness. These characteristics fall squarely within civic culture.

Notwithstanding the retributive characteristics the government has added to *Gacaca*, it remains a restorative instrument. Because of its restorative nature, it serves as a precedent for peaceful dispute resolution while engendering the civic engagement and empowerment that are necessary for civic culture to develop.

Restorative justice mechanisms are defined in terms of both procedure and values. Procedurally, rather than isolating the criminal and the State from the victim and the community, restorative mechanisms bring all stakeholders in an offense together for the purpose of reintegrating the accused into society. In *Gacaca*, the stakeholders include the accused, his or her family, the village, and the victims, as well as the government.

Rather than operating on the basis of retributive, eye-for-an-eye tactics, restorative values introduce to the justice process 'healing rather than hurting, moral learning, community participation and community caring, respectful dialogue, forgiveness, responsibility, apology, and making amends'. In *Gacaca*, great value is placed on the accused's admissions of guilt and on expressions of shame and regret. Punishments are significantly reduced to reward such restorative behavior. Similarly, *Gacaca* incorporates restorative punishment mechanisms, such as community service, for many lower-level crimes.

Restorative justice and democracy are conceptually linked. Anthony Alfieri, in arguing for community prosecution for politically isolated ethnic minorities in the United States, explains that '[t]he theory of restorative justice offers a model of democratic citizenship'. Restorative justice creates community networks of interdependence and develops a demand for accountability, thus engaging and empowering individuals in society and building a civic culture that promotes democracy.

Restorative justice is based on 'communitarianism, a belief that the rights of individuals cannot be preserved without citizens taking responsibility, both individually and collectively, for the good of the community as a whole'. However, the concept of community does not simply signify homogeneity of views. Rather, a closer assessment of community reveals that it actually connects groups of individuals with similar interests to groups of individuals with opposing interests.

At one level, when individuals meet in a restorative forum, they have the opportunity to find that their interests place them within a distinct stakeholder group. Finding safety and support in numbers, such 'common-interest' groups can begin to voice their concerns and interests more courageously and openly, even in the presence of other groups that may possess opposing interests. This phenomenon can occur in *Gacaca*, where Hutu villagers find that their sense of oppression by the government is shared by other villagers. Thus, restorative forums place individuals within common-interest groups that may oppose one another.

However, the restorative process also counterbalances stakeholders' common-interest positions by placing them in an interdependent relationship with opposing groups. This interdependence emerges from the fact that, to resolve a problem, opposing communities must come together and co-operate. Thus, in *Gacaca*, Hutu villagers, Tutsi victims, and Tutsi government officials must work together if they are to achieve justice. In order to achieve justice, groups that hold opposing views first must develop an egalitarian, deliberative, cooperative *modus operandi*. By fostering teamwork, restorative mechanisms allow stakeholders to learn that the concept of 'community' can, and indeed must, include the opposition. In this way, the concept of community in Rwanda can be transformed effectively from an ethnic, us-versus-them paradigm into a paradigm that includes all citizens.

Fundamentally, the experience of peaceful management of opposing interests should generate a public preference against violent resolution of schisms. It is this new preference for peace, coupled with practices of both contestation and participation that may emerge as a unifying force within Rwanda, thus creating a national community. The interdependence among contesting common-interest groups may effectively achieve the minimal national unity necessary for Rwandese society to coalesce into a democracy. Similar to the mission of nationally focused TRCs, the mission of the community-focused restorative justice experience is to redefine the relationship between opposing communities from violence that leads to disintegration to constructive engagement that leads to a polity and thus to a functioning democracy. Whereas the TRC achieves this linearly, prior to or distinct from the political process, a community-level restorative mechanism such as *Gacaca* develops commitment to the processes of democratic participation and contestation by engaging in them directly. As parties engage in these processes, the commitment to them emerges and feeds back into the processes themselves. In effect, *Gacaca's* democracy-engendering function may fulfil *Gacaca's* official goal of reconciliation, albeit in a circular way.

Experiencing interdependence with the opposition within a restorative context facilitates the development of a practice of peaceful dispute management that must exist for democracy to operate fully. Opposing common-interest groups balance power through the processes of participation and contestation. However, opposition is counterbalanced by the recognition that society is interdependent, thus preventing the disintegration of the common-interest communities' commitment to living together with their opposition in a cooperative and tolerant democratic state. Restorative mechanisms therefore highlight the interrelationship between these two seemingly opposing notions of community and demonstrate how opposition and co-operation function in tandem to drive the democratic process.

Beyond creating a network of communities, restorative mechanisms tie stakeholders, both citizen and state, into a system of mutual accountability. By seeking justice through participation and deliberation with state officials, the society creates 'an important restraint on state actions in this area'. In this way, accountability begins to flow in two directions: top-down from the State to the communities that remain closest to the criminals, and bottom-up from society to the State that may be dispensing punishment unjustly.

Finally, through encouraging and protecting participation, *Gacaca* ought to create a sense of empowerment among the people of Rwanda. Restorative justice mechanisms have been found to empower communities that are typically isolated from the democratic process. Alfieri reports that 'the enlargement of citizen participation, institutional decentralisation, and accountability of [government] prosecution offices to local communities stimulates citizen-state collabouration and grassroots equality initiatives broadly within the criminal-justice system, thereby ameliorating the conditions of poverty, disempowerment, segregation, and crime pervading communities of color'.

Similarly, beginning with community engagement on the subject of criminal justice, Rwanda's people can begin to develop a sense of empowerment that will allow further pursuit of 'citizen-state collabouration and grassroots ... initiatives aimed at alleviating ... powerlessness ... and ... violence', Rwanda's most pressing problems.

...

Gacaca in the transitional justice menu

Over the past fifty years, the international community has been developing a menu of transitional justice mechanisms and a body of international criminal law to fulfill its commitment to putting an end to crimes against humanity and systemic abuse of human rights. The *Gacaca* experiment serves to remind those involved in this continuing international effort that the primary recipient of transitional justice is not the international community, but the postconflict society – composed of both victims and perpetrators – that suffered during mass atrocities. As Neil Kritz, a leading authority in transitional justice, argues, 'it is essential that the needs of those people not be given short shrift for the sake of a feel-good international exercise in justice'. Kritz calls for bringing transitional justice mechanisms ever closer to the society that experienced conflict: 'From a pragmatic, political perspective, insofar as post-conflict justice is a necessary ingredient to successful peacebuilding and long-term stability in the country, ... ensuring a form of post-conflict justice that is maximally effective vis-à-vis the local population needs to be a higher priority ...'.

This issue has particular resonance in Rwanda's case. The measure of success of the ICTR as a transitional justice institution will not depend on whether it has provided international criminal law with a body of precedent, but on whether Rwanda will revert to mass murder. Should interethnic violence return to Rwanda, it will discredit not only the ICTR, but the entire transitional justice effort.

To be sure, the existing transitional justice mechanisms all play useful roles in promoting peace and democracy. However, no one mechanism suffices to address the complex undertaking of healing and transforming a post-conflict society. The recent coupling of a tribunal and TRC in Sierra Leone reflects an understanding within the transitional justice field that such mechanisms can complement each other and thus answer a post-conflict society's needs more thoroughly. In this context, a mechanism modelled on Rwanda's *Gacaca* – an indigenous, community-owned, restorative bridge between the people and the new State that fosters local participation and open management of conflict – emerges as an addition to the existing transitional justice menu. With this addition, transitional justice not only will be more effective, but will be recalibrated more closely to its preventative mission.

In addressing mass atrocities such as genocide, transitional justice scholars must remember that they are tackling society-wide calamities. Miriam Auckerman conveys this by arguing that mass atrocities are more akin to natural or humanitarian disasters than to crime. Such a conceptualisation of social conflict directs our responses away from punishment and toward 'rebuilding societies by developing shared histories, establishing democratic institutions, or ensuring greater economic and political equality'. With this understanding, transitional justice is seen less as a means of managing calamities and more as a means of altering their preconditions and thus preventing them from occurring again. This reasoning shifts the transitional justice field from the justice paradigm towards one of democratisation.

If democratisation requires a change in the political culture of a people, then, as Erin Daly submits, transitional justice is more appropriately called 'transformative' justice. 'Transition' refers to top-down processes, and 'it does not reach deep into the soil of the new society where the commitment to democratic values actually takes root'. Transformation, on the other hand, calls upon a society to 'reinvent itself'. As the field develops in light of experiments such as *Gacaca*, it may well seek to change even its very name to better reflect the scope of its mandate.

It remains to be seen whether *Gacaca* will bring about justice or truth in relation to the genocide of 1994. Nonetheless, *Gacaca* will serve the mission of transitional justice if it creates a forum through which democracy can take root in Rwanda. By engendering civic culture, *Gacaca* addresses the preconditions that have made violence part of Rwanda's history. Consequently, *Gacaca* can fulfill transitional justice's fundamental goal of preventing the events of 1994 from recurring.

...

The focus of the following extract is on the International Criminal Tribunal for Rwanda (ICTR) located in Arusha in Tanzania, which functions adjacent to the Gacaca *and other courts in Rwanda. The task of the ICTR is to prosecute alleged major perpetrators of genocide.*

HABIMANA, A 'WHAT DOES "INTERNATIONAL JUSTICE" LOOK LIKE IN POST-GENOCIDE RWANDA?' (2001)

Carnegie Council on Ethics and International Affairs *Human Rights Dialogue: Human Rights in Times of Conflict: Humanitarian Intervention* Series 2, No 5

When pressed, many Rwandans acknowledge the impartiality of the Arusha proceedings compared to those the Rwandan magistrates conduct. Along with my colleagues at LIPRODHOR, I have monitored both sets of proceedings for years. Rwandan jurisdictions would do well to adopt the practices of the Tribunal magistrates who utilise experts in trial proceedings, examine case files in depth, apply high standards for thorough evidence, and provide the full right to defense of the accused prior to judgment. The Rwandan public and genocide survivors also have a high regard for the Tribunal's witness-protection system, which helps to shelter survivors from potential intimidators; national tribunals have no such programme.

Still, public opinion of the Tribunal is overwhelmingly negative. The most recurrent criticism is linked to its perceived incompetence. People wonder how up until now the Tribunal has only managed to convict seven people and detain 39 in the Arusha facilities, given all the money it reportedly absorbs. It took over three years to arrive at a recent guilty verdict for Georges Rutaganda, the former leader of the infamous Interahamwe militia, which implemented the genocide.

Some Rwandan political activists and survivors' organisations adopt a hard line against the Tribunal, even rejecting its right to prosecute. They cynically declare that 'foreigners' have created the Tribunal 'to make business out of the genocide ... out of the blood of ours who passed away'. After the November 1999 decision to release the heinous génocidaire Jean Bosco Barayagwiza on a technicality, IBUKA, the most prominent of such organisations, accused the UN of denying the magnitude of the genocide. IBUKA also called the Tribunal a '*trompe l'oeil*' for survivors, which translates in our local language as a 'don't-cry-child toy'.

...

The Tribunal can make a difference for the future of human rights in Rwanda by exposing the truth of the genocide: It was not a result of ancient, tribal hatred, but rather a carefully planned exploitation of ethnic differences by rulers seeking to hold onto their power. With this truth, we may lay the groundwork for reconciliation, and through reconciliation, we can build understanding of each other's human rights.

Yet today, bitter perceptions among the public are severe enough to threaten the continued existence of the Tribunal. What saves it is Rwandan indifference. Victims of the genocide are much more concerned about what is happening in Rwandan courts, where over 125,000 detainees are held, the vast majority of those suspected of participation in the killings. These cases are more personal since the accused are those whom the victims saw breaking into their homes with machetes and clubs, not the masterminds who schemed to 'leave none to tell the story' in the distant state offices. Furthermore, unlike the Tribunal, the national courts compensate survivors for material losses.

To gain legitimacy in Rwanda the Tribunal needs to improve its work and efficiency while ameliorating its image. This is not to say that it should cave in to government and survivor-group criticism; it should do nothing that would threaten its independence and pursuit of justice. But it does need to improve its communication strategies with the Rwandan people to counter misperceptions of its role, procedures, and philosophy and to let the importance of its work be known. The longer the Tribunal keeps a distance from the people, the less it will appear to be serving the interests of Rwandans.

This will not be an easy task. Post-genocide Rwandan society is deeply divided. The war left behind not only chronic poverty, family dislocation, ethnic hatred, and trauma, but also a widespread legacy of negativism from which the Tribunal likely suffers. Even local human rights activists are confronted by the accusing fingers of their compatriots asking, 'What did you do during the genocide when innocent people were being butchered?'

Disillusionment mingled with trauma can constitute a great obstacle to any initiative, no matter how well intentioned. No institution can be expected to gain support from all strata of the population. Still, efforts must be made. If the Tribunal were to overcome these challenges, it would show that international justice can be more than just rhetoric.

This excerpt focuses on traditional African mechanisms of dealing with past suffering. The focus here is on Mozambique, and provides a critical assessment of the way in which this country has coped with its past.

GRAYBILL, LS 'PARDON, PUNISHMENT, AND AMNESIA: THREE AFRICAN POST-CONFLICT METHODS' (2004)

25 *Third World Quarterly* 1117

...

Yet another example of a post-conflict country is Mozambique, whose choice of 'amnesia' as a way of closing the book on the past has been less analysed. Mozambique was involved in a war of liberation against Portugal from 1964 to 1974. Following independence in 1975, it was embroiled in a civil war with Renamo forces pitted against the Frelimo government until 1992 when the General Peace Accord was signed, followed by multiparty elections in 1994.

Despite the fact that one million civilians were killed, thousands tortured, and some of the most horrendous acts of barbarism were committed, there were no calls for justice, punishment or accountability. There was never any serious thought given to establishing a South African styled truth commission, or holding international and local prosecutions as Rwanda did. Ten days after the peace accord was signed, the Frelimo government declared a general amnesty that would cover acts committed by both sides in the civil war. According to Harry West, powerful figures in each party feared opening up to pubic inquiry abuses of political opponents for fear opponents would charge them with similar crimes. West states that in Mozambique there was 'a broad constituency for public silence'. Prime Minister Pascoal Mocumbia told him, 'We thought it better to let time heal these wounds'.

African medicine and reintegration

There have been no truth commissions, or investigations into the past, to attribute blame. Neither have there been any trials arising out of the past civil war to hold any individuals accountable for human rights violations. Rather, Mozambicans have decided to deal with the past through traditional African ceremonies of healing at the local level. Part of the reason has to do with the Peace Accord, which never authorised commissions or tribunals. Another explanation is cultural. The notion of 'speaking out' is foreign to Mozambicans.

Edward Green and Alcinda Honwana explain: 'To talk and recall the past is not necessarily seen as a prelude to healing or diminishing pain. Indeed, it is often believed to open the space for the malevolent forces to intervene'. Absent as well is the notion of revenge. Mozambicans point out the folly of holding on to vengeful attitudes. If someone talks of wanting to avenge a violence done to him, listeners will remind him how revenge leads to counterrevenge and so forth. Whether this is absent from their culture, or the result of pragmatism – a lesson learned from years of conflict (ie that revenge leads to counter-revenge and more conflict) – is not clear. Whatever the reason, Mozambicans have chosen to move forward, to reintegrate perpetrators and victims into their communities, without dwelling on the past.

In Mozambique, violence was viewed as a pathology that needed to be cured like any other illness. Traditional healers, called *curandeiros*, were responsible for 'defusing the cultures of violence the war had wrought'. Traditional practitioners have played a role in purification ceremonies addressing both perpetrators and victims of violence. Examples abound of civilians kidnapping soldiers and taking them back to their villages for ceremonies to 'remove the war' from them. If someone finds a soldier wandering alone, we take him and bring him to a *curandeiro*. Most people do not really want to fight, these soldiers have done terrible things, but many of them were kidnapped and forced to fight ... The *curandeiros* take the war out of them, they uneducate their war education. They remind the person how to be a part of their family, to work their *machamba*, to get along, to be a part of the community.

Vengeance was forsworn; if they were to banish soldiers from the community, soldiers would continue to use violence to sustain themselves. Another reason for the interest in former soldiers is that they are vehicles through which the spirits of the war dead might enter and afflict the entire community. Ceremonies for returning soldiers are based on placating ancestors for bad deeds they may have committed. Reconciliation, then, is viewed primarily between the living and the dead – those who have been contaminated by war and bloodshed, and the spirits of the dead. The treatments involve a series of symbolic procedures aimed at cutting one's links with the past. Military clothes may be burned, and the soldier may be treated with water mixed with the leaves of the mululua tree splashed on his body. 'When he gets out of the river the young man cannot look back. Looking back is believed to open the door to the war spirits, inviting them to come and haunt him. The past, the war, has to flow away with the river'. Having placated the spirit of the person killed, the former warrior has removed the victim's spirit from sitting on his shoulder, and bringing him and the community bad luck. The ceremony re-humanises the former soldier, allowing him back into the community, where he is accepted, according to Priscilla Hayner, 'almost without question, even by the relatives of their victims'.

Community-based reintegration processes have also been conducted for victims. Carolyn Nordstrom describes a purification ceremony she witnessed involving a woman who had been sexually assaulted by soldiers. Members of the community helped her piece together decent clothing to wear on the special day. They told her stories of other atrocities as a reminder that she was not alone, nor responsible for her plight. On the day of the ceremony, food was prepared and musicians brought in. Highlights of the ceremony, which lasted through the night, included a ceremonial bath, accompanied by songs and stories about healing, dressing her in her new clothing, and feasting. The women then carried her into the hut, surrounding her and stroking her, and speaking encouraging words of healing and rebirth. They then picked her up, and returned to the crowd, who welcomed her back into the community. 'Throughout the ceremony, the woman was continually reassured with stories of ongoing support; of her need to place responsibility for her plight with war and not her own actions; and of her own responsibility to heal the war's wounds so she does not inflict the violence that she was subjected to on others'.

What is noteworthy is that the patient is not expected to speak, to articulate her trauma, which was so central to the work of the TRC's HRV hearings. Honwana argues that recent studies of war-affected populations in Mozambique ... show that talking about traumatic experiences does not necessarily help patients to come to terms with their distress. For Honwana, 'Recounting and remembering the traumatic past would be like opening the door for the harmful spirits to penetrate the communities'.

There is the danger, however, that these ceremonies, which are founded on the importance of an abrupt breach with the past, may lead to denial about the past. Based on his field work among women in Manica in 1992, an area with the longest exposure to violence in the country, Mark Chingono found: 'The most surprising thing to emerge from most of the life history narratives by women, especially young women, was that virtually none made a direct reference to the impact of war on their lives. They only mentioned the war in passing or when specifically asked'. Furthermore, not acknowledging the past, and not holding individuals accountable (blaming for instance not individuals, but 'the war'), may lead to a culture of impunity.

This method of dealing with the past – amnesia – seems to have worked for Mozambicans, at least in the short run. The civil war has not resumed. When Renamo leader Afonso Dhlakama did not win the presidency in the 1994 elections, Renamo did not return to the battlefield. The late United Nations Deputy High Commissioner for Refugees Sergio Viera de Mello praised 'the culture of reconciliation, the culture of peace' in Mozambique, stating there was 'no form of recrimination or hatred' there. Harrison's study of Mecufi (in northern Mozambique) also suggests that post-election conflict has subsided with time and that, despite political conflicts between Frelimo and Renamo, 'there was a basic mutual acceptance of the other party's presence'. The enduring peace is attributed by Nordstrom to the community-based conflict resolution strategies practised throughout the country that emphasised the reintegration of perpetrators and victims.

The peace, however, may not endure. The close 1999 election, with Frelimo barely wining, and the bitterness among Renamo supporters who felt the election had been stolen, led to demonstrations by Renamo supporters in 2000 in which 54 persons were killed. Ten years after the first post-peace accord elections, Renamo retains an armed group of former guerrillas in Sofala province, threatening a coup if the December 2004 elections do not go its way. If Frelimo wins, Dhlakama has threatened to seize power since 'any victory [of Frelimo] is the fruit of theft'. And if Renamo wins in 2004, it could mean 'payback' time. The constitution – lacking federalism, checks and balances, and separation of powers – 'is tailor made to become a charter of revenge, the sore winners lusting to punish their defeated rivals'.

There is peace – the absence of warfare – but the peace is precarious. And, if the civil war era generation has chosen to forego violence, there is no guarantee that their children will feel the same. Vamik Volkan argues that painful memories that are not adequately dealt with by one generation will infect future generations in cycles of violence and counter-violence. A 'chosen trauma' may lie dormant for years, ready to be rekindled by leaders to consolidate the group emotionally and ideologically, erupting finally in violence. This remains a real possibility in the absence of identifying individual perpetrators (rather than blaming 'the war'), or uncovering the truth about the past. The US State Department's annual Human Rights reports note that the fate of thousands of Mozambicans who disappeared during the civil war remains unresolved. The pact to 'let time heal all wounds' may overestimate people's capacity to let bygones be bygones. Recent events in Argentina and Chile, where the courts are overturning 30-year-old general amnesties, reflect the difficulty of 'sealing the book' on the past too quickly.

...

Truth commissions are being promoted increasingly in post-conflict situations around the world. The following two extracts elaborate on the nature of truth commissions and identify the contributions and limitations of truth commissions in the peace process.

FREEMAN, M AND HAYNER, PB 'TRUTH-TELLING' (2003)

in International Institute for Democracy and Electoral Assistance *Reconciliation after violent conflict: A handbook* Stockholm: International Institute for Democracy and Electoral Assistance

...

What is a truth commission?

Generally, the term 'truth commission' refers to bodies that share the following characteristics:

(1) are temporary bodies, usually in operation from one to two years;
(2) are officially sanctioned, authorised or empowered by the state and, in some cases, by the armed opposition as well as in a peace accord;
(3) are non-judicial bodies that enjoy a measure of *de jure* independence;
(4) are usually created at a point of political transition, either from war to peace or from authoritarian rule to democracy;
(5) focus on the past;
(6) investigate patterns of abuses and specific violations committed over a period of time, not just a single specific event;

(7) complete their work with the submission of a final report that contains conclusions and recommendations; and
(8) focus on violations of human rights and sometimes of humanitarian norms as well.

At least 25 official truth commissions have been established around the world since 1974, though they have gone by many different names. There have been 'commissions on the disappeared' in Argentina, Uganda and Sri Lanka; 'truth and justice commissions' in Haiti and Ecuador; 'truth and reconciliation commissions' in Chile, South Africa, Sierra Leone and now the Federal Republic of Yugoslavia; and most recently a 'commission for reception, truth and reconciliation' in East Timor. Although these commissions all fit within the definition above, it should be noted that some of them did not at the time of their operation consider themselves to be truth commissions, nor were they understood to be such by the wider public.

Potential benefits and risks

Potential benefits

Although truth commissions may not be appropriate in every context, they have the potential to generate many benefits for societies in transition. The following list of potential benefits may assist in initial reflections on the role and focus of a truth commission while a new commission is in development:

Commissions can help establish the truth about the past. They can establish a record of the past that is accurate, detailed, impartial and official. This record can serve to counter the fictitious or exaggerated accounts of the past that were propagated by the previous regime (or other parties to a past conflict) and bring the true scale and impact of a violent past to the public consciousness. In addition, commissions can locate the whereabouts of missing victims who may have been forcibly 'disappeared' or buried clandestinely.

Truth commissions can promote the accountability of perpetrators of human rights violations. They can complement the work of criminal prosecutors by gathering, organising and preserving evidence that can be used in prosecutions. They can also build a case for and recommend forms of accountability short of criminal sanction, such as civil liability, removal from office, restitution or community service schemes.

Commissions can provide a public platform for victims. They can put victims – long ignored and forgotten by the public – at the forefront and centre of the transition process. This can help to make victims whole again, both individually and as a group, and give them a sense of personal vindication. In addition, by providing a public platform for victims to speak in their own voices, commissions can help to educate the public about the individual human impact of past crimes and thereby build support for further victim-centred transitional justice initiatives such as reparation programmes.

Commissions can inform and catalyse public debate. They can help stimulate public deliberation on the complex array of moral, political and legal issues that must be addressed during a transition process. This can be achieved by engaging with the public through commission activities and encouraging broad media coverage. In addition, truth commissions can themselves serve as a model for the public, as the public begins to take up again the critical practice of discussing controversial political subjects without fear of recrimination or resort to violence. Commissions can also serve as independent, impartial and public arbiters if and when members of the previous regime grossly misrepresent or distort events of the past.

Commissions can recommend victim reparation. They can build a case for reparation as a necessary form of compensation for past abuses and for ongoing psychological, physical and economic injuries experienced by victims. They can also establish fair and effective definitions and categories of 'victim' for the purpose of financial reparation or benefits to follow. In addition, commissions can help to repair the moral dignity of victims by carrying out their work in a manner that is both sensitive to and acknowledges the harm suffered by them. Commissions can also make creative and appropriate suggestions regarding symbolic forms of reparation for victims, such as memorials, reburials and commemorative ceremonies.

Commissions can recommend necessary legal and institutional reforms. Through their investigations they can provide clear evidence of how particular institutions individually and collectively failed to uphold human rights protection in the past. In addition, commissions can identify and recommend specific legal and institutional reforms that will enable the country to achieve the long-term social, economic and political objectives that are essential to ensuring a better future. Such reforms may include, for example, strengthened civilian oversight of intelligence agencies and the military; new appointment, tenure and disciplinary rules for the judiciary; the establishment of an independent and well-financed prosecutor's office; redesign of the electoral and political system; land reform; and new human rights training programmes for the police and armed forces.

Commissions can promote reconciliation. They can promote tolerance and under standing by allowing conflicting parties to hear each other's grievances and suffering. This may help build empathy, thereby deterring acts of vengeance and countering the rivalries and hatreds arising from past events. Commissions can also provide a safe and impartial forum for direct restorative justice processes in which the victim, the offender and/or other individual or community members can actively participate in the mediation and resolution of past grievances of a less serious nature. In addition, commissions can recommend practical and fair measures for the necessary reintegration of certain categories of offenders back into society.

Commissions can help to consolidate a democratic transition. By all the above means, they can signal a formal break with a dark and violent past, and the transition to a more open, peaceful and democratic future. If they are successful, truth commissions can have the effect of weakening anti-democratic actors who might otherwise continue to pursue their goals outside the democratic process.

...

Principal activities of a truth commission during its lifetime

Outreach

Public outreach by a truth commission is critically important. The nature and the extent of a commission's outreach efforts will profoundly affect its access to information, its effectiveness in addressing the needs of victims, its ability to manage public expectations and its general reputation in the eyes of the public. Some of these efforts can be carried out directly by the commission through holding public information meetings and through the preparation, publication and dissemination of pamphlets, videos and publications in popular form about the role and mandate of the commission. The commission can also achieve its outreach goals by engagement with and effective use of NGOs, local grass-roots organisations and the media. Relations with civil society and the media can, however, be complicated by the fact that they will often play a dual role vis-à-vis the commission, working simultaneously as partner to it and as critical watchdog of its procedures and actions.

Statement-taking

Most truth commissions collect most of their information through private, closed-door meetings, usually by commission staff taking testimony from individual victims in one-to-one encounters. This process is referred to as 'statement-taking' and typically involves both a meeting and the filling out of a statement form by the deponent. Statement-taking is important in at least two ways: It furthers the goal of establishing the truth about the past; and it provides an opportunity for victims to come forward and recount their traumatic experiences in a sympathetic and generally safe environment. Because of the sensitive nature of the process and the often horrific character of the information involved, statement-taking requires staff to exhibit concentration, respect and emotional control, and should generally involve intensive training before it is undertaken. Statement-takers need to know when and how to listen and how to respect the often unexpected rhythm and logic of a person's memory. Although there can be a tension between the desire to focus only on the specific type of information being sought by the commission and the need to allow the deponent to tell the story in his or her own way, a statement-taker must find a way to strike the right balance. For most victims and witnesses, a statement-taker will be the only personal contact they have with the commission, and as a result the impressions they leave on deponents and communities are especially significant and enduring.

Research and investigation

Research units and police-like investigation units are increasingly becoming a part of the structure of truth commissions. Such units, however, tend to form only part of commissions with large budgets and robust mandates, such as the TRC in South Africa. Research units tend to be relatively small but staffed by persons with strong research skills and familiarity with national think tanks, NGOs, local archives and other key sources of information. In contrast, investigative units may include people with legal backgrounds or even experience in law enforcement. Many truth commissions combine research and investigation into one department, which has many advantages.

Data processing

Truth commissions have to deal with enormous volumes of information which must be organised and systematised. This requires, among other things, an effective database for the storage, organisation and retrieval of records and data. Generally speaking, commissions which do rigorous data collection and analysis will be better able to defend their findings on scientific grounds. A strong data management system will help arrive at a 'big picture' analysis of historical patterns that can show, for example, the exact ratio of violations committed by one side to those committed by the other. In terms of staffing, commissions should hire a programmer to write and maintain the basic software and to extract the data in formats appropriate for the analysts. They will also need professional statisticians (or social scientists fluent in statistical methods) to review the data before it is published, and a team of data processors to input all the information received by the commission.

Public hearings

Most past truth commissions have not held public hearings. There is, however, an increasing trend to give commissions a mandate to do this. This is the case for the new commissions in Peru, East Timor and Sierra Leone, to name only a few. There are persuasive reasons for a commission to hold public hearings. By giving victims and survivors a chance to tell their story before a public audience – particularly where the hearings are aired on television or the radio – a commission can formally acknowledge past wrongs, encourage public understanding and sympathy for victims, reduce the likelihood of certain sectors of society continuing to deny the truth, and enhance the transparency of its work. Public hearings can also help to shift a truth commission's focus from product (ie, its final report) to process, by engaging the public as audience, encouraging press coverage of its issues over a longer period of time and generally stimulating an authentic national discourse about the past. The truth commissions in Uganda, Sri Lanka and Nigeria have all held public hearings, but it was the public hearings of the South African TRC that had the greatest international impact. Not only were there hundreds of days of public hearings; there was also a unique diversity in the types of hearing held, including victim hearings, amnesty hearings, special thematic hearings (eg, on women and children), special event hearings (eg, on the 1976 Soweto student uprising), institutional hearings (eg, with the legal and health sectors) and political party hearings. Lured by the powerful example of South Africa, a number of analysts have recommended that all truth commissions should hold proceedings in public. There may, however, be legitimate reasons not to do so, including security risks for commissioners and victims, time and resource constraints, and concerns about 'judicialising' commission proceedings. At the same time, public 'truth' proceedings are potentially powerful enough to at least warrant consideration by all commissions.

Emotional support

Truth commissions seem to satisfy a clear need on the part of some victims to tell their stories, be listened to and ultimately be healed in some way. For others, however, the process can lead to re-traumatisation, which may in some cases have severe after-effects. Past truth commissions have not generally given this issue enough attention, but this is starting to change. For example, in South Africa, the TRC hired four mental health professionals, provided training in trauma counselling for staff and hired 'briefers' who had the job of providing constant support to those giving testimony at public hearings. It is worth noting that commission staff can themselves be traumatised by the process and require emotional support. In many societies, however, standard psychological counselling may not be the appropriate model for helping victims, for cultural reasons or because of resource constraints. The ideal source of support in some places, therefore, may be collaboration with community organisations, traditional healers, religious institutions or self-help support groups.

Final reports

Often the defining moment for a truth commission is the completion and publication of its final report. Final reports have often constituted the enduring legacy of commissions and have also been used as a resource for human rights education or for subsequent prosecutions. If they are well documented and methodologically sound, final reports can serve as a critical guard against revisionism. In many ways, however, the impact of a final report may depend less on its content than on a variety of surrounding factors, including when and how the report is publicised, how widely it is distributed, how much coverage it receives in the media and whether there are both traditional and alternative presentations of the findings.

Although the content and format of reports will vary, final reports usually contain a section on findings and a section on recommendations. The findings section will typically identify the causes and patterns of past violations, as well as the victims of those violations. In some cases, individual and/or institutional responsibility for violations may also be reported – a practice which is examined in greater detail in the subsection on *naming names and due process* below. There may sometimes be a tension within a commission between a preference for a legal or empirical approach and an emphasis on a narrative, historical account.

In addition to reporting findings, truth commissions usually make recommendations, aimed variously at providing assistance or redress to victims, making necessary constitutional, legal and institutional reforms in order to prevent future relapse into war or authoritarian rule, and facilitating the consolidation of democracy and the rule of law. In many cases, commissions have also made recommendations for follow-up measures to ensure their timely and effective implementation. Unfortunately, the record on implementation of commission recommendations is not encouraging.

Naming names and due process

A number of truth commissions have had the power to publicly name those individuals found to be responsible for human rights crimes. These include the commissions in El Salvador, Chad and South Africa. Others have not been expressly granted this power but have been creative in finding indirect ways of naming individuals. For example, some commissions have effectively identified individual perpetrators by printing (unchallenged) direct quotations of witnesses or victims that mention the perpetrators' names, or by identifying those who headed particular units or regions where particular violations took place, thereby making perpetrator identities easily discoverable. In other cases, attribution of individual responsibility has been effected through deliberate or unintentional press leaks by the commission.

Few of the issues surrounding truth commissions have attracted as much controversy as this question of 'naming names', and the issue remains a point of tension for those crafting new bodies. The disagreement is between two contradictory principles, both of which can be strongly argued by rights advocates. The first is that due process requires that individuals accused of crimes be allowed to defend themselves before being pronounced guilty. Due process is violated if a commission, which is different from a court of law and does not have the same strict procedures, names individuals responsible for certain crimes. The second principle is that telling the full truth requires naming persons responsible for human rights crimes when there is clear evidence of their culpability.

The question therefore becomes: What standards and procedures of due process should apply to individuals who may be named in a report? Should they be informed of the allegations against them and told that the commission intends to name them in a public report? Should they be given the opportunity to respond to the evidence against them and offer a defence? Should the commission be obligated to state clearly that its own conclusions about individual responsibility do not amount to criminal guilt? These are the sorts of issue that commissions must grapple with. Past experience seems to suggest that the best practice is to allow commissions to name names but ultimately to leave it at their discretion whether or not to do so. This is because there may be a range of legitimate reasons for not naming names. For example, there may be real security risks for commissioners, victims or witnesses, or there may be due process problems such as a lack of sufficient evidence to publicly condemn an individual, or an inability to afford proper notice or procedural safeguards for those accused of violations.

If a commission decides not to name perpetrators, it should at least be required to set out its reasons for not doing so, and these reasons must be politically, morally and legally defensible. Where a commission does decide to name names, it must clearly state that its findings do not amount to a finding of legal or criminal guilt. As to the due process entitlements that should apply, it seems that at a minimum persons who might be named should be (a) informed without undue delay of the allegations against them and of the intention to name them in a public report, and (b) given the opportunity to respond to the evidence against them and offer a defence, but not necessarily through an oral hearing. Additional due process entitlements, such as the right to counsel or the right to cross-examine witnesses, should be offered only in very exceptional circumstances.

As a general rule, it is both unnecessary and undesirable to burden truth commissions with due process requirements equivalent to those of a court. Burdening a commission in this way would seriously undermine its ability to carry out its most essential duties by considerably slowing down the investigation and hearing process, stifling its capacity to gather facts and evidence, and generally over-judicialising commission procedures. This is not to say that commissions ought to sacrifice the rights of perpetrators in the name of the victims. It is simply to emphasise that a rational balance must always be found between the dual interests of fairness and efficiency.

The challenge of engaging perpetrators in the process

One of the greatest shortcomings of past truth commissions has been their inability to secure meaningful co-operation from perpetrators, whether in the police, the military, the intelligence agencies or elsewhere. The one significant (and controversial) exception is the TRC in South Africa, which had the power to grant individual amnesty to perpetrators of politically motivated crimes. Amnesty was granted to those who fully confessed to their involvement in past crimes and showed them to be politically motivated. For particularly serious crimes, the applicant was required to appear in a public hearing to answer questions. Several thousand perpetrators came forward to the commission to disclose their involvement in and knowledge of past human rights violations under this process.

Of course, the use of a 'truth-for-amnesty' formula as a means to secure perpetrator co-operation raises difficult moral, legal and political issues. Amnesties generally violate the right of victims to redress and will generally be inconsistent with a state's obligation under international law to punish perpetrators of serious human rights crimes. They can also subvert the rule of law by allowing only certain groups of perpetrators to escape liability. They can undermine both specific and general deterrence, and promote cynicism and disillusionment among victims of human rights abuses, which in turn could cause them to take the law into their own hands and embark on acts of private vengeance.

On the other hand, a 'truth-for-amnesty' arrangement can be more defensible where: (a) the commission's power has been given reasonably democratically; (b) amnesty is given on an individual, not class, basis; (c) a form of public procedure is imposed on its recipients; (d) victims are given an opportunity to question and challenge an individual's claim to amnesty; and (e) reparation payments are made to victims. An amnesty's scope can also be narrowed by making the grant of amnesty reversible following the commission of a new and similarly grave offence. To date, only South Africa has used the 'truth-for-amnesty' formula. The example should be copied only with the greatest caution, and only where there are similarly compelling circumstances. First, in the absence of a credible threat of prosecution (a factor which is rarely present in transitional contexts), it is unlikely that perpetrators will feel compelled to apply for an amnesty. They are more likely to prefer to remain silent, thereby avoiding any risk of public shame or social ostracism. Second, a range of mechanisms to encourage perpetrators to come forward may be available that are more principled and practical than the granting of amnesty and could better serve the causes of truth and reconciliation. For example, commissions might offer mechanisms for testimony to be provided on an anonymous or confidential basis; they might use a subpoena power; or they might be able to offer a witness protection/relocation service. Another possibility is that truth commission sponsors could create a new punishable offence of failure by witnesses (other than victims) to come forward to the commission with information about past crimes. None of these alternative approaches will necessarily lead to extensive co-operation from perpetrators and reluctant witnesses. Without them, however, co-operation may be virtually non-existent.

Follow-up efforts

Once a truth commission submits its final report, archives its files and is formally dissolved, the task of carrying out its recommendations will naturally fall to others. Unfortunately, the implementation of recommendations has frequently been a major shortcoming for truth commissions, even where there has been a legal obligation on the part of government to implement them (as there was in El Salvador, for example). One of the main causes of non-implementation appears to be lack of political will; but even when sufficient political will is present, there may not be sufficient institutional capacity or funds. Whichever the case, it is critically important for truth commissions to suggest mechanisms that can ensure proper monitoring and follow-up. Sometimes truth commissions are fortunate in that a plan of follow-up is built into the mandate, as is the case in Sierra Leone. For most, however, a system of follow-up must be recommended. In Chile, the commission recommended the creation of a public commission to continue some of its own work and to facilitate compliance with reparation measures. In Guatemala, the commission recommended the creation of a follow-up institution (the Foundation for Peace and Harmony, *Fundación por la Paz y la Concordia*, to be made up of government and civil society representatives) to implement some recommendations directly and monitor the implementation of others.

...

MINOW, M 'TRUTH COMMISSIONS' (1998)

in Minow, M *Between vengeance and forgiveness: Facing history after genocide and mass violence* Boston: Beacon Press

...

Imprisoned for twenty-seven years for his political work, the freed Nelson Mandela then helped to negotiate the peaceful end of South Africa's apartheid. A crucial item in the negotiation was how the new government should deal with the events and consequences of the apartheid period. The outgoing leaders made some form of amnesty for those responsible for the regime a condition for the peaceful transfer to a fully democratic society. The interim constitution, a remarkable document of negotiated political transformation, called for a process for freeing participants in apartheid from prosecution. It gave explicit reference to the African concept, *ubuntu*, meaning humaneness, or an inclusive sense of community valuing everyone. Yet precisely the commitment to *ubuntu* made it urgent to establish human rights during the transition, and to help the entire nation confront its past.

The African National Congress (ANC), led by Mandela, wanted a truth commission, an official investigation into the facts of atrocities, tortures, and human rights abuses. The ANC had already launched two independent inquiries into human rights abuses committed by its own members, especially in ANC training camps in Angola. This process unearthed facts about tortures and deaths committed within ANC activities, embraced and elevated human rights standards, and set a tone concerning values that departed from those that prevailed under apartheid. Some ANC leaders thought a similar but more extensive truth commission to inquire into the massive atrocities committed by apartheid officials would help to honour victims and also offer some answers to burning questions about what really had happened under apartheid. The National Party, led by the old regime, advocated a reconciliation commission. The chief concern here was amnesty for participants in the activities approved and ordered by the apartheid government.

After a negotiated settlement between the major parties in the early 1990s, the world awoke on 27 April 1994, to globally transmitted pictures of the dramatic day of South Africa's first democratic elections. People of all colours and races waited patiently in massive lines to vote, and then hung around to celebrate the experience. The multiparty negotiating forum and the last apartheid Parliament adopted the Interim Constitution in 1993. It included in its final paragraphs an unusual self-reflection: A description of the document itself as a bridge from the past of a deeply divided society to a future committed to human rights, democracy, and peaceful coexistence. Toward those ends, the document directed the Parliament to adopt a law providing for the mechanisms and criteria for granting amnesty for conduct 'associated with political objectives and committed in the course of the conflicts of the past'.

On 19 July 1995, the Parliament fulfilled this charge in creating a Truth and Reconciliation Commission (TRC), with a Committee on Human Rights Violations, a Committee on Amnesty, and a Committee on Reparation and Rehabilitation. The Parliament's decision to create the TRC reflected a lengthy process of consultation with many different groups. This process built upon but also distinguished the South African effort from previous truth commissions undertaken elsewhere. Like a few other commissions, the TRC was launched by a democratic legislative act. Yet only the TRC grew from extensive public debate and involvement in its design.

...

After the transition to power in South Africa, national leaders and scholars joined with people drawn from the international community to study these and other previous truth commissions and conducted discussions in public hearings and other settings. Some people worried about this process. University of Cape Town professor Andre Du Toit, a long-time human rights activist in South Africa, has commented, 'as religious leaders and churches became increasingly involved in the commission's work, the influence of religious style and symbolism supplanted political and human rights concerns'. The language of forgiveness invoking religious community grew as the commission took shape.

Yet, when South Africa's justice minister Dullah Omar reflected on the goals embedded in the Act, he stressed the value of the process of public deliberation in creating legitimacy for the undertaking. He also emphasised how the drafters remained mindful of the larger context of negotiation and compromise between former adversaries, as well as theoretical analysis of principles of justice and international law. The religious and ethical commitments and standing of leaders in South Africa, such as Nelson Mandela and Archbishop Desmond Tutu, set the tone of reconciliation and forgiveness. The practical sense of security once the black majority obtained voting rights combined with the continuing recognition that whites retained vital power over economic resources to support a process for forging national unity.

Based on the experiences in other countries, South Africans concluded that 'to achieve unity and morally acceptable reconciliation, it is necessary that the truth about gross violations of human rights must be: Established by an official investigation unit using fair procedures; fully and unreservedly acknowledged by the perpetrators; made known to the public, together with the identity of the planners, perpetrators, and victims'. Crucially, Omar and others decided that the commitment to afford amnesty was the price for allowing a relatively peaceful transition to full democracy. Amnesty would be available but only conditionally to individuals who personally applied for it and who disclosed fully the facts of misdeeds that could be fairly characterised as having a political objective. Trading truth for amnesty, and amnesty for truth, the commission was intended to promote the gathering of facts and the basis for the society to move on toward a strong democratic future.

Members of Griffith Mxenge's family, Steve Biko's family, and other survivors of murdered activists joined to file a lawsuit challenging the TRC's very existence. They claimed that the amnesty provisions violated the rights of families to seek judicial redress for the murders of their loved ones. The newly created Constitutional Court heard the case, and rejected the claim. The court reasoned that neither the South African Constitution nor the Geneva Convention prevented granting amnesty in exchange for truth.

Stinging in the minds of many is the widespread practice of granting amnesty following collective atrocities. In Brazil, the armed forces granted themselves amnesty before permitting the civilian government to be restored; in Uruguay, the civilian government granted amnesty apparently after a private agreement with military leaders to do so. Against those images, amnesty seems closer to impunity than to justice or accountability.

Yet the amnesty process employed by the TRC, however contested and complex, is different. It is not a blanket grant. Prosecutions and civil suits remain potential options against any perpetrators who do not apply for amnesty, and against those whose applications are denied. There is an important difference between the TRC's individual grants of clemency or pardon that follow a finding of guilt, and other amnesties granted prior to prosecution, and often accorded to a group to wipe out the offenses entirely. The conditional amnesty process does not foreclose truth-seeking, but instead promotes it. The commission could secure statements and explanations of specific acts of torture and murder otherwise unavailable, especially because outgoing authorities destroyed records and closed ranks. Thus, as its name signals, the Truth and Reconciliation Commission combines a notion of restorative justice with the search for truth.

The commission is charged not only with obtaining the facts, but also with working to overcome ignorance or denial among the general community and among government officials. It turns the promise of amnesty, wrested from political necessity, into a mechanism for advancing the truth-finding process. The commission also aims to restore and devise recommendations for reparation. Its goal is to express government acknowledgment of the past, to enhance the legitimacy of the current regime, and to promote a climate conducive to human rights and democratic processes. Only if the recommendations for reparations are followed with concrete actions, though, will these aims promise to bear fruit.

Do the aspirations of the South Africa Truth and Reconciliation Commission represent 'second best' goals in the face of practical political constraints? Or do the TRC's objectives identify an admirable alternative to prosecutions needed to implement national and international norms in response to collective violence and state-sponsored atrocities? Does the TRC chart an exemplary path between vengeance and forgiveness? Or does this truth commission illustrate an inevitable residue – of feeling, moral outrage, and justice's demands – that exceeds the reach of legal institutions?

I suggest that even in light of some of the basic goals of prosecution, truth commissions can afford benefits to a society. If the goal of healing individuals and society after the trauma of mass atrocity is elevated, truth commissions could well be a better option than prosecutions, although limitations in the therapeutic value of commissions for individuals and limitations in our knowledge of societal healing make this a line of future inquiry rather than a current conclusion.

...

Healing a nation

Can a therapeutic process work for collectivities? Are truth commission mechanisms, which already fall short of the elements necessary for full therapeutic relationships and treatment for individuals, able to promote reconstruction of whole societies? National healing and reconciliation takes precedence over individual healing in the design of the TRC, but it would be wrong to suggest that a commission by itself could accomplish the reconstruction of a society devastated by violent and hostile divisions. Yet there are promising roles that a commission can play.

Father Bryan Hehir observes that truth commissions function at three levels: (1) personal catharsis through talking about terrible personal trauma; (2) moral reconstruction, by producing a social judgment and moral account of the historical record; and (3) political consequences, to take action such as prosecutions or instead to desist after assessing the risks of further violence and instability. In this view, the social reconstruction occurs as the commission provides an accounting of the atrocities and articulates the moral stance needed to name the horrors, and also to move on.

It remains an open question whether through taking testimony and publishing reports, a truth commission can also help to reconcile groups that have been warring or otherwise engaged in deep animosities. Even a minimal form of reconciliation would require capacities for constructive co-operation between those most victimised and those who committed, ordered, or countenanced their victimisation. Crucial here would be demonstrable evenhandedness and honest acknowledgment of injuries and wrongs committed by the competing sides without losing hold of the distinction between those who abused government power and those who resisted the abuses. The TRC is committed to exposing abuses by the liberation forces as well as by apartheid officials and supporters, and perhaps this commitment to the injuries on both sides can support reconciliation over time. Yet the very effort to articulate the moral baseline must treat the crimes of apartheid as worse than the crimes of the ANC or other antiapartheid activists in terms of scale and motive. Some observers object that the entire TRC operates as a political witch hunt designed to discredit the former National Party government even more than it has been already.

In addition, a truth commission focused on the experiences of victims may tilt the writing of history in terms of victimhood rather than rights in a democratic, political order. Andre Du Toit, an academic activist involved in the formation of the TRC, worries that the focus on victims, caregiving, and the Christian notion of forgiveness may lead some people to refuse to participate. The survivors [who do not identify as victims] do not relate to this situation. They respond by saying, 'we have had these experiences, but we do not want to present ourselves as victims in need of healing. We do not necessarily agree with the message of forgiveness. What political purpose does the story serve when it is framed in this way?'

Treating truth commissions as focused on therapy seems to ignore politics, short-change justice issues, and treat survivors and their recovery as a means toward a better society rather than as persons with dignity and entitlements to justice. Yael Tamir, an Israeli philosopher, listened to an exchange of views about the relative importance of victim testimony and common civic rights in truth commissions, and commented: 'I am uneasy about this psychological perspective because the catharsis of one person is the suffering of another. How does this work in cases where everybody has done something wrong to somebody else?'

Even where everyone has done something wrong to someone else, the wager of the TRC is that reconciliation can be better reached if the emphasis is on securing in public form the fullest possible truth. Then there is a chance to acknowledge human rights violations committed by each side rather than to blame and punish only those who devised and implemented apartheid.

Yet many long-time antiapartheid activists cannot accept the archbishop's call for reconciliation and forgiveness across South Africa. To Churchill Mzenge, the brother of Griffith Mxenge, and antiapartheid lawyer murdered under apartheid orders, the archbishop's stance seems a betrayal of his own promises made at Griffith's funeral to ensure that justice would be done. The surviving brother recounted to Tina Rosenberg, 'I try to put myself in Tutu's position ... Tutu is a man of the cloth, a man who believes in miracles. But I cannot see him being able overnight to cause people who are hurt and bleeding simply to forget about their wounds and forget about justice ... Unless justice is done it's difficult for any person to think of forgiving'.

Churchill Mxenge had the chance to convey his views to Archbishop Tutu directly on a television show with several family members of apartheid victims. Tutu offered the explanation of political necessity: Amnesty was extended to avoid military upheaval. When Tina Rosenberg later asked the archbishop whether he was honouring his commitment to justice, he replied by identifying different kinds of justice: 'Retributive justice is largely Western. The African understanding is far more restorative – not so much to punish as to redress or restore a balance that has been knocked askew. The justice we hope for is restorative of the dignity of the people'.

Archbishop Tutu does not speak for all black South Africans, and certainly not for all South Africans, in this aspiration. This very dissension, ideally, could be part of the story narrated by a truth commission. Honesty about the complexity of the past and transparency about the commission's own deliberations can help prevent the production of a victors' report. A fact-finding commission can expose the multiple causes and conditions contributing to genocide and to regimes of torture and terror, and it can distribute blame and responsibility across sectors of society.

Many in South Africa proudly embrace the TRC's search for nonviolent responses to violence. From their vantage point, it is an act of restraint not to pursue criminal sanctions, and an act of hope not to strip perpetrators of their political and economic positions. Yet it is also an act of judgment that prosecutions would impose too great a cost to stability, reconciliation, or nation building. Acknowledging the dimension of political necessity should not obscure the dimension of courage. When a democratic process selects a truth commission, a people summon the strength and vision to say to one another: Focus on victims and try to restore their dignity; focus on truth and try to tell it whole. Pursue a vision of restorative justice, itself perhaps a major casualty in the colonial suppression of African traditions. Redefine the victims as the entire society, and redefine justice as accountability. Seek repair, not revenge; reconciliation, not recrimination. Honour and attend in public to the process of remembering. Cynthia Ngewu, mother of one of the individuals known as the Guguletu Seven, expressed the vision beautifully:

> This thing called reconciliation ... if I am understanding it correctly ... if it means this perpetrator, this man who has killed Christopher Piet, if it means he becomes human again, this man, so that I, so that all of us, get our humanity back ... then I agree, then I support it all.

These bold ambitions may be doomed. To create such high expectations is to invite disappointment. Yet the wager is that setting these goals at least to some degree redirects people's understandable desires for vengeance and recrimination. The democratic origins of the TRC help to consecrate that redirection through a process of broad participation. A truth commission imposed by the nation's executive or an international body may have even more difficulty conveying the messages of reconciliation. It might instead seem merely an insincere or ineffective sop to those who demand some response to the atrocities. Articulating goals more modestly than the TRC's – such as gathering names and accounts of victims and documenting the scope of killings, torture, and other atrocities – could save truth commissions from generating cycles of high hopes and bitter disappointments.

The TRC's pursuit of restorative justice is also in jeopardy if it presages no changes in the material circumstances of those most victimised. Characterised as only one step in the process of reconciliation, the TRC is designed to propose specific economic reparations and also to assist the development of a society stable enough to pursue land reform, redesign of medical and educational systems, and other reforms to redress the massive economic imbalances in the country. The TRC committee on reparations will recommend to the president specific acts requested by the victimised, such as funds for gravestones, as well as collective reparations in the form of monuments, parks, and schools named for victims and survivors, and individual stipends to support medical and therapeutic treatment. Its Authorising Act also creates a special fund to meet the immediate needs of those who testify. The longer term vision of social transformation holds out the idea of redemption for suffering, and yet if progress toward this vision is not made, scepticism about the goals of healing and reconciliation will surely mount.

Justice requires at least particular truths. Truth-seeking may occur without the trials that can produce just punishments. Truth and justice are not the only objectives, or at least they do not transparently indicate the range of concerns they may come to comprise. Instead, I have identified twelve overlapping aspirations:

1. overcome communal and official denial of the atrocity and gain public acknowledgment;
2. obtain the facts in an account as full as possible in order to meet victims' need to know, to build a record for history, and to ensure minimal accountability and visibility of perpetrators;
3. end and prevent violence; transform human activity from violence – and violent responses to violence – into words and institutional practices of equal respect and dignity;
4. forge the basis for a domestic democratic order that respects and enforces human rights;
5. support the legitimacy and stability of the new regime proceeding after the atrocity;
6. promote reconciliation across social divisions; reconstruct the moral and social systems devastated by violence;
7. promote psychological healing for individuals, groups, victims, bystanders, and offenders;
8. restore dignity to victims;
9. punish, exclude, shame, and diminish offenders for their offenses;

10. express and seek to achieve the aspiration that 'never again' shall such collective violence occur;
11. build an international order to try to prevent and also to respond to aggression, torture, and atrocities;
12. accomplish each of these goals in ways that are compatible with the other goals.

In light of this list, truth commissions are not a second-best alternative to prosecutions, but instead a form better suited to meet many of the goals. Indeed, to serve the goals of healing for individuals and reconciliation across social divisions even better, truth commissions would need to diverge even more than they usually do from prosecutions, and to offer more extensive therapeutic assistance and relief from threats of prosecution.

When the societal goals include restoring dignity to victims, offering a basis for individual healing, and also promoting reconciliation across a divided nation, a truth commission again may be as or more powerful than prosecutions. The commission can help set a tone and create public rituals to build a bridge from a terror-filled past to a collective, constructive future. Individuals do and must have their own responses to atrocity, but the institutional framework created by a society can either encourage desires for retribution or instead strengthen capacities for generosity and peace.

This suggests that the most difficult aspiration is the last one: It is far from clear that a truth commission can achieve therapeutic and reconciliatory goals at the same time that prosecutions proceed. Although South Africa currently permits prosecutions of those individuals who do not obtain amnesty from the TRC, all of the practical dimensions of prosecutions could work against the goals of healing, reconciliation, and full truth-telling. Nonetheless, a rich understanding of healing from atrocity gives an important place to the operations of a justice system, including prosecution and punishment of perpetrators, if the process is not to unleash new violence and thirst for revenge. Prosecutions and truth commissions share, fundamentally, the effort to cabin and channel through public, legal institutions the understandable and even justifiable desires for revenge by those who have been victimised.

The repertoire of societal responses to collective violence must include prosecutions, but it must not be limited to them. Investigatory commissions, most fully developed in the South African Truth and Reconciliation Commission, challenge the assumption that prosecutions are the best form of response. Consider the story of General Magnus Malan, army chief and later defense minister. Charged with authorising an assassination squad that mistakenly killed thirteen women and children in 1987, General Malan was the subject of one of the few prosecutions before the completion of the work of the TRC in South Africa. The prosecution of Malan grew from nine months of investigation and trial took nine more, costing twelve million rand. In 1996, General Malan was found not guilty, despite numerous allegations that continued to be made after the trial ended. Then, in 1997, General Malan volunteered to speak before the TRC. He expressly did not seek amnesty but instead wanted the chance to tell his own story. He acknowledged cross-border raids; he described how he set up a convert unit to disrupt Soviet-backed liberations movements. He denied approval of assassinations or atrocities. He also made clear his opposition to the operation of the TRC itself, as a witch-hunt, but said that he came forward to take moral responsibility for the orders he had given.

Fact-finding commissions open inquiry into the varieties of possible responses and the multiple responses and the multiple purposes they may achieve. Truth commissions emphasise the experiences of those victimised; the development of a detailed historical record; and the priority of healing for victims and entire societies after the devastation to bodies, memories, families, friendships, and politics caused by collective violence. A truth commission could generate the evidence to support prosecutions. Or, when the fullest accounts and anticipation are sought in a nation marked by deep and historic divisions, a truth commission represents a potential alternative to prosecutions. Whether these implement or complement justice, they are worthy of human effort in the continuing struggles against mass atrocities.

...

Slye considers the nature and scope of the mandate of the International Criminal Court (ICC). He discusses the circumstances under which cases can be admitted by the ICC and the way in which investigations of serious crimes may be undertaken if not investigated or prosecuted by national courts.

SLYE, R 'THE INTERNATIONAL CRIMINAL COURT' (2004)

in Villa-Vicencio, C and Doxtader, E *Pieces of the Puzzle* Cape Town: Institute for Justice and Reconciliation

The International Criminal Court (ICC) was created by a treaty negotiated in Rome in 1998 (the Rome Treaty). The Rome Treaty required 60 ratifications before the Court could come into existence. These ratifications came far sooner than many had anticipated and on 1 July 2002, the ICC came into being. As of May 2004 94 countries had ratified the Rome Treaty. These include 8 states from Europe, including France, Germany and the United Kingdom; 24 states from Africa, including the Democratic Republic of the Congo, Namibia, Nigeria, South Africa and Sierra Leone; and other significant states from all regions of the globe, including Argentina, Australia, Brazil, Canada, Jordan and New Zealand. Significant states that have not ratified the treaty include China, Russia and the United States.

The Court's subject matter jurisdiction is limited to four of the most serious international crimes: genocide, crimes against humanity, war crimes and aggression. At the present moment, the Court has subject matter jurisdiction only over the first three of these crimes. The Court will have jurisdiction over the fourth crime, aggression, only after the states party to the Rome Treaty agree on a definition of aggression ... Under the terms of the Rome Treaty, the earliest period by which such a definition can be agreed is July 2009.

Personal jurisdiction

Only individuals may be prosecuted before the Court, although those who are under 18 years of age at the time they commit one of the enumerated crimes are explicitly excluded from the jurisdiction of the Court. Organisations, corporations and states are not subject to the jurisdiction of the ICC. This is in contrast to the International Court of Justice, which can only hear cases brought by one state against another, and in rare circumstances can hear a case brought by an agency of the United Nations. While other courts have suggested that certain high-ranking government officials may not be prosecuted while they are in office, the Rome Treaty is quite clear that such immunities do not hold with respect to the work undertaken by the ICC. Thus, any individual, regardless of his or her official status either at the time of the commission of the offence or at the time of the prosecution, may be brought before the ICC.

Military commanders and other superiors may be held responsible for the acts of their subordinates if they either ordered such acts or knew, or should have known, that their subordinates were committing such acts. Thus, a superior officer may not avoid criminal responsibility just because he or she did not engage in the torture, killing or other act that constitutes an international criminal offence. He or she may avoid responsibility if it can be shown that all necessary and reasonable measures within his or her power were taken to prevent the criminal activity, or that the matter was referred to the relevant authorities for investigation and possible prosecution.

In addition to being limited to crimes committed by natural persons, the ICC is subject to a number of other jurisdictional limitations. It is charged to hear only those cases that involve the most serious international crimes and only in circumstances where there is no other viable forum before which individual responsibility for such crimes can be adjudicated.

The Court does not automatically have jurisdiction over an individual suspected of committing one of the four enumerated crimes. To be subject to the Court's jurisdiction, an individual must either be a national of a state party to the Rome Treaty, or the act for which they are being prosecuted must have been committed on the territory of a state party. In other words, there must be a link between the individual suspected of committing the international crime and a state that has ratified the Rome Treaty. If there is such a link, then the Court has personal jurisdiction over the individual. Thus, if an individual who is either from a state that is not a party to the Court or who commits one of the enumerated crimes in the territory of a state that is not party to the Rome Treaty, then they fall outside of the personal jurisdiction of the Court. As of this writing, a US soldier who commits a war crime in Iraq would not be subject to the jurisdiction of the ICC, as neither the United States nor Iraq has ratified the Rome Treaty.

There is one significant exception to these requirements: The Court can assert jurisdiction over crimes committed by an individual who is not a national of a state party and when the offences are not committed on the territory of a non-state party if the United Nations (UN) Security Council refers the matter to the Court. Thus, the ICC has potential jurisdiction over every individual and territory in the world subject to the approval of the Security Council and the veto powers of the five permanent members (China, France, Russia, the United Kingdom and the United States of America).

Admissibility

The ICC's jurisdiction complements, rather than replaces, the jurisdiction of national courts. Even if an individual suspected of committing one of the covered crimes satisfies the linkage requirement of personal jurisdiction, the Court may still not have the power to hear the case. If the Court has personal jurisdiction over the individual for a crime that falls within its subject matter jurisdiction, the case may not be heard if it fails to meet certain admissibility requirements. A case is admissible and can proceed to trial only if all other states that also have jurisdiction over the individual for the same criminal activity choose not to prosecute. Thus, if an individual subject to the personal jurisdiction of the Court commits a war crime in the context of an armed conflict, the ICC will only be able to prosecute that individual if neither the state in which the crime was committed nor the state of which the individual is a national decides to prosecute.

The Rome Treaty mentions neither amnesty nor truth commissions. To the extent that they are used to protect an individual from accountability for an international crime, amnesty and truth commissions may raise questions about the admissibility of a case. If a state undertakes an investigation or prosecution of an individual suspected of a violation within the jurisdiction of the Court, the case may still be admissible if it can be shown that the investigation or prosecution were in fact designed to protect the individual from any liability for his or her crimes. Therefore, the question facing the Court will be whether a truth commission like the South African Truth and Reconciliation Commission (TRC) provides sufficient accountability for violations of international criminal law. If it does not, then the Court may hear a case even though it was the subject of such a commission.

Investigations

The Court has certain built-in checks and balances to ensure that only the most serious crimes that would otherwise not be addressed are investigated and prosecuted. There are three ways that the jurisdiction of the Court may be triggered (or an investigation for the purpose possible prosecution may be initiated): by a state party to the Rome Treaty, by the United Nations Security Council or by the prosecutor of the ICC. A state party may refer to the prosecutor for further investigation of a 'situation' in which crimes subject to the Court's jurisdiction are alleged to have occurred. Similarly, the Security Council may also refer a matter to the prosecutor for further investigation.

In addition to initiating investigations based on a referral by a state party or the Security Council, the prosecutor may under his own initiative investigate situations where one of the enumerated crimes is alleged to have occurred. The prosecutor's authority to initiate an investigation and eventual indictment is subject to the approval of a Pre-Trial Chamber of the Court. The prosecutor must have a 'reasonable basis' for initiating the investigation. Even if the prosecutor believes that they have a reasonable basis for proceeding with an investigation, they may not proceed unless the Pre-Trial Chamber agrees with their determination and assertion that the case does indeed fall within the jurisdiction of the Court. The decision at this initial stage by a Pre-Trial Chamber with respect to jurisdiction and admissibility is not binding on the Court.

In June 2004, the Prosecutor, Luis Moreno Ocampo, announced that he was initiating his first investigation of alleged violations under the Rome Treaty in the Democratic Republic of the Congo.

...

Kofi Annan considers the significance and potential of the International Criminial Court (ICC) in the promotion of international law.

INTERNATIONAL CRIMINAL COURT JUDGES EMBODY 'OUR COLLECTIVE CONSCIENCE' SAYS SECRETARY-GENERAL TO INAUGURAL MEETING IN THE HAGUE (2003)

United Nations Press Release SG/SM/8628
Also available at http://www.un.org/News/Press/docs/2003/sgsm8628.doc.htm

It has taken mankind many years to reach this moment.

By the solemn undertaking they have given here in open court, these 11 men and seven women, representing all regions of the world and many different cultures and legal traditions, have made themselves the embodiment of our collective conscience.

For centuries, and especially in the last century, that conscience has been shocked by unspeakable crimes: Crimes whose victims were counted not in tens, but in tens of thousands — even in millions.

By 1945, those crimes had cost humanity so dear that it was deemed necessary to set up special tribunals, in Nuremberg and Tokyo, to judge the main perpetrators. Those tribunals established a principle of vital importance: That those who take part in gross violations of international humanitarian law cannot shelter behind the authority of the State in whose name they did so. They must take personal responsibility for their acts, and face the consequences.

Ever since then, the international community has sought to establish a permanent international criminal court to try and punish those who commit genocide, war crimes and crimes against humanity. These include mass murder, enslavement, rape, torture, and other abhorrent crimes — not only against people of other nations, but also against their own.

A big step forward was taken in the past decade, with the establishment of the international criminal tribunals for the former Yugoslavia and for Rwanda. These have already shown that it is feasible to bring to impartial justice, before a judiciary representing the world's great legal systems, persons both high and low who are accused of crimes against humanity.

Yet it has taken 50 years to agree on the form this court should take, and the extent of its powers. There were many considerations that had to be carefully evaluated – in particular, the implications such a court might have for the delicate process of dismantling tyrannies and replacing them with more democratic regimes, committed to uphold human rights.

There are times when we are told that justice must be set aside in the interests of peace. It is true that justice can only be dispensed when the peaceful order of society is secure. But we have come to understand that the reverse is also true: Without justice, there can be no lasting peace.

Certainly there is a place in every court for mercy and compassion. But mercy can be shown only when guilt and responsibility have been clearly established and acknowledged.

And individual responsibility is of crucial importance, for two reasons.

First, persons who are tempted or pressured to commit unspeakable crimes must be deterred, by the knowledge that one day they will be individually called to account. That deterrence was missing in the past. It is needed today as much as ever, and it will be needed in the future.

And second, only by clearly identifying the individuals responsible for these crimes can we save whole communities from being held collectively guilty. It is that notion of collective guilt which is the true enemy of peace, since it encourages communities to nurture hatred against each other from one generation to the next.

As for compassion, those most entitled to it are, of course, the victims of crime.

For those who have been slaughtered, all we can do is seek to accord them in death the dignity and respect they were so cruelly denied in life.

To the survivors, who are also the witnesses, and to the bereaved, we owe a justice that also brings healing. And that means that you, the judges, will have to show great patience and compassion, as well as an unfailing resolve to arrive at the truth. There must be justice, not only in the end result, but also in the process.

Above all, however, this court is for those who might be victims in the future. If the court lives up to our expectations, they will not be victims, because would-be violators will be deterred.

That is why it is so important that you, the judges, and all the officials of the Court, demonstrate in all your actions and decisions an unimpeachable integrity and impartiality.

In all your functions – judicial, administrative and representational – you must act without fear or favour, guided and inspired by the provisions of the Rome Statute. The wisdom of your judgements must be such as to command universal respect for international justice and the force of law. The honesty and efficiency of the Court's administration must be beyond reproach.

All your work must shine with moral and legal clarity, bringing life to the provisions of the Rome Statute and helping the States parties to discharge their share of responsibility. That assistance will be an important part of your task.

Of crucial importance is one responsibility that States parties must discharge in the very near future: The choice of a prosecutor. The importance of that function can hardly be exaggerated. As we know from the experience of the international tribunals for the former Yugoslavia and Rwanda, the decisions and public statements of the prosecutor will do more than anything else to establish the reputation of the Court, especially in the first phases of its work.

It is, therefore, vital that a person of the highest calibre be found to undertake that grave responsibility. This surely is a time to set aside national interests, and focus exclusively on the qualifications of the individual candidates. Once that choice is made, States will also have a responsibility to co-operate with the Court – in effecting arrests of those indicted, in providing evidence, and in enforcing sentences once imposed. That co-operation is essential, if the Court is to succeed.

The commitment shown thus far augurs well for the future. The United Nations looks forward to working with the International Criminal Court in this cause, which is the cause of all humanity.

In this newspaper article, consideration is given to the complex situation prevailing in northern Uganda. The question is posed whether the arrest and prosecution of child killers will potentially facilitate peace or undermine initiatives aimed at bringing an end to the crisis.

'HUNTING UGANDA'S CHILD-KILLERS: JUSTICE VERSUS RECONCILIATION' (2005)

375 *The Economist* 57

No one doubts that terrible crimes have been committed in northern Uganda. The Lord's Resistance Army (LRA), a rebel group led by Joseph Kony, a man who thinks himself semi-divine, has spent the past 18 years slaughtering peasants, enslaving children and slicing off the lips and noses of conscripts it suspects of disloyalty. But does this mean that the newly established International Criminal Court (ICC) should be going after Mr Kony and his lieutenants? Several community leaders in northern Uganda think not.

As the ICC prepares to issue its first arrest warrants against the LRA's leaders, Rwot Acana II, the paramount chief of the northern Acholi people, who have borne the brunt of the rebels' atrocities, predicts that it will be 'the last nail in the coffin' of a fragile peace process. The threat of prosecution, he argues, will deter the rebels from accepting a government-offered amnesty, and therefore prolong the war. He and other Acholi leaders have been furiously lobbying the ICC to back off. They argue that it would be better to apply traditional Acholi justice. If the rebels confess their guilt and undergo cleansing rituals, they will be accepted back into their communities, say the ICC's critics.

The ICC was first invited to consider the northern Ugandan conflict in January 2004, by the Ugandan government. Earlier this year, the government appeared to be having second thoughts. President Yoweri Museveni spoke of 'convincing the ICC to drop their indictment if the LRA rebels surrender'. But Luis Moreno-Ocampo, the court's chief prosecutor, turned a deaf ear, and the government has now relented. Mr Moreno-Ocampo is expected to apply to the court's pre-trial chamber for arrest warrants against half a dozen rebel chiefs by the end of this month.

Mr Kony's gang has reportedly abducted more than 20 000 children. Some are forced to fight, some to carry bags, others to have sex with the fighters. By way of initiation, many are obliged to club, stamp or bite to death their friends and relatives, and then to lick their brains, drink their blood and even eat their boiled flesh.

Nearly 2 million people, representing some 90 per cent of the population of the three main Acholi provinces of Gulu, Kitgum and Pader, have fled their homes and now live in crowded and unhealthy camps. Even here, they are at risk. Every night, streams of bare-footed children trudge miles to sleep in the relative safety of the main towns, before returning home at dawn.

The force that terrorises them remains shadowy. Mr Kony, who was raised, like most Acholis, as a Catholic, claims to have been sent by God to save his people from evil, a heading under which he includes President Museveni and all forms of witchcraft. He says he wants to rule Uganda in accordance with the Ten Commandments, though he has at times made more prosaic demands, including education for all, an independent judiciary and policies to encourage foreign investment.

No one knows how many troops Mr Kony commands. Some say he once had as many as 10,000; others that he now has only a few hundred. Betty Bigombe, the chief mediator between the government and the LRA, reckons there are about 3 000 'rebels' left, of whom 800 are fighters. Since Mr Museveni's forces number 100 000 or so, including militias, many northerners wonder how hard the government is really trying to crush the rebellion.

That said, peace looks more likely now than for a decade. Pressure on the rebels has increased since the government of neighbouring Sudan agreed in 2002 to stop backing them. It has also allowed Ugandan forces to attack Mr Kony's bases in southern Sudan, and last month, the two countries mounted their first joint military operation against the LRA.

This, combined with the amnesty, has flushed thousands of rebels out of the bush. Despite the vaunted Acholi tradition of reconciliation, many have found it hard to rejoin their own communities. Hundreds have joined the army instead, and are now hunting their former comrades. Others have hidden to escape the wrath of their families. But Mr Kony and his top commanders have not been lured out – and many suspect they never will be.

The ICC's supporters argue that it can help end impunity, which was why it was first set up in 1998. If Mr Kony is brought to justice, it may deter others currently contemplating mass murder. And despite the fears of Acholi leaders – which not all Acholis share – it does not seem to have impeded the peace process in northern Uganda. Some argue that, on the contrary, it has increased the pressure on rank-and-file rebels to turn themselves in.

But the ICC has no police force. How, ask the sceptics, will it catch Mr Kony when he has evaded the Ugandan army for 18 years? The court's supporters retort that similar misgivings were voiced when the international tribunal for the former Yugoslavia was set up, yet Slobodan Milosevic, the former Serbian president, and most of his generals are now in the dock.

Since this is its first test case, the ICC is determined to succeed in northern Uganda. Its credibility is at stake. Catching Mr Kony may take years or even decades. But unlike other international tribunals, the ICC is permanent. There is no time limit for its work. Its indictments, once issued, remain in force until the indictee is either tried or dead. It can wait for Mr Kony, who may incidentally be running out of hiding places.

His fellow Acholis hate him. His friends in Sudan are turning their backs on him. Donors are pressuring Mr Museveni to pacify the north (and to abide by constitutional term limits, but that is another story). Mr Kony might hope to hide in a state that is not a party to the ICC. But who would want him?

The provisions for the Sierra Leonean Special Court to prosecute those primarily responsible for the atrocities committed in that country after 30 November 1996 are a major step forward in the advancement of international law. The question, however, remains how to deal with those guilty of crimes prior to that date. The need for reparations is discussed and the limitations of the amnesty clause in the 1999 Lome Peace Agreement are identified.

AMNESTY INTERNATIONAL 'SIERRA LEONE: ENDING IMPUNITY AND ACHIEVING JUSTICE' (2005)

Amnesty International's message to the National Victims Commemoration Conference

Also available at www.amnesty.org

...

The Statute of the Special Court provides a mandate to prosecute those *'who bear the greatest responsibility'* for crimes against humanity, war crimes and other serious violations of international law committed during Sierra Leone's armed conflict after 30 November 1996. Its jurisdiction therefore does not include all those who committed crimes under international law throughout the 10-year conflict. Only 11 of the very large number of people suspected of committing these crimes have been indicted. Two of them, including former Liberian President Charles Taylor, have yet to be arrested and surrendered to the Special Court.

Since August 2003 Charles Taylor has been harboured by the Nigerian government in violation of its legally binding obligations under international law. Its decision to grant refugee status to Charles Taylor violates Nigeria's obligations to surrender a person indicted for crimes under international law or to submit the case to its prosecuting authorities. The Nigerian government must arrest Charles Taylor and surrender him to the Special Court.

While prosecuting a few of those responsible for these crimes is a major contribution towards ending impunity in Sierra Leone, it is only a partial response. More needs to be done. While Sierra Leone's Truth and Reconciliation Commission (TRC) has been important in providing a forum for victims and perpetrators to recount their experiences, creating an impartial historical record of human rights abuses committed during the conflict, identifying the reasons for those abuses, and facilitating reconciliation, it cannot be a substitute for a court of law to try alleged perpetrators of serious violations of international law.

An essential element of providing justice to the victims of human rights abuses is the provision of reparations. Amnesty International was disappointed that the Statute of the Special Court did not follow the example of the Rome Statute of the International Criminal Court by authorising the Special Court to award reparations for victims of crimes within its jurisdiction, including restitution, compensation, rehabilitation, satisfaction and guarantees of non-repetition. Such reparations are integral to achieving justice for the victims and also assisting them to rebuild their lives.

The national justice system needs to be able to work to ensure that all those who committed horrific crimes during the conflict, but who are not among the small number indicted by the Special Court, are brought to justice and that their victims have access to reparations. In this, the 'legacy' bequeathed by the Special Court to the national justice system – which continues to face serious challenges in providing effective and efficient administration of justice – is crucial. Although the Special Court cannot by itself turn around the struggling national justice system, its presence, example and resources should be an important catalyst for and reinforce a committed, long-term strategy to end impunity and build an effective system of justice for the future.

A major stumbling block, however, is the general amnesty included in the 1999 Lomé peace agreement and subsequently enacted into national law. This amnesty, however, cannot apply to crimes against humanity, war crimes and other serious violations of international law. In a historic decision in March 2004 the Special Court refused to recognise the applicability of the amnesty provided by the Lomé peace agreement and concluded that it did not prevent international courts, such as the Special Court, or foreign courts from prosecuting crimes against humanity and war crimes. For impunity to be successfully challenged in Sierra Leone, the amnesty provision must be removed from the statute books.

A landmark and lasting legacy of the Special Court would be if its example were to be followed and the death penalty removed from Sierra Leone's statute books. The discrepancy between the Special Court, where the maximum penalty which can be imposed is a period of imprisonment, and the national courts, which continue to pass death sentences, needs to removed. The Sierra Leone government should follow the example of the Special Court, as well as implement one of the key recommendations of the TRC, and abolish the death penalty.

Women suffer specific crimes, such as rape, in a conflict situation. These crimes are often not adequately addressed through the justice process and need specific attention. The African Union mandate and role in the promotion of gender justice are considered.

JUMA, M 'THE ROLE OF THE AFRICAN UNION MACHINERY IN PROMOTING GENDER JUSTICE IN POST-CONFLICT SOCIETIES' (2005)

African Women for Peace Advocacy Magazine Special Edition

Gender in post-conflict societies

Post-conflict situations pose a number of challenges to the reconstitution of justice – broadly taken to encompass the set of norms and principles that assign rights and duties, and guarantee appropriate distribution of benefits and burden among societal members. Effective justice ensures due process, engenders a sense of fairness and forms a basis for public law and order, whose breakdown is a major source of conflict in the first place. In other words, attainment of justice and reconciliation guarantees the rule of law and the protection of private and collective property. Challenges relating to retribution, restoration and/or healing in post-conflict situations are compounded when viewed through a gender lens. This paper flags out, in a summarised form, some of these challenges and suggests ways in which the African Union (AU) can utilise its mandate to promote gender justice in post-war countries.

Usually, justice systems and structures are among the first to collapse at the onset of conflict. This reality accentuates the level of injustice that women confront during active conflicts. Disruption and break-up of familial, social and community structures of protection as well as the involvement men in prosecuting war, expose women to numerous levels of insecurity and injustices. Furthermore, efforts to deal with injustices committed during, or after, war are complicated by the heinous character and nature of violence perpetrated against women. In all major African conflicts from Liberia, Sierra Leone, Democratic Republic of Congo, Rwanda, Burundi, Northern Uganda, Southern Sudan to Somalia, women have been subjected to war crimes including rape, physical violence, assault, destitution and prolonged physical and psychological insecurity emanating from the loss of social networks and protection. In extreme situations, women have been targets of war, part of the war game and/or booty. No wonder statistics the world over indicate women to be the main victims of war. Attainment of justice in post-conflict situations therefore cannot escape dealing with gender specific crimes and injustices as a basis for consolidation of peace. Failure to do so meaningfully not only increases the vulnerability of women in 'peace' times, but also means violations against women could continue unabated.

Attention in addressing gender justice needs to focus at two levels: First are the issues in the normative realm that sets forth the norms, principles, standards and benchmarks that guarantee justice. In other words, what choice does a country emerging from conflict adopt in terms of the justice system? It is imperative that women effectively participate in determining the national choice; otherwise reconstruction runs the risk of excluding a large section of the population. A second set of issues relates to the transformation of institutions and ethos in ways that enable women to take full advantage of opportunities that the reconstruction agenda presents. The AU has the potential to reinforce both these levels of engagement in all aspects and activities of post conflict reconstruction.

AU mandate and role in promoting gender justice

The AU has a central role in the promotion of justice, including gender justice, in post-conflict societies. Broadly, this mandate is derived from article 5(2) of the Constitutive Act, which provides for the establishments of a Peace and Security Council (PSC). This Council is a standing decision-making organ for the prevention, management and resolution of conflicts, including post-conflict reconstruction. More specifically, the Protocol Relating to the

Establishment of the Peace and Security Council states the rationale for the creation of the PSC as, among other things:

> To promote and implement peacebuilding and post-conflict reconstruction activities and to consolidate peace and prevent resurgence of violence, as well as to promote and encourage democratic practices, good governance and the rule of law, protect human rights and fundamental freedoms, respect for the sanctity of human life and international humanitarian law, as part of the efforts for preventing conflicts.

This involves restoration of the rule of law, establishment and development of democratic institutions, consolidation of peace agreements, reconstruction of the society and government institutions, implementation of disarmament, demobilisation and reintegration of refugees and internally displaced persons, humanitarian action and disaster management. The manner in which these activities are conceived and implemented has implications for the extent to which women can claim and access justice in the post-war situations.

While the AU has a well-articulated mandate for post-conflict reconstruction, the Protocol makes flirting references to gender specific issues in post-war situations. Women are conceived as objectives of intervention and lumped with other categories of 'vulnerable' groups, namely children, the elderly and other traumatised groups (article 14 (3)). Although positive interpretation of this provision could address issues specific to gender injustice and needs, this is not provided for explicitly and remains as a matter of speculation.

The on-going work of crafting an AU framework for post-conflict reconstruction provides a great opportunity for the AU to promote gender justice. It should be recognised that war impacts differently on women and men. The reconstitution of a society, including its justice systems and practices, may require new and innovative frameworks and structures that differ from those in place before the outbreak of conflict. In other words, pre-war institutions may be incapable of addressing crimes committed during or after the war, as well as the consequences of such crimes. Experiences across the continent indicate a great desire to address gender (in)justice and inequality especially in areas that have traditionally been of concern such as participation in decision-making, economic empowerment, especially issues of property, access to credit, etc. While these are important and need to be pursued, it is critical to note that war experiences transform societies, and that communities seldom return to their exact pre-war order. Reconstruction should thus be conceived as an opportunity for innovative reconstitution or creation of structures that open up new horizons for women empowerment including enhancing gender justice.

...

Challenges for enhancing gender justice

There are three major obstacles to the enhancement of gender justice in post-conflict situations. Perhaps the greatest is the manner in which recovery is conceived and executed. Any post-war situation is characterised by immense pressure to turn a country around. However, the vision of this recovery is still dominated by development and securocrat perspectives, with the main actors being international (World Bank, Development donors etc) and the national political and security elite. This mind set obscures other critical aspects of recovery, including justice, which remain addendums to the 'main' programmes, namely economic development and security. Issues of fairness, due process, distribution or governance are seen as 'soft' areas. This poses a paradigmatic challenge especially because it diminishes the value of a more integrative human security approach to reconstruction.

Secondly, the lack of a normative framework for reconstruction leaves countries to muddle through reconstruction without a template to guide national processes that determine their priorities and design strategies for recovery. This void is often filled by international intervention in the form of expatriates or imposition of foreign models that may be irrelevant to the situation on the ground. More often than not these interventions fail to consolidate peace.

Thirdly, although women are increasingly playing critical roles in conflict resolution, peace building and post conflict reconstruction, they remain under-represented at decision and policy-making levels at both the national and multilateral levels. Women remain marginalised from the onset of peace processes. From Burundi, Sierra Leone, Liberia, DR-Congo and most recently in the Sudan, male securocrat types have dominated peace processes – this composition has undoubtedly shaped both the nature of negotiations as well as implementation practices. The need for adequate and effective women representation in thinking about, designing and implementing policies and programmes cannot be emphasised enough. If the experiences from the few peacekeeping missions where women have been deployed are anything to go by, then the involvement of women in post-conflict reconstruction, and especially in the area of justice which is a linchpin for co-existence and democratic practice, is an imperative.

Opportunities for the AU to promote gender justice

First, the AU has made some progress that should be consolidated as evidenced by its adoption of the Protocol on the Rights of Women. It has embraced the values of gender equality, democracy, human rights and good governance and made policy decisions to increase the participation of women at the continental, regional and national levels. The expansion of these values will be tested by the ability and commitment of the African Union to involve key constituencies, in this case women, in activities relating to the peace and security agenda in general and post-conflicts reconstruction specifically. Commitments need to be translated into frameworks and guidelines that ensure women contribute positively. In line with this, the AU can use its leverage to cascade these commitments to the regional and national levels. It could encourage member states to adopt parity with AU commitment on gender equality. This would greatly increase the opportunity for women to access and improve the justice in post-conflict situations.

Secondly, the AU could enhance gender issue within its mechanisms. Women should as a matter of right, rather than privilege, serve in key AU organs such as the Panel of the Wise, be appointed as special envoys or mediators and be offered an opportunity to engage in various processes of unpacking the different aspects of the peace and security agenda, including post-conflict reconstruction.

Thirdly, the AU can encourage women to take advantage of the provisions of the Protocol on Peace and Security to increase their influence in the Peace and Security Council. Using article 8 of the Protocol, the AU could establish a unit that monitors genders issues in post conflict situations. It is imperative that such a committee or unit is linked to the PSC and other AU structures. One way of attaining this immediately, would be to revive the defunct African Women Committee on Peace and Development and locate it within the AU structures rather than consulting it in an advisory capacity. The AU could also urge the Peace and Security Council to invite women groups, experts and organisations to address the Council on a regular basis, as provided for in article 20 of the Protocol on Peace and Security. In addition to providing women with an opportunity to influence the decisions of the PSC, such an arrangement would keep the Council well-informed on the issues relating to gender in any recovery situation.

...

QUESTIONS

(1) Do traditional justice systems, such as *gacaca*, provide distinct advantages or disadvantages when compared to international criminal law, such as the International Criminal Tribunal for Rwanda or the International Criminal Court?

(2) Is it justifiable to suspend prosecutorial justice, as was done to some extent in the case of the South African Truth and Reconciliation Commission, for the sake of peace?

(3) Can there be peace without justice? Choose an African country to illustrate your argument.

(4) When does a transitional period end, requiring a country to terminate transitional justice initiatives?

(5) What steps might a nation in transition be required to take to ensure economic growth?

(6) What form can reparations realistically take in a poor country such as Rwanda or Burundi?

FURTHER READING

Amadiume, I and An-Naim, A (eds) (2000) *The politics of memory: Truth healing and social justice* London: Zed

Biggar, N (ed) (2001) *Burying the past: Making peace and doing justice after civil conflict* Washington DC: Georgetown University Press

Bloomfield, D; Barnes, T and Huyse L (eds) (2003) *Reconciliation after violent conflict: A handbook* Stockholm: Institute for Democracy and Electoral Assistance

Boraine, A (2000) *A country unmasked: Inside South Africa's Truth and Reconciliation Commission* Oxford: Oxford University Press

Kritz, N (ed) (1995) *Transitional justice: How emerging democracies reckon with former regimes, Vol I-III* Washington DC: United States Institute of Peace Press

Lederach, JP (1997) *Building peace: Sustainable reconciliation in divided societies* Washington DC: United States Institute of Peace

Mani, R (2002) *Beyond retribution: Seeking justice in the shadows of war* Cambridge: Polity Press

Mani, R 'Restoring justice in the aftermath of conflict: Bridging the chasm between theory and experience' in Coates, T (ed) (1999) *International justice* London: Ashgate

Minow, M (1998) *Between vengeance and forgiveness: Facing genocide and mass violence* Boston: Beacon Press

Orentlicher, DF 'Settling accounts: The duty to prosecute human rights violations of a prior regime' (1991) 100 *Yale Law Journal* 2537

Penal Reform International (2002) *Access to justice in sub-Saharan Africa: The role of traditional and informal justice systems* London: PRI

5

MECHANISMS FOR THE ENFORCEMENT OF HUMAN RIGHTS AT THE INTERNATIONAL LEVEL

Because domestic systems often fail to protect human rights, international human rights mechanisms on the global as well as the regional level, have been developed to serve as 'safety nets'. International human rights law has made a huge contribution to the development of human rights as a universal concept. Some of the mechanisms currently in place are discussed here.

HUMAN RIGHTS IN THE UNITED NATIONS

This contribution provides a birds-eye view of the constantly changing United Nations system in respect of human rights. New developments, such as the replacement of the Commission on Human rights by the Council on Human Rights, are not reflected here.

SMITH, R 'THE UNITED NATIONS SYSTEM OF HUMAN RIGHTS PROTECTION' (2005)

in Smith, R and van den Anker, C (eds) *The essentials of human rights*
London: Arnold

...

The United Nations has, since its inception in 1945, pioneered international standard setting on human rights issues. Under its auspices, a number of human rights instruments have been adopted and a comprehensive monitoring system has been instituted with the aim of promoting compliance by states. A number of bodies are involved with human rights as the following diagram illustrates.

The principal UN institutions are the Security Council, the General Assembly and the International Court of Justice. These bodies were established in terms of the UN Charter which clearly explains their functions and powers. The Secretary-General is also included as his offices are central to the successful functioning of the United Nations. The Security Council, which operates at the highest level, has primary responsibility for the maintenance of international peace and security. It comprises five permanent members (France, People's Republic of China, Russia, United Kingdom and United States of America) and a further ten members drawn from other states. A range of enforcement measures may be applied against states by the Security Council, ranging from diplomatic pressure through sanctions to military action. Given the principle of non-intervention in internal affairs of any state, the Security Council is most likely to be involved in human rights issues when friction caused by human rights threatens international peace. Examples of this include intervention in the former Yugoslavia in the 1990s. Given the failure to intervene timeously in Rwanda, it is possible that the Security Council will prove more willing to act in the future when evidence of gross violations of rights emerge, even if there is no inter-state element. In its early years, the Security Council spearheaded decolonisation, transforming the map of the world in barely 30 years. At the heart of decolonisation is a belief of self-determination, one of the recognised fundamental rights. (Now with decolonisation almost complete, the scope of the right to self-determination is being explored in greater detail.)

The General Assembly comprises representatives of all member States of the United Nations. The Charter of the United Nations imbues it with responsibility in a number of areas including studies and making recommendations which promote the realisation of international human rights and fundamental freedoms. Probably the most significant success of the Assembly was the Proclamation of the Universal Declaration on Human Rights in 1948. In furtherance of the principles entrenched therein, the General Assembly has been instrumental in proclaiming a series of profile-raising international decades, not least that on human rights education. It has also instituted special investigations into areas of concern, for example reform of the UN Human Rights system. A number of resolutions on human rights issues have been adopted by the General Assembly. Although not legally binding, such resolutions have strong moral force, representing as they do the expressed will of the majority of the international community. Such mechanisms are sometimes termed 'soft law' by international lawyers.

The International Court of Justice is the principal court of the UN system. However, it does not have competence to hear complaints from individuals. Its primary objective is as a venue for inter-state complaints. In a few occasions, this has overlapped with human rights issues – most notably in the proceedings brought by Croatia and Bosnia-Herzegovina against Yugoslavia concerning alleged violations of the Genocide Convention. The jurisdiction of the Court can be contrasted with the International Criminal Court which entered operation in July 2002. Individuals alleged to have been involved in war crimes could be brought to justice through this avenue. Obviously the crimes are serious infringement of human rights. Not all states have agreed to the terms proposed in the Statute of Rome.

As a figurehead of the United Nations, the Secretary-General, at the time of writing currently Kofi Annan, can perform a valuable function raising the profile of human rights issues. Moreover, the current Secretary-General has also been instrumental in introducing the current reform agenda for the United Nations and human rights.

In addition to these principal bodies, a number of other bodies were created under the auspices of the United Nations. The various councils and commissions with responsibility for human rights will be considered next. In each instance, the functions and powers of the body can be traced through to the UN Charter.

Turning to specific human rights bodies, the United Nations has one Council and two Commissions with particular responsibility for human rights. Thereafter, a number of lesser bodies are established with specific responsibility – most notably monitoring the compliance of contracting states with various human rights treaties. The Economic and Social Council has 54 individual members, elected by the General Assembly. It can initiate reports on a range of issues and make recommendations for, *inter alia*, the purpose of promoting respect for, and observance of, human rights and fundamental freedoms (article 62, UN Charter). In general, the Council coordinates activities within its area of competence. For human rights, it thus receives reports from the Treaty monitoring bodies and from the Commissions. It also delegates areas for investigation to its Commissions and associated sub-bodies.

Two of the Council's Commissions impact on human rights: The Commission on the Status of Women and the Commission on Human Rights. Established in 1946, the Commission on the Status of Women has expanded from 15 to 45 members, imbued with responsibility preparing recommendations and report to the Council on the promotion of women's rights globally. The Commission on Human Rights, in contrast has a broader remit. Originally its goal was to draft the Universal Declaration of Human Rights (adopted 1948). Since then, its role has been redefined. Today, it has power not only to organise technical assistance for those states in need and appoint rapporteurs to investigate areas of concern, it also can action individual complaints. Should a pattern of systematic or gross violations of human rights emerge from studies, the Commission may investigate the matter further through a specific procedure (Resolution 1503 (XLVIII) 1970). The investigation is carried out in private but the names of states involved are published: Vietnam and Zimbabwe are recent examples. Perhaps the greatest problem with the system is that the consent of the state concerned is required for a full investigation. However, as the United Nations is based on a principle of respect for the sovereignty of states, such a requirement is perhaps inevitable. Under the auspices of the Commission on Human Rights is the Sub-Commission on the Promotion and Protection of Human Rights, originally with a remit restricted to minority rights — a throwback to the system advocated by the League of Nations.

International human rights exists in its present form through a range of international treaties. Compliance with each of the principal UN treaties is monitored by a special committee. These committees only enjoy such powers and functions as are specified in the treaty concerned. In addition to these organs and bodies, a number of treaty-monitoring bodies have been established, essentially to oversee the implementation of specific treaties. For example, the Human Rights Committee was established to oversee the implementation of the International Covenant on Civil and Political Rights. All these committees, known as conventional mechanisms as they are established pursuant to specific instruments (the terms treaties and conventions can be used almost interchangeably), report to the Economic and Social Council and the General Assembly.

Finally, the 'public face' of international human rights in the UN is the High Commissioner for Human Rights. Just as the Secretary-General is the figurehead of the United Nations, the High Commissioner for Human Rights, an appointment at the level of Under-Secretary-General, has primary responsibility for human rights activities. The Office of the UN High Commissioner for Human Rights was created to protect and promote human rights for all. Based in Geneva, the Office now coordinates and provides secretarial support for much of the UN's human rights activities. The fourth High Commissioner, Louise Arbour, assumed the post in summer 2004.

...

This report of the 637th and 638th meetings of the Committee tasked with the supervision of the Convention on the Discrimination Against Women illustrates how state reporting is used in the UN treaty system.

COMMITTEE ON THE ELIMINATION OF DISCRIMINATION AGAINST WOMEN (20 JANUARY 2004)

...

Acting in their personal capacities, the Committee's 23 expert members monitor compliance with the Convention on the Elimination of All Forms of Discrimination against Women, which entered into force in 1981. Nigeria ratified the Convention in 1985 and signed its Optional Protocol, which allows individual women or groups of women to petition the Committee, in 1999.

Expressing concern about contradictions and inconsistencies created by the application of Nigeria's three legal systems, namely, Islamic *Shari'a*, customary law and common law, in its six geopolitical zones, experts cautioned against the perpetuation of customary and religious practices which negatively affected the situation of Nigerian women. Given the country's size, complex political system and rich cultural heritage, experts stressed the need for Nigeria to set the example for neighbouring African nations by fully implementing its obligations under the Convention.

Many experts emphasised the need for the Government to take urgent action to harmonise its legal framework to ensure the uniformity of human rights protections. Noting that harmonising the legal system was complicated by customary, religious and common law practices, the expert from Benin asked if the Government intend to adopt uniform laws with respect to marriage and family. She also asked whether diversity took precedence over international rights and commitments, and if the legislative reforms would be only partial.

The slow process of domesticating the Convention in Nigeria's national legislation was delaying women's rightful enjoyment of their human rights, experts stated. Noting that the situation of Nigerian women did not require gradual, but fast and radical change, the expert from the Republic of Korea, commenting on the recent acquittal of women in danger of being stoned to death for adultery, said it was the Government's obligation to ensure that states did not have those discriminatory laws in the first place. The acquittals were not, in her view, a question of 'celebration', but of shame.

Responding to experts' comments, Rita Akpan, Nigeria's Minister for Women Affairs, noted that the Government had taken some concrete steps to realise its commitments under the Convention.

Recent examples included the passage, in 2003, of the Trafficking in Persons Law Enforcement and Administration Act and the Child Rights Act. Acknowledging the slow pace of domesticating the Convention, she added that although Nigeria had ratified the Convention in 1985, during the time of the military government, it had been taboo to discuss the Convention. With the start of a democratic process, she believed that it would not be long before the Convention was fully implemented in Nigeria's legislation.

...

THE AFRICAN REGIONAL HUMAN RIGHTS SYSTEM

Here the African human rights landscape and the main role-players are introduced, including the new African Court on Human and Peoples' Rights and the African Peer Review Mechanism of the New Partnership for Africa's Development.

HEYNS, CH AND KILLANDER, M 'THE AFRICAN REGIONAL HUMAN RIGHTS SYSTEM' (2006)

in Gomez Isa, F and de Feyter, K (eds) *International protection of human rights: Achievements and challenges* Deusto: University of Deusto-EIUC

INTRODUCTION

While the term 'human rights' is of relative recent currency on the continent, people have been struggling for freedom, dignity, equality and social justice for centuries in Africa. In Africa, as is the case elsewhere, that which is now called human rights finds its foundations in the struggle to assert these core values of human existence.

Today, the term human rights is used widely in the African context. The written constitutions of every country in Africa recognise the concept; the inter-governmental organisation of African states, the African Union, regards the realisation of human rights as one of its objectives and principles; and the record of ratification of the human rights treaties of the United Nations by African countries is on a par with practices around the world. There is wide acceptance that the security and development of Africa — as in the world at large — will have to be based on human rights.

Not surprisingly, given the history of exploitation of Africa, the struggle roots of the concept of human rights are clearly visible in the human rights documents of the continent. The African Charter on Human and Peoples' Rights also reflects in many ways a reaction to the continental experience of slavery and colonialism, for example by recognising a 'peoples'' right to self-determination. The excesses of some post-independence leaders are reflected in the fact that a significant number of African constitutions explicitly recognise a direct right, located in the people, to protect constitutional and human rights norms, if need be through political struggle, should they be violated. The Constitutive Act of the African Union uniquely provides for a right of humanitarian intervention in member states by the Union, in cases of grave human rights violations.

As is well known, the struggle for human rights on the African continent is far from over or complete. The continent is plagued by widespread violations of human rights, often on a massive scale. The process to establish effective institutional structures, that will help to consolidate and protect the hard earned gains of the freedom struggles of the past, has become a struggle in its own right. No doubt, the most important task in this regard is to establish legal systems on the national level that protect human rights. At the same time regional and global attempts to change the human rights practices of the continent, and to create safety nets for those cases not effectively dealt with on the national level, are assuming increased importance.

This contribution first introduces the main legal instruments relevant to the continental protection of human rights in Africa, then discusses the norms recognised (individual and peoples' rights and duties etc) and thereafter turns to the regional institutional structures set up to achieve the implementation of the norms. This institutional overview focuses primarily on four important pillars of the African human rights system: The organs of the African Union, the African Commission on Human and Peoples' Rights, the yet to be established African Court on Human and Peoples' Rights and the newly established African Peer Review Mechanism.

THE AFRICAN UNION AND HUMAN RIGHTS

Background

The African regional system has been developed under the auspices of the Organization of African Unity (OAU), established in 1963, which was transformed in 2001 into the African Union (AU). All the states of Africa are members of the AU, except Morocco which withdrew in 1984 when the OAU recognised Western Sahara bringing the membership to 53. While the Charter of the OAU of 1963 made only passing reference to the concept of human rights, the Constitutive Act of the AU of 2000 (entered into force 2001) has now placed human rights squarely on the agenda of the new regional body.

The Constitutive Act

The Constitutive Act of the AU, in its Preamble, refers to the African struggles for independence and human dignity 'by our peoples' and the determination of the Heads of State and Government 'to promote and protect human and peoples' rights'. Article 3 sets out the 'Objectives' of the AU as follows: 'The objectives of the Union shall be to ... (e) encourage international co-operation, taking due account of the Charter of the United Nations and the Universal Declaration of Human Rights;' and to '... (h) promote and protect human and peoples' rights in accordance with the African Charter on Human and Peoples' Rights and other relevant human rights instruments ...'.

Article 4 deals with 'Principles', and provides that:

> The Union shall function in accordance with the following principles: ... (g) non-interference by any member state in the internal affairs of another; (h) the right of the Union to intervene in a member state pursuant to a decision of the Assembly in respect of grave circumstances, namely war crimes, genocide and crimes against humanity; (i) peaceful co-existence of member states and their right to live in peace and security; (j) the right of member states to request intervention from the Union in order to restore peace and security ... (l) promotion of gender equality; (m) respect for democratic principles, human rights, the rule of law and good governance; (n) promotion of social justice to ensure balanced economic development; (o) respect for the sanctity of human life, condemnation and rejection of impunity and political assassination, acts of terrorism and subversive activities; (p) condemnation and rejection of unconstitutional changes of governments.

There are no entry requirements in terms of their human rights records and practices for states to join the African Union (as is the case for example with the Council of Europe), and all the members of the OAU became members of the AU without scrutiny of their human rights records. There is, however, at least a theoretical chance that violations of AU human rights standards may lead to suspension from the AU; certainly lesser forms of sanctions are possible.

According to article 23(2):

> ... any member state that fails to comply with the decisions and policies of the Union may be subjected to ... sanctions, such as the denial of transport and communications links with other member states, and other measures of a political and economic nature to be determined by the Assembly.
>
> Art 30 provides: 'Governments which shall come to power through unconstitutional means shall not be allowed to participate in the activities of the Union.'
>
> The African Union has seen the establishment of a number of new institutions, many with relevance for the implementation of human rights, which will be discussed below.

African human rights instruments

The central document of the African regional human rights system, the African Charter on Human and Peoples' Rights (African Charter), was opened for signature in 1981 and entered into force in 1986. It has been ratified by all 53 member states of the OAU/AU. The sole supervisory body of the African Charter currently in existence is the African Commission on Human and Peoples' Rights (African Commission). The African Commission was constituted and met for the first time in 1987. The Commission has adopted its own Rules of Procedure (amended in 1995). The work of the African Commission will be discussed later in this article.

The Protocol to the African Charter on Human and Peoples' Rights on the Establishment of the African Court on Human and Peoples' Rights (African Human Rights Court Protocol) was adopted in 1998 and entered into force in January 2004, but as of February 2006 the Court had not yet been established.

The African Charter has further been supplemented by the Protocol to the African Charter on Human and Peoples' Rights on the Rights of Women in Africa, adopted in 2003, which entered into force in November 2005.

In addition to these instruments the African regional human rights system is comprised of the OAU Convention Governing the Specific Aspects of Refugee Problems in Africa of 1969 which entered into force in 1974 (45 ratifications); and the African Charter on the Rights and Welfare of the Child (African Children's Charter) of 1990, which came into force in 1999 (38 ratifications). A special monitoring body for the African Children's Charter, the African Committee on the Rights and Welfare of the Child, discussed further below, held its first meeting in 2002.

The relatively unknown Cultural Charter for Africa of 1976 came into force in 1990. Another treaty with relevance for human rights is the Convention on Preventing and Combating Corruption adopted in 2003. This Convention has as of February 2006 not entered into force. The Convention for the Elimination of Mercenarism in Africa was adopted in 1977 and entered into force in 1985. The OAU Convention on the Prevention and Combating of Terrorism of 1999 entered into force in 2002. There are also two African regional treaties dealing with the environment.

THE NORMS RECOGNISED IN THE AFRICAN CHARTER ON HUMAN AND PEOPLES' RIGHTS

As alluded to earlier, the 1963 OAU Charter did not recognise the realisation of human rights as such as one of the objectives of that body. It would only be in 1979 that a meeting of experts was gathered by the OAU in Dakar, Senegal, to prepare a preliminary draft of an African human rights charter. This culminated in the Draft African Charter on Human and Peoples' Rights, finalised in Banjul, The Gambia in 1981 (resulting in the name 'Banjul Charter', which is sometimes used for the African Charter). The African Charter was formally adopted by the OAU in Kenya later that year.

A number of reasons have been advanced why the OAU changed its approach and gave the concept of human rights the prominence offered by the Charter during the late 1970s and the early 1980s. These include the increased emphasis on human rights internationally at the time (as in the foreign policy of President Carter of the United States of America), the use to which the concept of human rights was put in international bodies such as the UN and the OAU to condemn the apartheid practices in South Africa, and abhorrence at the human rights violations that had taken part in some member states in particular Uganda, Central Africa and Equatorial Guinea.

The African Charter recognises a wide range of internationally accepted human rights norms, but also has some unique features. The Charter recognises not only civil and political rights, but also economic, social and cultural rights, not only individual but also peoples' rights, not only rights but also duties, and it has a singular system for the restrictions on rights. The Charter also contains provisions concerning interpretation which are very generous towards international law.

Civil and political rights

The civil and political rights recognised in the African Charter are in many ways similar to those recognised in other international instruments, and these rights have in practical terms received most of the attention of the African Commission.

The Charter recognises the following civil and political rights: the prohibition of discrimination (article 2); equality (article 3); bodily integrity and the right to life (article 4); dignity and prohibition of torture and inhuman treatment (article 5); liberty and security (article 6); fair trial (article 7); freedom of conscience (article 8); information and freedom of expression (article 9); freedom of association (article 10); assembly (article 11); freedom of movement (article 12); political participation (article 13); property (article 14); and independence of the courts (article 26).

A number of possible shortcomings in respect of civil and political rights in the African Charter could be noted. There is for example no explicit reference in the Charter to a right to privacy; the right against forced labour is not mentioned by name; and the fair trial rights and the right of political participation are given scant protection when measured against international standards. However, the Commission has in resolutions and in cases before it interpreted the Charter protection to encompass some of the rights or aspects of rights not explicitly included in the Charter.

An overview of some Commission decisions in respect of individual communications provides a sample of the Commission's approach:

- In a number of cases the Commission has held that there is a positive duty on state parties to protect those in their jurisdictions against violations by non-state actors. In a case concerning Mauritania, the Commission found that, although slavery had officially been abolished in that country, this was not effectively enforced by the government. In a case involving Chad, the Commission likewise held that the state's failure to protect people under its jurisdiction during a civil war against attacks by unidentified militants, not proven to be government agents, constituted a violation of the right to life.
- The imposition of *Shari'a* law on non-Muslims in Sudan has been held to violate freedom of religion.
- In *Media Rights Agenda and Others v Nigeria* the Commission ruled against the Abacha government's clampdown on freedom of expression, and determined that politicians should be provided less protection from free expression than other people. As with many of the seemingly more bold decisions of the Commission, this decision was unfortunately handed down only after the Abacha regime had fallen. Nevertheless, a positive precedent was set.
- The suspension of national elections was held to violate the right to political participation in *Constitutional Rights Project and Another v Nigeria*.
- The Commission has held that decrees ousting the jurisdiction of courts to examine the validity of such decrees, violate the fair trial provision of the Charter, and also that the creation of special tribunals, dominated by members of the executive, violated the same right.

- The Commission has held that an execution after an unfair trial is a violation of the right to life, but that the death penalty in itself does not violate the African Charter.
- A constitutional amendment providing that anyone who wanted to stand for office in the presidential election in Zambia would have to prove that both parents were Zambians by birth or descent was found to be in violation of the Charter in *Legal Resources Foundation v Zambia*.

Socio-economic rights

A unique feature of the Charter is the inclusion of socio-economic rights in a regional human rights treaty, alongside the civil and political rights mentioned above. The inclusion of socio-economic rights in the Charter is significant, in that it emphasises the indivisibility of human rights and the importance of developmental issues, which are obviously important matters in the African context.

At the same time, the fact that only a modest number of socio-economic rights are explicitly included in the Charter, should be noted. The Charter only recognises 'a right to work under equitable and satisfactory conditions' (article 15), a right to health (article 16) and a right to education (article 17). Some prominent socio-economic rights are not mentioned by name, such as the right to food, water, social security and housing.

The socio-economic rights in the Charter have received scant attention from the Commission, but in one case the Commission has dealt extensively with the issue, and has in effect held that some internationally recognised socio-economic rights which are not explicitly recognised in the Charter should be regarded as being implicitly included.

The so-called *SERAC v Nigeria* decision dealt with the destruction of part of Ogoniland by Shell, acting in collabouration with the government of Nigeria. The Commission held that the presence of an implicit right to 'housing or shelter' in the Charter has to be deduced from the explicit provisions on health, property and family life in the Charter. Similarly, a right to food has to be read into the right to dignity and other rights. It was accepted, without argument or reasoning, that the Ogoni's constituted a 'people'.

The approach of the Commission of filling in the gaps in the Charter as was done in the *SERAC* case could be seen as a creative and bold move on the part of the Commission, but it could also be argued that a too wide divergence between the Commission's interpretation of the Charter and the Charter itself could compromise legal certainty.

Women's rights

The way in which the Charter deals with gender issues has been a bone of contention. Article 18(3) provides as follows:

> The state shall ensure the elimination of every discrimination against women and also ensure the protection of the rights of the woman and the child as stipulated in international declarations and conventions.

This lumping together of women and children, in an article which deals primarily with the family, reinforces outdated stereotypes about the proper place and role of women in society and has been partially responsible for the drive to adopt the Protocol to the African Charter on the Rights of Women in Africa. The Protocol was adopted by the AU Assembly in 2003 and received the required 15 ratifications on 26 October 2005 thereby entering into force on 25 November 2005.

The Protocol on the Rights of Women is detailed with 24 substantive articles, some dealing with specific issues affecting women, while others deal with rights that should apply equally to men and women, some of which are not included in the African Charter. The rights in the Protocol include elimination of discrimination against women (article 2); right to dignity (article 3); right to life, integrity and security of person (article 4); elimination of harmful practices (article 5); marriage (article 6); separation, divorce and annulment of marriage (article 7); access to justice and equal protection of the law (article 8); political participation (article 9); peace (article 10); protection of women in armed conflict (article 11); education (article 12); economic and social welfare rights (article 13); health and reproductive rights (article 14); food security (article 15); adequate housing (article 16); positive cultural context (article 17); healthy and sustainable environment (article 18); right to sustainable development (article 19); widows' rights (article 20); inheritance (article 21); special protection of elderly women (article 22); women with disabilities (article 23); and women in distress (article 24).

The African Commission (and after its establishment also the African Court) is responsible for monitoring the implementation of the Charter and as a result also for the Protocol, thereby avoiding the duplication that exists with regard to children's issues, where as mentioned above a separate Committee on the Rights and Welfare of the Child has been established.

Peoples' rights

In its protection of peoples' rights the Charter goes further than any other international instrument.

All 'peoples', according to the Charter, have a right to be equal (article 19); to existence and self-determination (article 20); to freely dispose of their wealth and natural resources (article 21); to economic, social and cultural development (article 22); to peace and security (article 23); and to a satisfactory environment (article 24). Clearly part of the motivation for the recognition of 'peoples' rights' lies in the fact that entire 'peoples' have been colonised and otherwise exploited in the history of Africa.

The concept of 'peoples' has been referred to in some of the cases before the Commission, including the following:

- In a case concerning Katangese secessionists in the former Zaire, a complaint was brought on the basis that the Katangese people had a right, as a people, to self-determination in the form of independence. The Commission ruled that there was no evidence that a Charter provision had been violated, because widespread human rights violations or a lack of political participation by the Katangese people had not been proven. This could be understood to suggest that if these conditions were met, secession by such a 'people' could be a permissible option. On the other hand the Commission was careful to emphasise that self-determination can also take forms other than secession, such as self-government, local government, federalism, or confederalism.

- In a case concerning the 1994 *coup d'état* against the democratically elected government of The Gambia, the Commission held that this violated the right to self-determination of the people of The Gambia as a whole. The same conclusion was reached when the Abacha government in Nigeria annulled internationally recognised free and fair elections.
- In the abovementioned *SERAC* case the Commission held that the right to a satisfactory environment in article 24 requires the state 'to take reasonable ... measures to prevent pollution and ecological degradation, to promote conservation, and to secure an ecologically sustainable development and use of natural resources'. Significantly, here the rights of peoples are also used outside the context of self-determination.

Limitations, derogation and duties

The way in which the African Charter deals with restrictions on all rights, including civil and political rights, presents a significant obstacle. The African Charter does not contain a general limitation clause (although, as is noted below, article 27(2) is starting to play this role). This means that there are no general guidelines spelled out in the Charter on how its rights should be limited — no clear 'limits on the limitations', so to speak. A well-defined system of limitations is important. A society in which rights cannot be limited will be ungovernable, but it is essential that appropriate human rights norms be set for the limitations.

A number of the articles of the Charter setting out specific civil and political rights do contain limiting provisions applicable to those particular rights. Some of these internal limitations clearly spell out the procedural and substantive norms with which limitations should comply, while others only describe the substantive requirements which limitations must meet.

A last category of these internal limitation clauses merely poses the apparently procedural requirement that limitations should be done 'within the law'. An example of this category of internal limitations is article 9(2), which provides as follows: 'Every individual shall have the right to express and disseminate his opinions within the law'. This kind of limitation is generally known as a 'claw-back clause'. They seem to recognise the right in question only to the extent that such a right is not infringed upon by national law.

If that was the correct interpretation, the claw-back clauses would obviously undermine the whole idea of international supervision of domestic law and practices and render the Charter meaningless in respect of the rights involved. Domestic law will in those cases have to be measured according to domestic standards; a senseless exercise. What is given with the one hand is seemingly taken away with the other.

As has been noted above, however, the Charter has a very expansive approach in respect of interpretation. In terms of articles 60 and 61, the Commission has to draw inspiration from international human rights law in interpreting the provisions of the Charter. The Commission has used these provisions very liberally in a number of instances to bring the Charter in line with international practices, and the claw-back clauses are no exception.

In the context of the claw-back clauses, the African Commission has held that provisions in articles that allow rights to be limited 'in accordance with law', should be understood to require such limitations to be done in terms of domestic legal provisions, which comply with international human rights standards.

Through this interpretation, the Commission has gone a long way towards curing one of the most troublesome inherent deficiencies in the Charter. However, it remains unfortunate that the Charter, to those who have not had the benefit of exposure to the approach of the Commission, will continue to appear to condone infringements of human rights norms as long as it is done through domestic law.

The African Charter does not contain a provision either allowing or disallowing derogation from its provisions during a state of emergency. This has led the Commission to the conclusion that derogation is not possible. This could mean that in real emergencies the Charter will be ignored, and will not exercise a restraining influence.

The Charter recognises, in addition to rights, also duties. For example, individuals have duties towards their family and society, and state parties have the duty to promote the Charter.

Perhaps the most significant provision under the heading 'Duties' is article 27(2), which reads as follows: 'The rights and freedoms of each individual shall be exercised with due regard to the rights of others, collective security, morality and common interest'. This provision has now in effect been given the status by the African Commission of a general limitation clause. According to the Commission: 'The only legitimate reasons for limitations of the rights and freedoms of the African Charter are found in article 27(2) ...'.

The Commission's use of article 27(2) as a general limitation clause seems to confirm the view that the concept of 'duties' should not be understood as a sinister way of saying rights should first be earned, or that meeting certain obligations is a precondition for enjoying human rights. Rather, it implies that the exercise of human rights, which people have simply because they are human beings may be limited by the duties which they also have. Rights precede duties, and the recognition of certain duties is merely another way of signifying the kind of limitations that may be placed on rights.

NORMS RECOGNISED IN OTHER TREATIES

OAU Convention Governing Specific Aspects of Refugee Problems in Africa

The definition of refugee in article 1 of the OAU Refugee Convention is broader than in the UN Refugee Convention. In addition to 'well founded fear of being persecuted for reasons of race, religion, nationality, membership of a particular group or political opinion' the OAU Convention also stipulates that anyone who is compelled to leave his country because of 'external aggression, occupation, foreign domination or events seriously disturbing public order' shall be considered a refugee. The OAU Convention does not provide for any supervisory system but the African Commission has considered a number of communications dealing with refugees.

African Charter on the Rights and Welfare of the Child

The African Children's Charter, adopted in 1990, in many respects has similar provisions to the UN Convention on the Rights of the Child (CRC), adopted less than a year prior to the African instrument. In some respects the African Children's Charter goes further than the CRC. No person under 18 years should be recruited or take part in direct hostilities. The CRC sets the age-limit at 15 years, though a Protocol adopted in 2000 raises it to 18 years. The African Children's Charter goes further than the CRC also in other aspects, for example in prohibiting child marriages. The implementation of the African Children's Charter lies with the African Committee of Experts on the Rights and Welfare of the Child, discussed further below.

AU Convention on Preventing and Combating Corruption

Corruption depletes the resources necessary for a state to be able to fulfil its human rights obligations. This is recognised in the AU Convention on Preventing and Combating Corruption which provides as one of the objectives of the Convention to '[p]romote socio-economic development by removing obstacles to the enjoyment of economic, social and cultural rights as well as civil and political rights'. The Convention also provides for rights linked to the fight against corruption such as access to information. The Convention provides for an Advisory Board on Corruption as a follow up mechanism.

ORGANS ESTABLISHED FOR THE ENFORCEMENT OF HUMAN RIGHTS

The establishment of the African Union has seen an unprecedented institutional proliferation of bodies with a human rights mandate.

...

The role of the main organs of the AU in protecting human rights

The African Union has the following main organs: The Assembly of Heads of State and Government, the Executive Council, the Permanent Representative Committee, the Pan-African Parliament, the African Court of Justice, the AU Commission, Specialised Technical Committees, the Economic, Social and Cultural Council, financial institutions and the Peace and Security Council.

The Pan-African Parliament shall 'ensure the full participation of African peoples in the development and economic integration of the continent'. The Parliament has as one of its objectives to 'promote the principles of human rights and democracy in Africa'. The Parliament held its first session in 2004. Each state party to the Protocol establishing the Parliament sends five national parliamentarians to the Parliament that meets twice a year in Midrand, South Africa. Currently its powers are purely consultative and advisory.

The Economic, Social and Cultural Council (ECOSOCC) is 'an advisory organ composed of different social and professional groups'. Its purpose is to provide a role for civil society in the AU. ECOSOCC has as one of its objectives to 'Promote and defend a culture of good governance, democratic principles and institutions, popular participation, human rights and freedoms as well as social justice'. The statutes of ECOSOCC were adopted by the AU Assembly in July 2004 and the Council held its first meeting in Addis Ababa in March 2005.

The African Court of Justice, one of the main organs of the AU, has not yet been established as the Protocol setting up the court had only received eight of 15 ratifications required to enter into force by November 2005. The Court of Justice will be further discussed below in relation to the African Court on Human and Peoples' Rights.

The attempts to develop mechanisms to deal with conflict in Africa are also of importance in trying to prevent massive human rights violations. The Protocol on the Peace and Security Council (PSC), adopted in 2002, entered into force in 2003. The PSC is composed of 15 members. The criteria for membership include 'respect for constitutional governance ... as well as the rule of law and human rights ...'.

Article 4 of the PSC Protocol provides that the Council shall be guided by the AU Constitutive Act, the UN Charter and the Universal Declaration of Human Rights. The Protocol further provides as one of the objectives of the Council to:

> promote and encourage democratic practices, good governance and the rule of law, protect human rights and fundamental freedoms, respect for the sanctity of human life and international humanitarian law, as part of efforts for preventing conflicts.

Article 19 of the Protocol provides that:

> The Peace and Security Council shall seek close co-operation with the African Commission on Human and Peoples' Rights in all matters relevant to its objectives and mandate. The Commission on Human and Peoples' Rights shall bring to the attention of the Peace and Security Council any information relevant to the objectives and mandates of the Peace and Security Council.

From its Annual Activity Reports it appears that the Commission has not made use of this provision, though it has made reference to PSC resolutions in its own country specific resolutions.

The development programme of the AU, the New Partnership for Africa's Development (NEPAD), links human rights to development and provides for the African Peer Review Mechanism, (APRM), discussed below.

The African Commission on Human and Peoples' Rights

As was mentioned earlier, the African Charter, as adopted in 1981, provided only for the creation of a Commission and not a Court on Human Rights, in contrast with the other two regional systems in the world – in Europe and in the Americas, which, at the time, had both. The Commission is not formally an organ of the AU, as it was created by a separate treaty.

The commissioners

The African Commission consists of 11 commissioners, who serve in their individual capacities. The Commission meets twice a year in regular sessions for a period of up to two weeks. They are nominated by state parties to the Charter and elected by the Assembly. The Secretariat of the Commission is based in Banjul, The Gambia. The Commission alternates its meetings between Banjul and other African capitals. The Commission has a protective as well as a promotional mandate.

Although the Charter provides that the Commissioners should be independent there have been many instances were the independence of individual Commissioners has been questioned. The fact that many Commissioners have been serving civil servants or ambassadors has received criticism. For example a Commissioner from Mauritania elected in 2003 became a minister in his home country shortly thereafter. An important step was, however, taken when the AU requested nominations to fill the post of four Commissioners in 2005. In a *note verbale* to the member countries in April 2005 the AU Commission provided guidelines that excluded senior civil servants and diplomatic representatives. The four new Commissioners elected at the July 2005 summit all hold positions which are independent from government.

The main mechanisms employed by the Commission to fulfil its task of supervising compliance with Charter norms by state parties are the following:

The complaints procedure

Both states and individuals may bring complaints to the African Commission alleging violations of the African Charter by state parties.

The procedure by which one state brings a complaint about an alleged human rights violation by another state is not often used. Currently one such case is pending before the Commission, between the Democratic Republic of Congo and three neighbouring countries.

The so-called individual communication or complaints procedure is not clearly provided for in the African Charter. One reading of the Charter is that communications could be considered only where 'serious or massive violations' are at stake, which then triggers the rather futile article 58 procedure, described below. However, the African Commission has accepted from the start that it has the power to deal with complaints about any human rights violations under the Charter even if 'serious or massive' violations are not at stake, provided the admissibility criteria are met.

The Charter is silent on the question who can bring such complaints, but the Commission practice is that complaints from individuals as well as NGOs are accepted. From the case law of the Commission it is clear that the complainant does not need to be a victim or a family member of a victim. The Commission in the *SERAC* case expressed its thanks to:

> The two human rights NGOs which brought the matter under its purview ... This a demonstration of the usefulness to the Commission and individuals of *actio popularis*, which is wisely allowed under the African Charter.

The individual complaints procedure is used much more frequently than the inter-state mechanism of the African Charter, although not as frequently as one would have expected on a continent with the kind of human rights problems that Africa has. This could to some extent be attributed to a lack of awareness about the system, but even where there is awareness, there is often not much faith that the system can make a difference.

According to a recent study on the compliance of states with the findings of the Commission there has been full state compliance in six of the 44 cases where the Commission found state parties in violation of the African Charter. The study finds that there has been non-compliance in 13 cases, partial compliance in 14 cases, seven cases of situational compliance (through change of government) and unclear compliance in four cases. Viljoen and Louw finds that:

> In the analysis of cases of full and clear non-compliance, it appears that the most important factors are political, rather than legal. The nature of the case, the elabourateness of reasoning or the type of remedy required seems to have little bearing on the likelihood of adherence by states. The only factor of relevance that relates to the treaty body itself is follow-up activities undertaken by the Commission.

As with other complaints systems, the African Charter poses certain admissibility criteria before the Commission may entertain complaints. These criteria include the requirement of exhausting local remedies. The Commission may be approached only once the matter has been pursued in the highest court in the country in question, without success, or a reasonable prospect of success.

The Commission has stated that for a case not to be admissible local remedies must be available, effective, sufficient and not unduly prolonged. In *Purohit and Moore v the Gambia,* a case dealing with detention in a mental health institution, the Commission gave a potentially far-reaching decision on the exhaustion of local remedies when it held that:

> The category of people being represented in the present communication are likely to be people picked up from the streets or people from poor backgrounds and as such it cannot be said that the remedies available in terms of the Constitution are realistic remedies for them in the absence of legal aid services.

The Charter also has a requirement that the communications are 'not written in disparaging or insulting language directed against the state concerned and its institutions or to the Organization of African Unity'.

When a complaint is lodged, the state in question is asked to respond to the allegations against it. If the state does not respond, the Commission proceeds on the basis of the facts as provided by the complainant. If the decision of the

Commission is that there has indeed been a violation or violations of the Charter, the Commission sometimes also makes recommendations that continuing violations should stop (for example prisoners be released); or specific laws be changed, but often the recommendations are rather vague, and the state party is merely urged to 'take all necessary steps to comply with its obligations under the Charter'. Sometimes there is no provision at all as to remedies, while in other cases the remedies provided are elaborate. Recently the Commission required some states to report on measures taken to comply with the recommendations in their state reports to the Commission.

Article 58 provides that 'special cases which reveal the existence of serious or massive violations of human and peoples' rights' must be referred by the Commission to the Assembly, which 'may then request the Commission to undertake an in-depth study of these cases'. Where the Commission has followed this route, the Assembly has failed to respond, but the Commission has nevertheless made findings that such massive violations have occurred. Today, the Commission does not seem to refer cases anymore to the Assembly in terms of article 58.

The Charter does not contain a provision in terms of which the Commission has the power to take provisional or interim measures requesting state parties to abstain from causing irreparable harm. However, the Rules of Procedure of the Commission grant the Commission the power to do so. The Commission has used these provisional or interim measures in a number of cases. One such case concerned Ken Saro-Wiwa and other Ogoni activists, who had been sentenced to death by a special tribunal, set up by the military government in Nigeria. In that particular case, the interim measures requesting the Nigerian government not to execute them were ignored. The execution of Saro-Wiwa and the others caused a worldwide outcry. The Commission said in its decision that it had tried to assist Nigeria to meet its obligations under the Charter by means of the interim measures, and the execution in the face of the interim measures consequently violated article 1.

Consideration of state reports

Each state party is required to submit a report every two years on its efforts to comply with the African Charter. Although it is not provided for in the African Charter that the reports should be submitted specifically to the African Commission, the Commission recommended to the Assembly that the Commission be given the mandate to consider the reports. The Assembly has endorsed this recommendation. NGOs are allowed to submit shadow or alternative reports, but the impact of this avenue is diminished by the lack of access of NGOs to the state reports to which they are supposed to respond. The reports are considered by the Commission in public sessions. Reporting by state parties should be done in accordance with guidelines adopted by the Commission. Currently there are two sets of guidelines; one, adopted in 1988 is long and complex and one, adopted in 1998 which is overly brief. The relationship between these guidelines is unclear and it should be a priority of the Commission to clarify the situation as regards guidelines on state reporting.

Reporting under the Charter, as in other systems, is aimed at facilitating both introspection and inspection. 'Introspection' refers to the process when the state, in writing its report, measures itself against the norms of the Charter. 'Inspection' refers to the process when the Commission measures the performance of the state in question against the Charter. The objective is to facilitate a 'constructive dialogue' between the Commission and the states.

Reporting has been very tardy, and 18 of the 53 state parties to the African Charter have never submitted any report. In 2001 the Commission started to issue concluding observations in respect of reports considered. Their usefulness is diminished by the fact that neither the state reports nor the concluding observations are published by the Commission.

Special rapporteurs and working groups

The Commission has appointed a number of special rapporteurs, with varying degrees of success. There is no obvious legal basis for the appointment of the special rapporteurs in the Charter; it has been described as another innovation of the Commission. The special rapporteurs are all members of the Commission.

There has been widespread criticism of the lack of effective action on the part of the Special Rapporteur on Summary, Arbitrary and Extrajudicial Executions, while the same is true of at least the first incumbent of the position of Special Rapporteur on the Conditions of Women in Africa. In contrast, the Special Rapporteur on Prisons and Conditions of Detention in Africa has set the standards for years to come.

The Commission has recently appointed special rapporteurs on freedom of expression; refugees and internally displaced persons; and human rights defenders. The Commission has also established a committee to monitor the implementation of the Guidelines and Measures for the Prohibition and Prevention of Torture, Cruel, Inhuman or Degrading Treatment or Punishment in Africa (Robben Island Guidelines). In addition a Working Group on Indigenous People or Communities and a Working Group on Economic, Social and Cultural Rights have been established. Some of the members of these working groups are not members of the Commission.

On-site visits

The Commission has since 1995 conducted a number of on-site visits. These involve a range of activities, from fact finding to good offices and general promotional visits. Many mission reports have never been published.

Resolutions

The Commission has adopted resolutions on a number of human rights issues in Africa. In addition to country-specific and other more *ad hoc* resolutions, they have adopted resolutions on topics such as the following: Fair trial; freedom of association; human and peoples' rights education; humanitarian law; contemporary forms of slavery; anti-personnel mines; prisons in Africa; the independence of the judiciary; the electoral process and participatory governance; the International Criminal Court; the death penalty; torture; HIV/AIDS; and freedom of expression.

Relationship with NGOs

NGOs have a special relationship with the Commission. Large numbers have registered for observer status. NGOs are often instrumental in bringing cases to the Commission; they sometimes submit shadow reports; propose agenda items at the outset of Commission sessions; and provide logistical and other support to the Commission, for example by placing interns at the Commission and providing support to the special rapporteurs and missions of the Commission. NGOs often organise special NGO workshops just prior to Commission sessions, and participate actively in the public sessions of the Commission. NGOs also collaborate with the Commission in developing normative resolutions and new protocols to the African Charter.

Interaction with AU political bodies

The Annual Activity Reports of the Commission, which reflect the decisions, resolutions, and other acts of the Commission, are submitted each year for permission to publish to the meetings of the Assembly of Heads of State and Government ('Assembly') of the OAU/AU that have traditionally taken place in June or July of the following year. The Assembly has now delegated the authority to discuss the Activity Report to the Executive Council. However, it is still formally adopted by the Assembly as this is required by the Charter. The AU has recently started to have summits twice a year and it remains to be seen whether the African Commission will submit a report to each summit.

In practice the Assembly has served as a rubber stamp for the publication of the report by the Commission containing its decisions, but the principle that the very people in charge of the institutions whose human rights practices are at stake – the heads of state – should take the final decision on publicity undermines the legitimacy of the system. When the 17th Annual Activity Report was considered by the Executive Council at the AU summit in July 2004, Zimbabwe complained that it had not had the opportunity to respond to allegations contained in the report concerning a fact-finding mission undertaken by the Commission to Zimbabwe. The Council suspended the publication of the report and its publication was only finally authorised at the summit in January 2005.

Information on the Commission

The decisions of the Commission are published in the *African Human Rights Law Reports* (AHRLR). A small but growing number of secondary publications on the work of the Commission have appeared. Information on the work of the Commission is available on a number of websites. It is unclear why the Commission makes little use of its own web site which should be the main resource on information on the work of the Commission. In December 2005 the Commission published the18th Annual Activity Report, adopted by the AU Assembly in July 2005 on its web site. However, the 17th Annual Activity Report, adopted by the AU Assembly in January 2005 had as of February 2006 not been published on the web site.

The African Court on Human and Peoples' Rights

Several reasons have been advanced why only a Commission, and not a Court, was provided for in the African Charter in 1981 as the body responsible for monitoring compliance of state parties with the Charter. On the one hand there is perhaps the more idealistic explanation that the traditional way of solving disputes in Africa is through mediation and conciliation, not through the adversarial, 'win or lose' mechanism of a court. On the other hand there is the view that the member states of the OAU were jealous of their newly founded sovereignty.

The notion of a human rights court for Africa would be taken up by the OAU 13 years after the adoption of the African Charter when, in 1994, the Assembly adopted a resolution requesting the Secretary-General of the OAU to convene a Meeting of Experts to consider the establishment of an African Court on Human and Peoples' Rights.

Ostensibly, the concept of human rights was accepted widely enough in Africa in the early 1990s for the decision to be taken to give more 'teeth' to the African human rights system, in the form of a Court. This came in the wake of the different waves of democratisation on the national level, epitomised by the watershed elections in Benin in 1991, and the advent of democracy in South Africa in 1994. Worldwide, of course, the idea of human rights also gained prominence after the end of the Cold War.

The Protocol on the African Court on Human and Peoples' Rights was adopted in Addis Ababa, Ethiopia, in 1998. The Protocol entered into force in January 2004 and by February 2006 had received 22 ratifications.

The AU Assembly decided at its summit in July 2004 that the African Human Rights Court should merge with the African Court of Justice. The protocol establishing the latter court had been adopted by the Assembly in July 2003, without any reference to a merger with the human rights court. The Protocol on the African Court of Justice had as of February 2006 not received the required 15 ratifications to enter into force. A draft merger protocol has been circulated and at the AU summit in July 2005 the Assembly decided that:

> ...
> (2) ... a draft legal instrument relating to the establishment of the merged court comprising the Human Rights Court and the Court of Justice should be completed for consideration by the next ordinary sessions of the Executive Council and the Assembly ...
> (3) ALSO DECIDES that all necessary measures for the functioning of the Human Rights Court be taken, including particularly the election of the judges, the determination of the budget and the operationalisation of the Registry;
> (4) FURTHER DECIDES that the Seat of the merged court shall be at a place to be decided upon by the member states of the Eastern Region, which shall also serve as the seat of the Human Rights Court pending the merger.

Once the African Human Rights Court is in place, it will 'complement' the protective mandate of the Commission under the Charter. Under the 1998 Protocol the Court will consist of 11 judges, serving in their individual capacities, nominated by state parties to the Protocol, and elected by the Assembly. Only the president will be full-time. The judges were elected by the Assembly in January 2006. The seat of the Court is still to be determined, but as is clear from the above resolution it will be in the Eastern Region.

The Protocol provides that the judges will be appointed in their individual capacities, and their independence is guaranteed. Special provision is made that '[t]he position of judge of the Court is incompatible with any activity that might interfere with the independence or impartiality of such a judge ...'. Judges will not be allowed to sit in a case if that judge is a national of a state which is a party to the case.

In respect of the Court's findings, the Protocol determines that '[i]f the Court finds that there has been a violation of a human or peoples' right, it shall make appropriate orders to remedy the violation, including the payment of fair compensation or reparation'. The Court is explicitly granted the powers to adopt provisional measures.

By ratifying the Protocol, states accept that the Commission and the states involved will be in a position to take a case that has appeared before them to the African Human Rights Court, to obtain a legally binding decision. Individuals and those who act on their behalf will be able to take cases to the Court only in respect of those states that have made an additional declaration specifically authorising them to do so. In such instances the case will have to be taken 'directly' to the Court, presumably bypassing the Commission or, if the Commission was approached first, the case can be taken to the Court without requiring the authorisation of the Commission.

Article 3(1) reads as follows:

> The jurisdiction of the Court shall extend to all cases and disputes submitted to it concerning the interpretation and application of the Charter, this Protocol and any other relevant human rights instrument ratified by the states concerned.

The phrase 'any other relevant human rights instrument ratified by the states concerned', according to most commentators, means that adjudication in respect of even UN and sub-regional human rights instruments will fall within the jurisdiction of the African Human Rights Court, provided that such treaties have been ratified by the states concerned.

It is submitted that nothing is wrong with the African Human Rights Court interpreting the Charter in view of international standards. Advisory opinions could also deal with other treaties. However, if contentious cases could be brought to the African Human Rights Court on the ground that for example UN treaties have been violated, with no reference to the African Charter, this could lead to conflicting decisions in the different systems.

The jurisdiction of the African Human Rights Court to give advisory opinions was mentioned above. In addition to member states and AU organs any 'African organisation recognised by the [AU]' can request an advisory opinion from the Court. Advisory jurisdiction has proved useful in the Inter-American human rights system and could potentially play a similar role in the African system.

African Committee on the Rights and Welfare of the Child

The African Children's Charter adopted in 1990 entered into force in November 1999. The 11 members of the African Committee on the Rights and Welfare of the Child, provided for under the Charter were elected in July 2001. The Committee held its first meeting in 2002. The Committee has adopted its Rules of Procedures and Guidelines for State Reports. States shall report to the Committee within two years from the entry into force of the Convention for the state party concerned and thereafter every three years. Apart from state reporting the African Children's Charter, uniquely among international instruments for the protection of the rights of children, also provides for a communication procedure. The Committee has recently received one communication but it remains unclear how the Committee will handle this.

The Committee does not have its own secretariat, and is serviced by the Department for Social Affairs. The AU is in the process of recruiting a Secretary to the Committee. The Committee suffers from a serious lack of resources and the question could be asked whether the Committee should not be merged with the African Commission.

The African Peer Review Mechanism

In July 2002 in Durban the OAU/AU Assembly of Heads of State and Government adopted the Declaration on Democracy, Political, Economic and Corporate Governance (Governance Declaration). The Governance Declaration provided for the establishment of an African Peer Review Mechanism (APRM) 'to promote adherence to and fulfilment of the commitments' in the Declaration. The initiative grew out of the New Partnership for Africa's Development (NEPAD), adopted by the AU in 2001 as the development framework for the Union.

The Governance Declaration in section 10 provides as follows:

> In the light of Africa's recent history, respect for human rights has to be accorded an importance and urgency all of its own. One of the tests by which the quality of a democracy is judged is the protection it provides for each individual citizen and for the vulnerable and disadvantaged groups. Ethnic minorities, women and children have borne the brunt of the conflicts raging on the continent today. We undertake to do more to advance the cause of human rights in Africa generally and, specifically, to end the moral shame exemplified by the plight of women, children, the disabled and ethnic minorities in conflict situations in Africa.

Under the heading 'Democracy and Good Political Governance', section 13 provides:

> In support of democracy and the democratic process, We will: ensure that our respective national constitutions reflect the democratic ethos and provide for demonstrably accountable governance; promote political representation, thus providing for all citizens to participate in the political process in a free and fair political environment; enforce strict adherence to the position of the African Union (AU) on unconstitutional changes of government and other decisions of our continental organisation aimed at promoting democracy, good governance, peace and security; strengthen and, where necessary, establish an appropriate electoral administration and oversight bodies, in our respective countries and provide the necessary resources and capacity to conduct elections which are free, fair and

> credible; reassess and where necessary strengthen the AU and sub-regional election monitoring mechanisms and procedures; and heighten public awareness of the African Charter on Human and Peoples' Rights, especially in our educational institutions.

At the Durban summit the Assembly also adopted a document specifically dealing with the APRM process, the so-called APRM Base Document:

> The process will entail periodic reviews of the policies and practices of participating states to ascertain progress being made towards achieving mutual agreed goals and compliance with agreed political, economic and corporate governance values, codes and standards as outlined in the Declaration on Democracy, Political, Economic and Corporate Governance.

The APRM process consists of a self-evaluation by the country that has signed up to being reviewed and a review by an international review team. It is in this respect similar to the state reporting under the African Charter. However, there are also clear differences such as country visits by the APRM review team and the political stage, when the leader of the country discusses the outcome of the review with his peers in other participating countries.

The highest decision making body in the APRM is the APR Forum consisting of the heads of state and government of the participating states. A panel of eminent persons with seven members oversees the review process and a member of this panel is chosen to lead the review team on its country mission.

The international review process consists of five stages. First a background study is carried out by the secretariat assisted by consultants. This stage also includes a support mission to the country that will be reviewed. In the second stage a review team led by one of the eminent persons visits the country for discussions with all stakeholders, after which the team prepare its report (third stage). A number of partner institutions and independent consultants assist in the process. The fourth stage consists of the submission of the report to the APRM Forum and the discussion among the peers. The last stage is the publication of the report and further discussion in other AU institutions such as the Pan-African Parliament.

The APRM deals with political, economic and corporate governance and socio-economic development. Initially, there was some debate as to the inclusion of political governance aspects, including human rights, but as pointed out by Cilliers: 'Without making political governance the core focus of NEPAD, the Partnership is unlikely to make an impact on the continent'.

The APRM is voluntary and as of February 2006, 26 out of 53 AU member states have signed the Memorandum of Understanding (MOU) that forms the legal basis for the review. In paragraph 24 of the MOU the signatory state agrees to 'take such steps as may be necessary for the implementation of the recommendations adopted at the completion of the review process ...' The MOU does not deal with the substantive undertakings of the signatories, but instead refers to the Governance Declaration. The Governance Declaration makes reference to standards that have already been accepted by the participating states in other declarations and treaties, including global and regional human rights instruments. The Governance Declaration comprises of only 28 paragraphs and covers all the areas that are being reviewed, ie political, economic and corporate governance as well as socio-economic development. Further documents have been developed with regard to standards and indicators, including a questionnaire to help participating states complete their self-assessments.

Many observers have emphasised the necessity for civil society to engage the APRM if the mechanism is to make any difference on the ground. The possibilities for such engagement varies greatly between participating countries, as do the approaches to the independence of the national process from government interference.

The APRM integrates the political level of the AU/NEPAD in a way that other parts of the African human rights system have not done. The situation could to some extent be compared to the role, by many perceived as successful, of the Committee of Ministers of the Council of Europe with regard to the European Convention on Human Rights and the European Social Charter. However, as shown by the activities of the political bodies of the United Nations involved with human rights, the direct involvement of other states in the protection of rights is not without its problems.

As in other parts of the world African leaders have not shown a great interest in criticising their peers. Hence there are reasons to be sceptical about whether 'peer pressure' will be employed in the process. However, to solely focus on the pressure exercised at this level would be to underestimate the process as a whole. The APRM Base Document provides for sanctions as a last resort if peer pressure is not enough to convince governments with a lack of political will to rectify identified shortcomings.

There has not been much co-operation between the APRM and the African Commission, which is unfortunate. A look at the composition of the missions to Ghana and Rwanda, the first two states to be subject to the APRM process, also makes it clear that the focus is more on economic than political governance.

CONCLUSION

It is not difficult to criticise the African regional human rights system, and many have done so. Some have argued that given the fact that the African Charter was adopted 25 years ago and the African Commission has been in operation for 20 years, the track record of the Commission is less than impressive. The Commission has been poorly managed by its Secretariat for many years. The Commission suffers from a lack of resources, but questions have been asked about the way in which available resources have been managed.

The perceived lack of impartiality of some Commissioners has been a constant bone of contention, as has been the lack of political will in the OAU/AU on a political level to ensure the effectiveness of the Charter system.

The Charter itself has its own internal limitations and thus has required extensive creative interpretation by the Commission. For example, the main mandates of the Commission – receiving individual communications and state reports – are not clearly recognised in the Charter. Some of the internationally accepted rights are recognised only in a cursory form in the Charter.

Moving beyond the Charter system, the need to have established a separate system for the protection of children's rights (complete with a complaints and reporting mechanism) has been questioned. There is a danger of a proliferation of mechanisms, each one depleting the scarce resources even further, instead of establishing one or two truly effective mechanisms before more are created.

Some commentators have also focused on the potential weaknesses of the APRM, which relies on heads of state – who often don't have much interest in promoting a system of finger-pointing about human rights violations – to police each other.

There is undeniably some truth in these criticisms, and much room for improvement. At the same time the merits of the African regional human rights system also need to be recognised.

The fact that Africa has a regional human rights system in the first place – only one of three regions to have that – provides an entry point for international human rights to play a role which would otherwise not have existed. The arguments about a possible 'African exception' to the concept of human rights – the idea that human rights is a foreign concept with little applicability to the African situation – are considerably weaker than they would otherwise have been. The regional human rights system provides the possibility of imminent critique through a mechanism created by African states themselves, which cannot be shrugged off as easily as critique expressed by far-away capitals.

The current make-up of the African regional system in terms of the norms recognised and the enforcement mechanisms followed – largely the result of recent changes to the system – are probably well suited to the African environment. The fact that the norms recognised also reflect socio-economic rights, duties and people's rights does not detract from the recognition of civil and political rights, and the rights of individuals, in the system. Their addition ensures that norms that play a strong role on the continent are also reflected. It should be noted in this regard that the jurisprudence of the African Commission so far by and large reflects internationally accepted standards, and constitutes a valuable point of reference also for national courts.

A wider range of enforcement mechanisms than that which is used elsewhere is followed in Africa. While the European regional human rights system places a strong emphasis on the judicial enforcement of individual civil and political rights through the European Court of Human Rights, the African system, operates on a number of levels simultaneously. While the African Human Rights Court (under whatever name that may be used) will provide for a component of judicial suspension, the APRM on the other side of the spectrum has a more political character. This is complimented by the quasi-judicial mechanism of the African Commission, which occupies a place somewhere between the other two mechanisms.

On a continent as diverse as Africa, with its multi-layered landscape of human rights issues, employing an enforcement mechanism with such diverse components seems to be a wise approach. Each component of the collective mechanism plays a different and equally important role. Courts can address individual cases in a strong and decisive manner, but they have a more limited role to play in respect of mobilising a political consensus or dealing with widespread human rights violations. A commission on human rights, which can consider state reports and conduct on site visits, can play an important role in identifying human rights issues that need to be addressed in a systematic way and in working towards negotiated solutions which courts cannot always do. To the extent that such a commission functions and is perceived as an independent body, it can to some extent play a role which those placed inside the confines of power politics will have difficulty in playing.

At the same time there is also a role for human rights supervision in the political processes of the continent. A mechanism such as the APRM, although it has limitations because of its political nature, can also precisely for that reason have an impact on aspects of political life which the other mechanisms cannot reach. Standing alone the APRM would probably not have made much of a difference, but as part of a broader network of mechanisms aimed at the protection of human rights the APRM has the potential to play a significant role – and the same probably applies also to the Court and the Commission.

The issue of political will remains, and it cannot be denied that much remains to be done to turn the potential offered by the available systems and mechanisms into reality. At the same time, the new institutional focus of the African Union on human rights, as reflected in its Constitutive Act, and in the mandates of its organs provides a starting point. Increasingly, individuals are encountered within the system in governments and in civil society in Africa who take this orientation seriously. Clearly, it is on their input that the full implementation of an effective African regional human rights system will depend. Much will depend in this regard on the increased realisation of human rights on the domestic level – an international human rights system cannot survive without a critical mass of building-blocks of state parties that take human rights seriously internally at home.

...

The African Commission on Human and Peoples' Rights faces many challenges, some of which are set out in this Report. The Commission has established a working group to study its working methods.

REPORT OF THE RETREAT OF MEMBERS OF THE AFRICAN COMMISSION ON HUMAN AND PEOPLES' RIGHTS (2003)

Facilitated by the Office of the High Commissioner for Human Rights
Full report available at http://www.nhri.net/pdf/ACHPR-Retreat-Report-Final.pdf

...

The African Commission is faced with problems of lack of capacity. The current number of commissioners (11 members) is too small and their meeting period of 30 days per year is grossly inadequate to meet the responsibilities linked to the mandate of the African Commission.

The African Union's responsibility for ensuring that the African Commission functions in an autonomous and sustainable way has not been fully met.

In the election of commissioners the provisions of the African Charter relating to possession of human rights knowledge, expertise and incompatibility, which have a bearing on the independent functioning of the African Commission have not been coherently adhered to by member states.

The level of expertise and number of legal staff in the African Commission's Secretariat is inadequate to meet the expected level of efficiency and professionalism ...

The budgetary allocation to the African Commission from the AU is grossly inadequate and extra-budgetary funds are not properly planned for or managed ...

The relationship between the African Commission and its Secretariat, between the African Commission and the AU Commission, and between the Secretariat of the African Commission and the AU Commission are not clearly defined. This affects co-ordination, transparency and accountability as well as efficiency of the African Commission and its Secretariat.

Secretariat services provided to backstop the Commission have been inadequate. For example, there are no regular minutes of meetings of the Commission.

...

A number of evaluations and studies have been conducted on the African Commission and its management in the past but their recommendations have not been fully implemented.

...

The Commission normally meets only twice a year, but it can also hold extraordinary sessions. Viljoen looks at how the Commission responded to the deteriorating situation in Darfur, Sudan.

VILJOEN, F 'RECENT DEVELOPMENTS IN THE AFRICAN REGIONAL HUMAN RIGHTS SYSTEM' (2004)

4 *African Human Rights Law Journal* 344

...

At its 35th ordinary session, in May to June 2004, the African Commission considered the second state report of Sudan ... [T]he examination of the report lacked focus and consideration for the urgency of the situation in Darfur. Instead, detailed technical and routine questions were posed about issues such as institutional mechanisms, for instance the Civil Service Board, freedom of expression, personal status laws and the rights of prisoners to vote. Although some incisive questions were also posed about Darfur, the misallocation of time caused these to be neglected: It took the commissioners about two and a quarter hour to ask questions, but after less than an hour the Sudanese representative was asked to wrap up and summarise his answers. As a result, a number of questions were left unanswered, allowing the representative to brush over alleged government involvement in the Darfur conflict.

Significantly, though, the Sudanese representative invited the Commission to undertake a mission to Sudan, and undertook to provide the mission with every possible aid and assistance. In its private session, the Commission decided to send a fact-finding mission to the region. This fact-finding mission visited Sudan from 8 to 18 July 2004 ...

At the end of the mission, the Chairperson of the African Commission sent a request to President Bashir of Sudan, regarding the necessity to take urgent provisional measures in respect of security, the protection of women, access to displaced persons and the supply of humanitarian assistance, the need to reassure a safe return of displaced persons to their villages, the deployment of human rights observers and to ensure the right to fair trial for political prisoners.

The Commission met in Pretoria on 19 September 2004 for its extraordinary session. The main purpose of the meeting was to discuss and adopt the report of the Commission's fact-finding mission to Darfur. This report also remains confidential until adoption by the Assembly. Even if it agreed on the report, and made recommendations, the Commission interpreted its mandate to mean that it can only make this report public once it has been contained in the Annual Activity Report, and once the Assembly has adopted that report.

...

Motala sets out the important role played by NGOs in the work of the African Commission. On the one hand the Commission is seen as uniquely open to NGO interventions, perhaps to a larger degree than other international human rights bodies. On the other hand, access to Commission documentation is limited, making it difficult for NGOs to make meaningful contributions, for example in relation to state reporting.

MOTALA, A 'NON-GOVERNMENTAL ORGANISATIONS IN THE AFRICAN SYSTEM' (2002)

in Murray, R and Evans, M (eds) *The African Charter on Human and Peoples' Rights: The system in practice, 1986-2000* Cambridge: Cambridge University Press

Throughout its existence over little more than a decade, non-governmental organisations (NGOs) have provided crucial support in strengthening the mandate of the African Commission on Human and Peoples' Rights (the Commission) and in improving its efficiency. Even prior to the establishment of the Commission, NGOs played a role in the drafting of the African Charter on Human and Peoples' Rights (the African Charter), its adoption by the Organization of African Unity (OAU) and its ratification by African States.

...

The African Charter recognises the role of NGOs in the work of the Commission, albeit without specifically referring to NGOs. Article 45(1)(a) of the African Charter requires the Commission to promote human and peoples' rights by encouraging (national and local institutions concerned with human rights), and article 45(1)(c) requires the Commission to (co-operate with other African and international institutions concerned with the promotion and protection of human rights). The important role of NGOs in bringing complaints of human rights violations before the Commission is given recognition in article 55 of the African Charter, although the drafters of the treaty refer to 'communications other than those from States Parties to the present Charter'. The Rules of Procedure of the Commission are explicit about the role to be played by NGOs in its work from proposing items for the agenda of its sessions, to the granting of observer status, and consultations with NGOs. Although the previous Rules of Procedure of the Commission specifically referred to the submission of complaints by NGOs, the current Rules of Procedure make no reference to NGOs in its provisions relating to 'other communications'.

The African Commission clearly recognises the excellent relationship it has with NGOs and the important contribution that they provide to its work. Its plan of action for 1996-2001 includes the establishment of an exchange and communications network and the strengthening of links with NGOs. In its most recent report the Commission acknowledges the contribution of NGOs to its work including through the provision of funding for additional staff and promotional visits of Commissioners and the organisation of meetings and seminars.

...

An NGO seeking observer status applies in writing to the Commission providing information about its constitution, by-laws, a list of officers, sources of funding, publications and other relevant information. While well-known African and international organisations may not require scrutiny, with the proliferation of NGOs it became necessary for the Commission to scrutinise the applications being presented. The Commission often considered applications for observer status without a representative being present to answer questions or present additional information that may be required. In some instances, representatives of NGOs simply handed to a member of the Commission all the relevant documents during a session and had their applications granted during the session without the information being processed by the Secretariat, whereas in other instances applications have been inexplicably lost or the granting of observer status delayed without reasons.

...

The most visible role of NGOs has been during the sessions of the Commission. They have availed themselves of the provision of the Rules of Procedure of the Commission that permits NGOs to suggest items for the agenda of the Commission and have suggested topics pertaining to human rights situations in African countries, for example Sierra Leone, and thematic issues such as economic, social and cultural rights. Besides presenting information on the agenda item they have suggested, NGOs often make concrete proposals to the Commission on measures it could adopt to investigate the specific country situation or violations or mechanisms it could establish to deal with thematic issues. Examples of such initiatives include urging the Commission to undertake investigative missions to countries where serious human rights violations have been occurring, and the establishment of the mechanism of Special Rapporteur to investigate specific recurring human rights violations NGOs have identified.

...

International organisations such as Amnesty International present an oral statement at each session in which they highlight the human rights situation in a few African countries and address a thematic issue. African NGOs often deal with the human rights situation in their own countries and make recommendations to the Commission to adopt resolutions or undertake investigative missions. The close co-operation among NGOs ensures that they present different perspectives of the same message, which results in greater impact on the Commission. For example, at the 26th Session in November 1999 in Rwanda, Amnesty International, Human Rights Watch, Interights and representatives of the Sierra Leone Bar Association teamed up to present information to the Commission on the serious human rights situation in Sierra Leone. The Commission acted upon that information by undertaking a mission to Sierra Leone in February 2000. Although the representatives of several Nigerian NGOs attend each session of the Commission, there is always a collaborative effort among them and they often present a single joint statement. While the relationship between most NGOs that attend the Commission's sessions is cordial and co-operative, sometimes competitiveness and confrontation between NGOs from the same country is also evident. Such confrontations emanate from some NGOs seeking legitimacy, competition for funding and the stance of the NGO, especially those that may be perceived to be pro- or anti-government. Many resolutions adopted by the Commission have been the result of the close collaboration between NGOs and the Commission. Even in instances where draft resolutions have not been proposed by NGOs, representatives of NGOs have assisted in the drafting of resolutions. For example, at the 26th Session representatives of Amnesty International, the African Society for International and Comparative Law and Prisoners Rehabilitation and Welfare Action assisted the Special Rapporteur on extrajudicial, summary or arbitrary executions in drafting a resolution on the death penalty which was adopted by the Commission. Since its 17th Session, the Commission has tried to act independently of NGOs in the drafting of resolutions after the Government of Algeria protested against a resolution on that country and as more governments began sending representatives to the Commission's sessions. While it is important that the Commission acts independently from NGOs as much as it does from governments, the expertise and often firsthand experience of NGOs proves invaluable in encapsulating in a resolution the concerns regarding human rights in a particular African country or human rights theme.

The Commission's sessions provide the ideal opportunity for NGOs to share their information with members of the Commission, other NGOs and government representatives. The information, in the form of documents, reports and press releases, is presented mainly in English and French and sometimes in Arabic and languages indigenous to Africa. The array of publications distributed at each session of the Commission attests to the efforts being made by NGOs to promote and protect human rights in Africa. Many publications promote the African Charter and the work of the Commission, while others report on the human rights situation in different African countries. The Commission has on several occasions called on NGOs to create a body to ensure better co-ordination of their activities at each session. While there has been informal co-ordination among NGOs at each session, many NGOs, especially African ones, have been reluctant to form a body for co-ordination of their activities. This reluctance is based on several uncertainties: Whether the Commission would communicate with NGOs only through the co-ordinating body; whether NGOs would be required to present a composite oral statement to each session; whether northern NGOs would play a dominant role in the co-ordinating body; and whether the co-ordinating body would assist the Commission in the consideration of applications for observer status. Some NGOs such as the International Commission of Jurists (ICJ) have suggested that in order to improve the relationship between the Commission and NGOs a specific post for liaison with NGOs should be established within the Secretariat, similar to that in the UN and the Council of Europe. The Commission has yet to act on this suggestion.

THE IMPORTANCE OF INTERNATIONAL HUMAN RIGHTS LAW

A major theme in the current discussion about international human rights law is whether it actually makes a difference on the ground. In this extract it is argued that the impact of international human rights treaties has been more significant through their use at the national level than through the supervisory measures that they provide for, such as state reporting and individual complaints. They argue that the main function of the treaty system is to affect the human rights situation in the countries that are not engaged with the system.

HEYNS, CH AND VILJOEN, F 'THE IMPACT OF THE UNITED NATIONS HUMAN RIGHTS TREATIES ON THE DOMESTIC LEVEL' (2001)

23 *Human Rights Quarterly* 483

The success or failure of any international human rights system should be evaluated in accordance with its impact on human rights practices on the domestic (country) level. At the beginning of the new millennium, it is clear that the concept of human rights is widely accepted as the 'idea of our time'. The conceptual battle is over, and the focus has shifted to the implementation of human rights. Universal ratification of the main human rights treaties might be appearing on the horizon, but ratification in itself is largely formal, and in some cases an empty gesture. The challenge now is to ensure that the promises contained in the treaties and affirmed through ratification are realised in the lives of ordinary people around the world. A paradigm shift to the true 'customers' of the system is necessary.

...

All the available evidence suggests that the treaties have had an enormous influence in shaping the present understanding throughout the world of what are to be regarded as basic human rights and the limits of these. The influence of the treaties is likely to increase in the future. The new generation of lawyers, government officials, and human rights activists are more aware of the treaties, and the conditions under which the treaties operate have improved dramatically over the last decade. These include rapid advances in the dissemination of information and the formation of strong international NGOs in the context of a shrinking world.

Nevertheless, two aspects regarding the influence of the treaty system are particularly striking. The first is the fact that the international system has had its greatest impact where treaty norms have been made part of domestic law more or less spontaneously (for example as part of constitutional and legislative reform), and not as a result of norm enforcement (through reporting, individual complaints, or confidential inquiry procedures). The second is that insofar as international norm enforcement plays a role, its influence is very unevenly spread among countries that are part of the system. These aspects pose important challenges and questions.

Beginning with the first point, the treaties have had their greatest influence domestically in shaping the understanding of government officials and members of civil society as to what is to be considered basic human rights. Although a causal link cannot always be proven, it could hardly be considered coincidental that the very language of human rights in the parliaments and courts of the surveyed countries is largely that which the treaty system has been introducing and reinforcing since the middle 1960s. As will be pointed out, even in cases in which the treaties have not yet been ratified, they have informed processes in which human rights provisions of new constitutions were drafted. The treaty system has largely defined the international consensus on human rights norms, which in many instances are simply adhered to because they are considered to be appropriate.

Continuing with the second point, international enforcement mechanisms used by the treaty bodies appear to have had a very limited demonstrable impact thus far. This is partly due to the fact that the system has taken a number of decades to develop to its present level and partly the result of inefficiencies in the system (backlogs, overlaps, vagueness in findings, etc). However, it is also true that focused and relevant concluding observations and views still are routinely ignored when domestic convenience so requires.

One obvious response to this state of affairs would be to focus on ways to strengthen the monitoring mechanisms in order to ensure greater efficiency and to attempt to turn the international enforcement screws tighter. However, it will be a central thesis of this study, however, that such attempts, although important, must be supplemented by creative efforts to ensure that treaty norms are internalised in the domestic legal and cultural system, and that they are enforced on that level. The challenge is to harness the treaty system to domestic forces – 'domestic constituencies' – that will ensure its realisation.

The second aspect mentioned above is the discrepancy in the actual and potential impacts of the system of international norm enforcement (insofar as it does play a role) with respect to the state parties to the treaties. Some countries are highly engaged with the system. They submit substantial reports, their NGOs bring individual complaints, their newspapers and academics publish information on the system, etc. With respect to these countries, the enforcement system can and does have an impact. However, other countries do very little of the above, and as a result, the system has a very weak hold on them. Disengaged countries – those that do not submit reports, discuss concluding observations, or allow an environment in which individual complaints can be lodged – can largely escape criticism from the treaty system, which is, after all, based on consent. The unfortunate result is that the countries that most often end up being singled out as human rights violators are those that are engaged. Within the system, more criticism seems to be the reward for a higher level of engagement.

The question will have to be asked whether under such circumstances, one could expect the international enforcement system to be strengthened. Disengaged countries will obviously not pursue such a result – they are already shying away from what little pressure the system exercises. It is also unrealistic to expect the countries that are engaged to push very hard for a stronger line to be taken with respect to violations, as they are the ones who are most likely to be singled out as human rights violators, and when they know worse perpetrators get away virtually without punishment.

...

There are two possible ways of moving forward on this issue. One is to argue that the focus should be on moving forward with those who are engaged. The other approach is to focus specifically on those who are not engaged, in order to get them to become engaged, so that the entire system may move forward.

...

Cassel further explores the difference between the direct and indirect impact of international human rights law.

CASSEL, D 'DOES INTERNATIONAL HUMAN RIGHTS LAW MAKE A DIFFERENCE?' (2001)

2 *Chicago Journal of International Law* 121

...

International articulation of rights norms have reshaped domestic dialogues in law politics, academia, public consciousness, civil society, and the press. International human rights law also facilitates international and transnational processes that reinforce, stimulate and monitor these domestic dialogues. While reliable quantitative measurement is probably impossible, by strengthening domestic rights institutions, international human rights law has brought incalculable benefits for rights protection.

In addition, international enforcement mechanisms have more limited, but nonetheless important, direct benefits for right protection. They protect lives, free prisoners, rescue reputations, prompt legislative reform, and afford otherwise unattainable justice in the form of truth telling, reparations, and condemnation and punishment of rights violators. Still, direct international interventions are limited in impact. Over time, the extent to which international law serves as a useful tool for protection of human rights will depend mainly on its contribution to a broader set of transnational processes that affect the ways people think and institutions behave – whether governments, state security forces, guerrilla groups, or corporations.

...

The 'rope' that pulls human rights forward

As one strand in the rope that pulls rights forward, the value of international human rights law depends mainly on its interaction with the other strands. The central strand in the rope is the global growth in human rights consciousness. This in turn interweaves the concept of rights, as entitlements of individuals or groups on which claims or demands may be based, together with the notion that some rights are so fundamental they are inherent birthrights of all human beings, regardless of nationality or culture.

Other strands of the rope include non-governmental human rights organisations, whose numbers, activities, and sophistication in international human rights law norms and institutions have grown dramatically at both national and international levels and rapidly evolving communications and transportation technology that makes possible far more effective transnational organising by these human rights groups than was possible only two decades ago. Both communications and faster and lower cost transportation technology, by making possible frequent, well attended international conferences, have contributed to the growth of another strand in the rights revolution, transnational issue networks, energised by 'epistemic communities' of like-minded rights advocates in non-governmental groups, sympathetic governments, academia, and the media, who work together across national and professional boundaries to promote shared values and agendas.

Some remaining strands include domestic constitutions and laws, which increasingly incorporate international norms, national human rights institutions, established in dozens of countries in the last fifteen years, spreading democratisation, and gradually extended rule of law. This list is not all-inclusive but merely points out some of the strands comprising this 'rope'. The purpose here is to recognise how international human rights law interweaves with these other strands, all growing both independently and in their relations with each other, to create an ever stronger rope that pulls international human rights forward. Other strands in the rope include the growing levels of affluence and education in most parts of the world, expansion in the number and reach of non-binding international norms, and, of course, the explosive growth of international human rights law itself.

Indirect effects of international human rights law on rights protection

Does the necessity to bring in other factors suggest that international law, by itself, counts for little? For that matter, with all these other rights-protecting processes, who needs international law?

What such questions overlook is that all the foregoing processes of rights protection – including international human rights law – are interrelated and, over time, growing stronger. All the others are strengthened by international human rights law, which in turn is strengthened by each of them. Human rights groups, for example, make constant use of international human rights law in their organising. National human rights ombudsmen regularly appeal to international norms in opposing local efforts to legislate lower standards. Constitutional courts increasingly look to international treaties and the jurisprudence of international courts in interpreting national constitutional rights.

In this process of mutual reinforcement, international law plays several distinctive roles:

(A) Provides a common language. Rights groups in Thailand and Chile, New York and Johannesburg, can invoke the same set of rights expressed in the same language, interpreted by the same UN human rights bodies. In theory, this function could be played by non-legal instruments. Indeed, at the outset of the modern rights revolution, it was played by the Universal Declaration, that instrument arguably evolved into customary international law. This function, then, is a by-product rather than a necessarily unique function of international human rights law. Nonetheless, in practice, the instruments of international law supply most of the vocabulary for transnational rights discourse.

(B) Reinforces the universality of human rights. Three quarters or more of all governments accept the main international human rights treaties: The International Covenant on Civil and Political Rights; UN treaties on rights of women and children and against racial discrimination; basic ILO treaties on labour rights; and the Geneva Conventions and Protocols on international humanitarian law. The numbers grow every year. Such broad participation in formally binding international instruments reinforces the claim that human rights are universal. This, in turn, strengthens their claim to being fundamental and hardens their currency in domestic and international political debate.

While most widely adopted instruments are legally binding, not all are. For example, the Universal Declaration not only asserts its universality, but has repeatedly been adopted without formal dissent, first by the UN General Assembly in 1948, and later by widely attended, UN-sponsored diplomatic conferences in 1968 and 1993. Thus, again, the contribution of international human rights law to universality, even if not unique, is an important by-product.

(C) Legitimises claims of rights. Because international human rights treaties are adopted by governments, usually after prolonged and contested negotiations and followed in many countries by lengthy processes of ratification, they confer legitimacy on claims of rights, especially when those claims are asserted (as they usually are) against governments. Human rights groups can (and regularly do) say to governments, 'It is not we who say that torture is illegal and must be investigated and punished; it is you who so declare, as parties to the Convention Against Torture'.

(D) Signals the perceived will of the international community. Because of broad participation by governments, via formally serious processes of negotiations and ratifications, international human rights treaties are often perceived as expressing the will of the international community. While that perception may matter little in a powerful country such as the United States, it often carries considerable weight in smaller and weaker countries – which is to say, most of the world's nations.

During peace negotiations in Guatemala in the mid-1990s, for example, the military pressed for a blanket amnesty for its wartime violations of human rights. Human rights groups had few cards to play in opposition, other than the argument that under international law, amnesties could not be conferred for certain crimes against humanity. In need of international approval and financial support for post-war recovery programmes, the government ultimately agreed to leave such crimes out of the amnesty. The perception that violating international law would flout the will of the international community – or at least that it could be so characterised by opponents – was a major factor in this decision. Only crimes whose prosecution is arguably required by international law were exempted. Those for which amnesty would merely offend international sensibilities were not exempted.

Perceived international will also plays a role in the tendency of newly democratic regimes to ratify human rights treaties and accept international enforcement mechanisms, as a kind of insurance policy against the return of authoritarian rule. Most recently, no sooner did Peru oust the regime of President Alberto Fujimori, who had purported to withdraw the country from the contentious jurisdiction of the Inter-American Court of Human Rights, than the new government promptly re-joined the Court.

(E) Provides juridical precision. Especially when international human rights law is put in treaty form, by which governments expect to be bound, negotiators strive to give it a degree of juridical precision generally lacking in political declarations and philosophical pronouncements. The room for debate as to its meaning – and hence pretense for evasion, or grounds for needless disagreement – is narrowed.

(F) Creates increased expectations of compliance. Because international human rights law is expressed as law, it generates increased expectations of compliance. This gives human rights claimants stronger ground to demand compliance, and narrows the defenses available to violators: They may deny that violations were committed, but they cannot easily deny their obligation to respect the relevant norm. A government may well have accepted an international obligation with no intention to comply, but this is a difficult thing to admit publicly. The government may find itself trapped by its own hypocrisy.

(G) Encourages domestic judicial enforcement. International human rights law, especially in treaty form, is susceptible to domestic judicial enforcement, whereas non-legal instruments generally are not. Many constitutions, for example, expressly incorporate treaties into domestic law, and some accord special, higher domestic legal status to human rights treaties.

(H) Encourages enforcement by international courts or agencies. Because international human rights law is couched as law, it also lends itself to potential enforcement by international courts or agencies – a trend growing in practice. Outside Europe such enforcement is rare and even more rarely effective. Still, the mere threat or perception (even mistaken) of its potential gives human rights groups added leverage. Indeed, the very uncertainty of enforcement makes governments nervous. The uncertainty is aggravated by the trend toward increasing enforcement in new and unexpected ways – witness the surprise arrest of Chile's General Pinochet on a Spanish arrest warrant in London, or credit denials by the World Bank on human rights grounds, after decades of contending that the Bank could not consider human rights. Risk-averse diplomats and bureaucrats often treat slaps on the wrist, administered by toothless international human rights bodies, as if they were matters to be taken seriously, precisely because they never know when such seemingly empty words may come back to haunt them.

(I) Creates additional stigma. International human rights law, especially international criminal law norms such as those proscribing crimes against humanity, adds to the moral sting and shame of violation. Granted, atrocities generate broad condemnation on moral grounds alone. Even so, in many cultures – including the culture of international diplomacy – criminal conduct carries its own, additional stigma, undermining the capacity of violators to defend their conduct, while enhancing the force of condemnations.

(J) Avoids moral relativism. State violence does not always provoke moral outrage. Populations victimised by opposing ethnic or rebel groups may tolerate, if not applaud, brutal retaliation. Yet in such situations international law, written for universal application, can keep its bearing. Even while few Peruvians, for example, protested the prison massacre of rebellious Shining Path guerrillas, the Inter-American Court of Human Rights ruled against Peru's resort to excessive force. Similarly, after the Knesset failed to stop torture of Palestinian security suspects, the Israeli Supreme Court finally ended the practice. And while few Israelis today protest their government's selective assassinations of security suspects, Amnesty International rightly denounces these violations of international law. Where moral clarity may be lost in the passions of the moment, international law can not only condemn, but also teach, helping morality to regain its compass.

...

Direct impact

Account should also be taken of the growing, non-negligible, direct impact of international human rights law. Unquestionably the direct impact has been greatest in Europe, where it has grown recently and rapidly in a hospitable climate of democratic values and regional unification.

In the Council of Europe, which has grown from the post-war democracies of Western Europe to its current embrace of some forty European states, the European Convention on Human Rights was adopted in 1950 and came into force in 1953. Not until the 1970s, however, did its enforcement institutions – the European Commission and Court of Human Rights – have much business. After gaining public and governmental trust, they expanded their dockets and effectiveness from the mid-1970s on. By 1990 the European Court had come to play for Europe approximately the same role in safeguarding approximately the same set of basic rights, as the US Supreme Court plays in enforcing constitutional rights among the fifty states, with comparable substantive outcomes and degrees of compliance.

As a result of judgments of the European Court of Human Rights, not only have individual plaintiffs been awarded damages, but European governments have revised legislation on such sensitive matters as media criticism of judicial proceedings, national security measures against terrorists, gay rights, family rights, and criminal justice procedures. The direct impact of international human rights law in Europe is not only comparable to that of domestic constitutional law in developed democracies, but greater than that of domestic law in nations where the rule of law has yet to take hold or is crippled by corruption.

While the European Court of Justice of the European Union mainly deals with economic and regulatory issues, it, too, has rendered important and effective rulings on such matters as gender discrimination and rights of immigrants.

Outside Europe, however, the direct impact of international human rights law has been sporadic. The UN human rights system – developed largely since the mid-1970s through state reporting requirements, special rapporteurs and experts who investigate and publish reports, and individual complaint procedures under several treaties – has been a useful strand in the rope of human rights protection. It indirectly protects rights by reinforcing public awareness, exposing violations, legitimising efforts by non-governmental organisations and keeping issues of human rights on diplomatic agendas. Beyond a few exceptions – its contribution to the fall of apartheid in South Africa; human rights components of peacekeeping missions in countries ranging from El Salvador to East Timor; *ad hoc* international or partly international criminal tribunals for the former Yugoslavia, Rwanda and Sierra Leone; and occasionally successful interventions in individual cases by rapporteurs and treaty committees – the UN's direct impact on rights protection has been exceedingly modest.

Two other regional systems merit mention. During the Cold War it could fairly be said that the Organization of American States had an ineffectual human rights declaration since 1948, a mostly ineffectual Inter-American Commission on Human Rights since 1959, and an Inter-American Court of Human Rights with no contentious caseload since 1979. Such successes as the system could claim – for example, documentation and exposure of Argentina's 'dirty war' in 1980 – were more diplomatic than legal in nature.

By the late 1980s, however, the Inter-American Human Rights legal system began to make claims of direct impact. In 1988, ruling under the American Convention on Human Rights, the Inter-American Court delivered the first of what are now a score of significant damage awards against states for violations of the right to life, and there are many more cases currently on its docket. Governments also began to accept substantial damage awards in settlement negotiations with the commission. In the 1990s the commission and court began regularly to issue requests and orders for 'precautionary measures' by governments to protect the lives of dozens of human rights defenders and witnesses. In nearly all these cases, security measures were taken or offered, and in nearly all, the intended beneficiaries were not thereafter killed.

Conclusion

The direct impact of international human rights law on practice in most of the world remains weak and inconsistent. But both this incipient body of law, and to a lesser degree its direct and even more its indirect influence on conduct, have grown rapidly in historical terms, and appear to be spreading in ways that cannot be explained by a worldview based solely on state power and rational calculations of self-interest. To appreciate its effectiveness and potential, international human rights law must be understood as part of a broader set of interrelated, mutually reinforcing processes and institutions – interwoven strands in a rope – that together pull human rights forward, and to which international law makes distinctive contributions. Thus understood, international law can be seen as a useful tool for the protection of human rights, and one which promises to be more useful in the future.

QUESTIONS

(1) Is it fair to say that human rights are a Western invention and imposition?

(2) Some writers see a direct link between human rights on the one hand and conflict on the other. Do you agree?

(3) The idea that human rights are entitlements of individuals limiting the power of the state is challenged when consideration is given to economic and social rights as well as cultural and so called 'third generation' rights, normally said to be 'collective' in their content and orientation. Elaborate on this dichotomy.

(4) Identify, if possible, some human rights norms that you think may be amenable to characterisation as 'relative or particular' and those that are clearly universal. Motivate.

(5) A bid to protect some of the norms recognised by the modern concept of human rights, for example, the rights of women in Africa, could lead to conflict with time-tested traditions, beliefs and practices. How are such clashes to be resolved?

(6) Some argue that there is a proliferation of terms in the field, causing confusion. Do the terms 'human security' and 'good governance', for example, add anything not covered by the concept 'human rights'?

(7) What are the comparable advantages and added value of having an international system for the protection of human rights in addition to a domestic system? Does a regional system for the protection of human rights offer anything that cannot be achieved through the United Nations system? Is the global, regional or domestic protection of human rights more important?

(8) Is there a proliferation of supervisory mechanisms within the African Union? Motivate.

(9) In the *Fawehinmi* case the Nigerian Supreme Court states that 'the rights ... in the Charter are not new to Nigeria as most of these rights and obligations are already enshrined in our Constitution'. What are the additional benefits of the inclusion of international human rights in a domestic legal system?

(10) Professor An-Na'im talks of the paradox of the state as one of the main perpetrators of violations of human rights also being the main protector. Do you agree?

(11) In some countries there is an increased reliance on courts to take decisions with far-reaching social consequences. It has been argued that such decisions should be left to the legislature, as representatives of the people. In light of this, discuss the advantages and disadvantages of the justiciability of socio-economic rights. Also, should parliament and the courts decide whether the death penalty is permissible?

(12) Discuss the performance of the national human rights institution in your country, if such an institution exists. Is it a 'pretender' or a 'protector'?

(13) Odinkalu argues that human rights NGOs in Africa exclude the 'participation of the peoples whose welfare it purports to advance'. In your opinion, is this a correct description, and if so, what can be done to achieve a more inclusionary approach? Are the measures as set out in the Kampala Declaration sufficient?

(14) What international instruments have been ratified by your country? Can you point to any results they have achieved in relation to your country? Try to find some of the concluding observations of treaty bodies regarding state reports submitted by your country, and investigate which of those recommendations have been implemented. Follow up on the views expressed by treaty bodies in terms of some individual complaints - have they been given effect?

(15) Do you think the judicial approach to human rights issues of a human rights court for Africa, the *quasi* judicial approach of the African Commission on Human and Peoples' Rights, and the political process of the African Peer Review Mechanism is more likely to yield results in Africa?

(16) The number of complaints received by the African Commission on Human and Peoples' Rights is very small in comparison with other regional human rights systems. At the same time there is no lack of human rights violations to report. Discuss possible explanations for the limited use made of the individual complaint mechanism of the Commission. Will the establishment of a human rights court for Africa improve the situation?

(17) Propose how the work of the African Human Rights Commission within the African Union can be made more effective.

(18) To what extent are Kennedy's criticisms — which have largely emerged in the North American context where there is a general acceptance of the idea of rights and specifically human rights — applicable in other societies where this is not necessarily the case?

FURTHER READING

Aidoo, A 'Africa: Democracy without rights' (1993) 15 *Human Rights Quarterly* 703

Ankumah, E (1996) *The African Commission on Human and Peoples' Rights: Practice and procedures* The Hague: Martinus Nijhoff

An-Na`im, A (ed) (1992) *Human rights in cross-cultural perspectives: A quest for consensus* Philidelphia: University of Pennsylvania Press

An-Na`im, A (ed) (2003) *Human rights under African Constitutions: Realizing the promise for ourselves* Philidelphia: University of Pennsylvania Press

Baimu, E 'Human rights in NEPAD and its implications for the African human rights system' (2002) 2 *African Human Rights Law Journal* 301

Brems, E (2001) *Human rights: Universality and diversity* The Hague: Martinus Nijhoff

Cherubin-Doumbia, G (2004) *African commitments to human rights: A review of eight NEPAD countries* Pretoria: African Human Security Initiative

Elsheikh, I 'The future relationship between the African Court and the African Commission' (2002) 2 *African Human Rights Law Journal* 252

Evans, M and Murray, R (eds) (2002) *The African Charter on Human and Peoples' Rights: The system in practice 1986 - 2000* Cambridge: Cambridge University Press

Heyns, CH and van der Linde, M (eds) (2004) *Human rights law in Africa* Leiden: Martinus Nijhoff

Heyns, CH; Baimu, E and Killander, M 'The African Union' (2003) 96 *German Yearbook of International Law* 252

Hannum, H (ed) (2004) *Guide to international human rights practice* Philidelphia: University of Pennsylvania Press

Lloyd, A and Murray, R (2004) 'Institutions with responsibility for human rights protection under the African Union' 2 *Journal of African Law* 48

Mamdani, M (ed) (2000) *Beyond rights talk and culture talk: Comparative essays on the politics of rights and culture* Cape Town: David Philip

Manby, B 'The African Union, NEPAD, and human rights: the missing agenda' (2004) 26 *Human Rights Quarterly* 983

Murray, R (2000) *The African Commission on Human and Peoples' Rights and international law* Oxford: Hart Publishing

Murray, R (2004) *Human rights in Africa: From the OAU to the African Union* Cambridge: Cambridge University Press

Nnaemeka, O and Ezeilo, JN (eds) (2005) *Engendering human rights: Cultural and socio-economic realities in Africa* New York: Palgrave Macmillan

Nyamnjoh, F and Englund, H (eds) (2004) *Rights and the politics of recognition in Africa* London; New York: Zed Books

Odinkalu, CA and Christensen, C 'The African Commission on Human and Peoples' Rights: The development of its non-state communication procedures' (1998) 20 *Human Rights Quarterly* 235-280

Onoria, H 'The African Commission on Human and Peoples' Rights and the exhaustion of local remedies under the African Charter' (2003) 3 *African Human Rights Law Journal* 1

Österdahl, I (2002) *Implementing human rights in Africa* Uppsala: Iustus Förlag

Ouguergouz, F (2003) *The African Charter on Human and Peoples' Rights: A comprehensive agenda for human rights* The Hague: Kluwer Law International

Quashigah, K 'The African Charter on Human and Peoples' Rights: Towards a more effective reporting mechanism' (2002) 2 *African Human Rights Law Journal* 261

Umozurike, O (1997) *The African Charter on Human and Peoples' Rights* The Hague: Kluwer Law International

Van der Linde, M and Louw, L 'Considering the interpretation and implementation of article 24 of the African Charter on Human and Peoples' Rights in light of the *SERAC* communication' (2003) 3 *African Human Rights Law Journal* 167

Viljoen, F 'A human rights court for Africa, and Africans' (2004) 1 *Brooklyn Journal of International Law* 30

The decisions of the African Commission on Human and Peoples' Rights may be found in the *African Human Rights Law Reports*. Journals such as the *African Human Rights Law Journal* and the *African Journal of International and Comparative Law* carry articles on human rights law in Africa.

6

APPROACHES TO PEACE IN AFRICA

TRADITIONAL CONFLICT RESOLUTION

What were the traditional conflict resolution mechanisms employed in Africa? Can they still be used?

In the following article, Mazrui identifies four African sources that, in his view, need to be tapped for future conflict resolution and for the enhancement of peace in Africa. These are: Africa's limited memory of animosity; the value of elders; Africa's ecumenical spirit; and African women.

MAZRUI, A 'TOWARDS CONTAINING CONFLICT IN AFRICA: METHODS, MECHANISMS AND VALUES' (1995)

2 *East African Journal of Peace and Human Rights* 81

...

Relevant African values and ethics

Short memory of hate

What cultural resources or traditional mores does Africa have which may be tapped to help contain or resolve conflict? Perhaps the most important is Africa's short memory of hate. Africans have frequently displayed a remarkable capacity to 'let bygones be bygones'.

Jomo Kenyatta was imprisoned for years by the British and denounced by a British Governor as a 'leader unto darkness and death'. However, when he was finally released from detention to lead a newly emerging independent Kenya, Kenyatta became one of the country's leading Anglophiles. He turned the foreign policy of independent Kenya towards Britain and the West, and crowned his metamorphosis with the publication of a book entitled *Suffering without bitterness*.

Nelson Mandela lost nearly three decades of the best years of his life imprisoned under the white man's laws. But he came out of prison in 1990 ready to forgive and forget provided apartheid was ended. Mandela was even capable of feeling compassion for three white terrorists ostensibly 'fasting unto death' in protest against their own white government. Mandela personally visited the white terrorists to beg them to eat. A short memory of hate indeed.

Ian Smith in the old Rhodesia unleashed the horrors of a Unilateral Declaration of Independence (UDI) upon his people, and was therefore instrumental in initiating a war in which thousands of Africans were killed. When the war ended, and Zimbabwe became independent in 1980, this architect of the blood-letting UDI was not tried before the equivalent of a Nuremburg trial, but became a member of parliament of the new Zimbabwe and proceeded to abuse the new Black government of the day. In some parts of the world Ian Smith would have been killed or assassinated as a 'war criminal'. In Africa he became a beneficiary of the African's short memory of hate.

As the Nigerian civil war was coming to an end, many people expected 'rivers of blood' in the former Biafra resulting from vengeance perpetrated by the victorious Federal side. The Pope in the Vatican was among those who were deeply concerned about the likely fate of the Catholics in Iboland. Moreover, Nigerians generally were not known for exceptional discipline or self-restraint. Would the euphoria of military victory result in an orgy of blood-letting? None of these fears were borne out by what happened. Unruly as Nigerians sometimes can be, they found self-restraint at the supreme moment of the conclusion of the civil war. There was no free-for-all orgy of revenge. There were no Nuremburg trials. On that occasion, Nigerians were tested for moral discipline-and they were not found wanting. They were the carriers of Africa's short memory of hate.

Interestingly, while African civil wars and fratricide receive considerable global attention from the international media, Africa's rapid moments of forgiveness are not a matter for headlines. From the point of view of global journalism, to kill is news, to forgive is not. A shot is a story, an embrace seldom worth recounting. Africa's short memory of hate is therefore not celebrated internationally. Nevertheless, this limited memory of animosity is an important cultural resource, a valuable traditional more, for future conflict resolution. Africa should find ways of tapping it to enhance the consolidation of Pax Africana.

Ecumenicalism and the elder tradition

Another cultural resource and value worth tapping is the elder tradition in Africa. The proposed Pan-African Senate of Elders consisting of former presidents who voluntarily stepped down to give way to democratically selected successors such as Kenneth Kaunda, Leopold Senghor, Julius K. Nyerere and Olusegun Obasanjo, could be requested from time to time to serve as mediators or conciliators in certain conflicts. General Olusegun Obasanjo is already performing some of those mediating tasks outside the purview of the Organization of the African Unity. Former US President Jimmy Carter has also attempted comparable mediating roles from time to time. If a Pan-African Senate of Elders is institutionalised, it could provide a pool of roving conciliators and mediators. Africa's respect for elders could be tapped to help the success of such roles.

The third cultural resource which may be tapped for conflict prevention, containment, or resolution is Africa's ecumenical spirit. On the whole, religion in Africa is divisive only when it reinforces other divisions. In Nigeria almost all Hausa are Muslims, almost all Igbo are Christians, while the Yoruba are split between the two religions. Christianity thus tends to reinforce Igbo identity while Islam tends to reinforce Hausa identity. The imported religions help to sharpen pre-existent differences. In the Sudan, Islam and Christianity also reinforce other immense ethno-cultural differences between the north and the south of the country. The two Semitic religions (Christianity and

Islam) are additional catalysts to regional discord, rather than being the main causes of differentiation.

Senegal, on the other hand, is over 80 per cent Muslim. And yet for twenty years the country had a Roman Catholic President (Senghor) without Islamic fundamentalist riots in the streets of Dakar protesting 'Christian minority domination'. Senegal was at once one of the most open African countries and one of the most ecumenical. Since Leopold Senghor voluntarily retired from power, Senegal at last had a Muslim President. But even then, the First Lady of Senegal was a Roman Catholic. This is a record of presidential ecumenicalism which has no equivalent in the Western world or anywhere else outside Africa.

In Tanzania the Muslim half of the population had a better record of accepting the leadership of Julius K Nyerere (a Roman Catholic) than the Christian half have had of accepting the leadership of Ali Hassan Mwinyi (a Muslim). However, on balance Tanzanians are still a fairly good illustration of the ecumenical spirit at work in Africa. Indeed, many African families in several parts of the continent are multi-religious without breaking up — a Sunni father, a Unitarian mother, a Catholic uncle, an Ahmadiyya son, an Anglican daughter, perhaps all of them with a partial allegiance to African traditional religion.

If the ecumenical spirit is indeed one of Africa's cultural resources, how can it be employed in the struggle for containment or conflict resolution in the continent? There has been an under-utilisation of religious leaders in Africa even in those conflicts which are perceived as being, in part, sectarian.

Until the visit of Pope John Paul II to the Sudan in 1993, there had in fact been very limited participation by major religious leaders in finding a solution to the Sudanese problem. The tendency was to look almost exclusively towards such political mediators as Ibrahim Babangida of Nigeria, Yoweri Museveni of Uganda, and Jimmy Carter of the United States. Should there not be a more systematic use of Africa's religious wisdom in the quest for a solution to Africa's sectarian problems? Archbishop Desmond Tutu has been used to help resolve political problems as far away as Thailand and Burma.

But has his wisdom been used to help solve problems in the Sudan and Nigeria? Is Desmond Tutu a prophet in Asia, but not in Africa? The proposed Pan-African Senate of Elders should include a few select religious figures from Africa such as Bishop Tutu, or the Sheikh of Al-Azhar University (the most senior representative of the Islamic wing of this ancient University), the most senior Roman Catholic Cardinal in Africa, the Head of the Orthodox Church of Ethiopia, and a distinguished exponent of the indigenous religions of Africa. Just as the House of Lords in Britain includes Bishops as members, the Pan-African Senate of Elders should include a selection of Africa's religious leaders.

Women in warfare

The traditional involvement of women in consultations about war and peace is yet another cultural or traditional more which may be relevant for conflict resolution. The liberation wars in Southern Africa in the second half of the twentieth century produced many strong women, both among fighters in the bush and political activists. In spite of her subsequent legal and political setbacks, Nomzamo Winifred Mandela of South Africa was often a beacon of hope and struggle especially in the 1980s. A less controversial but equally militant activist was Nohtsikelelo Albertina Sisulu, who was also subjected by the apartheid regime to recurrent harassment, banning, and detention.

In recent indigenous culture, some women became soldier-priestesses, leading men into battle. In the late 1980s the Government of Yoweri Museveni in Uganda had to contend with the rebellion led by Alice Lakwena, who had convinced tough Acholi warriors that she had religious powers that would protect them from bullets. Alice Lakwena was briefly the Joan of Arc of the Acholi and, like Joan of Arc, she was defeated. But it was sociologically significant that a woman could convince members of one of the most martial 'tribes' in Uganda to follow her into battle.

In the 1960s it was Alice Lenshina in Zambia who was leader priestess in defiance of the government of President Kenneth Kaunda. Although she and her Lumpa Church were militarily defeated, her leadership role was manifest. Are there ways of tapping Africa's female wisdom towards prevention, containment or resolution of conflict? Again at this stage we can only make a start. So far we have mentioned two categories of members of the proposed Pan-African Senate of Elders comprising of democratically replaced former presidents and major religious leaders. The third category of members should be outstanding African women, such as Angie Brooks of Liberia, who in 1969 served as one of the first women presidents of the United Nations General Assembly. How such women will be chosen to serve on the Pan-African Senate of Elders is something yet to be thought through. One possibility would be for the OAU Summit of Heads of State to create an electoral college consisting exclusively of independent women, which would then elect women to serve on the Senate of Elders. Members of the electoral college would themselves be disqualified from being elected to the Senate.

...

Malan highlights the necessity of examining conflicts within their social contexts. Such an approach would provide deeper understanding of the origin and nature of conflict, the role of elders, and social involvement throughout the process of resolving the con-flict.

MALAN, J *CONFLICT RESOLUTION WISDOM FROM AFRICA* (1997)

Durban: ACCORD

...

Taking the social context of conflicts seriously

When Africa's ways of dealing with conflicts are studied, most of the attention of researchers is almost magnetically attracted to real life. This does not only apply to researchers from Africa itself, but also to those from abroad.

Theoretical approaches seem to be out of place on African soil. Nothing can prevent games theorists from calculating statistical scenarios and from including Africa in their experiments. Other theorists, like those in the fields of bargaining or decision making, may also apply their paradigms to examples from Africa. Researchers in the entire field of the human sciences may rightfully use the theoretical approaches of their various disciplines when examining relevant topics in Africa. In all these ways meaningful insights and recommendations may indeed be reached. But still, when focusing on Africa, theorists should respond as far as possible to the pull towards real life in all its vibrant practicality. Abstract ideas (whether they originate from left-hand or right-hand sectors of researchers' brains) may be harboured and explored, but preferably not in life-estranged ways.

One of the major lessons the rest of the world may learn from Africa is precisely that social reality should be taken seriously. To call this a mere lesson, is an understatement, however. Many people, in many parts of the world, may need a long-term course in order to unlearn their inherited and indoctrinated individualism. People who tend to opt for the line of least resistance may prefer to avoid the challenge of wider social thinking. They may therefore need persistent encouragement to take the extra 'trouble' of getting themselves, or their research project, involved in a network of social complexities.

There is also the possibility, however, of learning this 'lesson' in a moment of sudden insight. After all, it is not a matter of acquiring knowledge. Essentially it is a breakthrough to a social way of thinking and living. It is like learning to swim in the sea of social life. When this skill has once been mastered, one's social orientation is no longer a duty that has to be remembered and observed from day to day. It has become a permanent ingredient of one's entire mode of thinking, speaking and acting.

For Conflict Studies the obvious implication is to view conflicts as non-isolated events in their social context. Such a perspective is not narrowly focused on a conflict and its resolution. It takes into account the cultural context setting and the social context. It looks at the history of preceding events which have led up to the conflict concerned. And while concentrating on the conflict itself and the process of resolving it, it takes possible implications for the future seriously. A wider look is taken than one which just includes the disputing parties. Possible consequences for others in their families and social networks are also taken into consideration. Potential effects on relationships and interests are envisaged.

This way of viewing conflicts and their resolution as events in the comprehensive continuum of social life is definitely distinctive of Africa. When Africans sit down to talk about a conflict, the talking usually covers all sorts of relevant background. It also explores the thoughts and intentions of others. Those taking part in the talks normally try to gauge how others are perceiving and interpreting their own actions. When an elder from a family, village or clan becomes involved in the talks, the traditional objectives are to move away from accusations and counter-accusations, to soothe hurt feelings and to reach a compromise that may help to improve future relationships. Precisely in this characteristic spirit of Africa the secretary-general of the Organization of African Unity recently emphasised the broader set of goals of which negotiations form part: political reform, economic development and greater social opportunities for all. With regard to the social context he also highlighted the important aspects of values and aspirations, perceptions and visions.

This earnestness about the social context of conflicts is not only practised and proclaimed by the people and leaders of Africa. It is emphatically endorsed by researchers in the fields of both sociology and anthropology. In fact, the need to take the social context of conflicts seriously should be absolutely self-evident to anyone who surveys the elements operating in the social dimension.

Social life is the area in which values and norms function. It is the environment in which cultural traditions are formed and handed down from generation to generation. Often, however, the cultural milieu is not just monopolised by one set of values, principles, norms and customs. It may be filled by a bi-, tri- or multi-cultural complexity, and the adherents of the various traditions may tend either to segregate or to integrate themselves. When it comes to religious beliefs, cults and prescriptions, differences (sometimes peripheral distinctions, but sometimes core contrasts) may lead to tensions or hostilities.

It should be obvious that the specifically religious or the wider cultural setting of a conflict deserves proper recognition and attention. This may be easier when the values are explicitly mentioned and discussed. It becomes more complicated when values, especially contradicting ones, are implicitly assumed. Values should never be ignored, however. All over Africa people have deeply rooted cultural commitments, and in many of the conflicts in Africa this cultural heritage may form at least a noteworthy background, or may even play a decisive role.

The other key element functioning throughout all social life is the fascinating network of human relations. This is obviously a world-wide phenomenon, but in Africa it has always received special attention. Family ties and community networking are constantly respected, maintained and strengthened. Whenever kinship or social relationships are disturbed by a dispute, priority is given to their restoration. When the disputing parties, their supporters and the elders concerned engage in talking a matter through, it is usually the issue of relationships which receives prime attention. The relationships of the past are reviewed, the tense relationships of the current conflict are investigated, and a settlement is sought that would improve future relationships. Not only direct and obvious relationships are taken into account, but also the more indirect relationships that may have a cross-stitching potential. If, for instance, each of two divergent groups happens to have members with a strong interest in music, this commonality may be utilised as a converging factor.

A noteworthy leadership policy of reaching out to the group or individual farthest from the leader concerned, is well described and discussed by Deng. The idea behind this approach is that the interests of the culturally or ethnically distant, even of strangers, should be duly considered. Their interests should be safeguarded as far as possible, without contravening justice of course. When such a method is followed from a position of strength and magnanimity, it cannot be interpreted as weakness or meekness.

Such reaching out is a striking example of an essential part of the orientation towards human relations: a special sense for interests and attitudes. These inner elements of our human existence are not always readily discernible by others. Usually a keen sensitivity and a genuine interest are needed to fathom and identify them. In a conflict situation, as in any situation, they are of vital importance, however. Like values and beliefs, interests and attitudes function at deep levels, either to draw different people closer together or to drive them further apart. As mentioned above, similar interests can help to merge groups or individuals. But conflicting interests can exaggerate already existing divisions.

Attitudes too, can be of an integrative or a segregative nature. In a typical African community, where social solidarity is highly valued, all signs of tolerance and co-operativeness will be observed and nurtured. When settlement-directed talks take place in such a community, the attitude of reconciliation will be promoted as far as possible.

We have to be honest, however, about divisive attitudes which are also found in socially-minded Africa. There are traditions which are centred on a preoccupation with honour. In such a context attitudes of competitiveness and retaliation are obviously taken for granted. Attitudes are not easily changed, however. Neither are traditions. Both are deeply embedded in the social and individual life of the people concerned. Still, it can make an important difference if such attitudes, as well as the traditions on which they may be based, are duly recognised as part of the social context of a particular conflict.

Another attitude that can help cause and intensify a conflict situation is fear. Here too, we have to admit frankly that, in spite of all the social cohesiveness found in Africa, the people of Africa are not exempt from fear. In some cases people seem to be living in fear of being rejected. The prospect of being excluded from association and co-operation in the social group you belong to, is indeed intimidating. But it can become even more frightening when it is coupled with a threat of sorcery or divine punishment.

When all these ethical, relational and attitudinal elements of a social setting are taken into consideration, it can provide a meaningful, comprehensive perspective of a conflict. But such a sensitivity for social phenomena may and its stages also be a valuable asset at all stages in the process of resolving a conflict.

From the very beginning of trying to approach and identify the root cause of a conflict, the involvement of the social context can make a crucial difference. A professional conflict resolver from abroad, using a well designed method of conflict analysis, may begin the exploration by retracing the steps of the parties to the point of initial tension. But an experienced elder from Africa, thinking along the life-related lines of social reality, may begin from a vantage point further back and try to form a frame of social reference. From this perspective questions like the following may be put to the individuals concerned (or the key members of the parties): Who are you, and where are you from? How do you form part of your (close and extended) family? In which environment did you grow up? What do you like doing? What are you living for?

Approaching a conflict from such a background may provide important clues, not only about immediate causes, but also with regard to long-standing grievances. Such a probing into the social context may lead to a wider and deeper insight into differences and similarities between the parties. Parties often have fairly similar needs, but rather different interests. Parties may be adherents of similar or different ideologies, and of similar or different beliefs. There may be important age and power differences, which have to be taken into account.

In all these ways insights derived from the social context may greatly increase the understanding of the origin of a conflict. A further advantage is that this understanding can develop as a shared understanding. If the exploring of the social context takes place in a genuinely social way, which is properly transparent and participatory, it helps all who are involved in the discussion to experience a growing awareness of remote and immediate causes.

It is not only the beginnings of a conflict that are illumined by the social context. The social context can also play its role to improve the end of the conflict resolution process. It can make an important difference if the purpose of the process is formulated in social, relational language. Both short-term objectives and long-term aims may benefit from Africa's concern with relationships.

A typical immediate goal is to reach an agreement which includes more than merely solving the problem or rectifying the injustice. What is specifically aimed at in the search for durable peace, is genuine reconciliation and, where necessary, restitution and rehabilitation.

Relationships that have been broken or damaged should be repaired. Wrongs should be rectified, and justice restored. After their conflict the parties should be fully integrated into their community or communities again. If they have been in competition with each other, they should adopt the mood of co-operation again. In societies where reciprocal obligations are expected to be honoured, such responsibilities should be resumed. Usually reciprocal goodwill is also hoped for, in spite of the general knowledge that it can never be instilled into a stubborn party.

Aims for the longer term are usually centred on an *ubuntu* nurturing harmony in the community. Such an aim may be regarded as superfluous in societies who take the social context seriously. The realities of 'human-natured' behaviour, also in Africa, deprive us of this illusion, however. Experience teaches us the lesson that even in socially oriented communities tolerance is not maintained automatically. It should purposefully be aimed at and worked for. Conditions that are favourable for sustaining and promoting a forbearing co-existence should be promoted. In this regard four extremely relevant objectives were highlighted in the Kampala Document: Security, stability, development and co-operation. To these socio-political and socio-economic key words a few others, having a more specific social thrust, may be added: mutual understanding, mutual respect, and constructive interaction.

When a conflict resolution process is directed toward short- and long-term goals which really extend into the field of human relations, at least a double advantage can result. Not only will the eventual stages of implementation and follow-up be more far and wide-reaching. The whole procedure of resolving the conflict will also be regarded to be what it actually is: an event in the continuum of social life.

This broad, socially minded perspective on the complex realities of life has important implications for any actual process of conflict resolution. It prevents us from having convenient illusions about straightforward methods of resolving conflict. Africa does not provide us with any simple recipe, nor with a recipe book. What does happen, however, is that Africa's orientation towards the social context makes us aware of a whole variety of approaches which are indeed found in societies of people with their respective histories, traditions and inclinations. Here too we may think in terms of a continuum of methods, ranging from violent fighting to gentle talking.

After all, on a continent which always had a large and growing number of nations or groups, and which currently accommodates more than 500 million people speaking over 800 languages and co-existing in 53 countries, one could expect quite a diversity of methods.

We have to be honest, therefore, about the fact that not all these methods have been versions of talking. The history of Africa does include examples of regulated fighting. As elsewhere in the world, fighting as an organised method is a rare exception, however.

We also have to admit that some ways of talking found in Africa differ from the way we usually have in mind nowadays when we refer to 'talks'. Past and present practices of conflict resolution in Africa include examples of adjudication and arbitration. In cases of adjudication the social context may not figure prominently. Some form of court proceedings is usually followed, in which an appointed 'judge', or perhaps a judicial panel, hears a case and decides about right and wrong, vindication and punishment. When arbitration is used, however, the social environment often plays an important role. After all, an arbitrator has to maintain the support of the community concerned, and therefore has to be more sensitive to the assessment of his or her decisions by others.

Examples are also found of adjudication and/or arbitration as one option, linked to a second option of informal talking. Here the classic example seems to be the two methods of the Kpelle in West Africa: institutionalised courts making and enforcing arbitral verdicts, and *ad hoc* local meetings ('moots' or 'house palavers') arriving at mediated settlements. In another classic example from Africa (the Ndendeuli of Tanzania) these two methods have been combined into one: Mediators play an active role by suggesting an agreement and even pressurising the parties to accept it.

Africa's emphasis on attitudes validates the use of two other ways of pressurising by talking and singing: shaming and ridiculing. Such special methods can obviously only be used in contexts where they are acceptable, and in cases where the cause of a dispute is self-evident. Either in a ritualised way or through ordinary conversation the persons guilty of anti-social and conflict-causing conduct are put to shame. Or individuals gifted with the knack of poking fun at others play their jocular role in an effort to change the behaviour of the trouble makers.

Apart from such more coercive modes of talking, however, the method of talking generally used in Africa is the one of negotiation in the neighbourhood. It is a method which can be most effective, and therefore duly deserves the attention of the whole world.

Much of its success may be ascribed to its elemental simplicity, participatory involvement, adaptable flexibility and complete relevancy. Its common-sensical beginning is usually that individuals within their social context start discussing an emerging dispute. According to the circumstances the context can be a condensed family or an extended family, immediate neighbours or a larger neighbourhood, or a combination of family and neighbourhood. It can also be a smaller or larger organisation, like a school or a religious grouping. Since all the people involved happen to be human-natured individuals, they will always have to contend with the temptation to degrade the discussion to ill-disposed gossip. If the social context is indeed taken seriously, however, this danger may be diminished. Instead of steering the discussion towards spite, or the apportioning of blame, it may be directed at a solution.

From its very beginning this process may be kept moving in a direction which differs from both adjudication and arbitration. Judges and umpires make decisions based on rules. They investigate past events, and their whole orientation is towards the past. But concerned family members and neighbours could envisage outcomes based on interests. They could maintain an orientation towards the future, looking forward to improved relations — not only between the disputants but also in the whole community who happens to be involved. And in most cases they will grant the disputing parties scope to make their own decisions. This forms a marked contrast with the judgemental procedure of imposing decisions on the parties.

Such interest related and forward looking discussions can move quite naturally into the mode of negotiating. But, just as the initial discussions, negotiation itself can begin and continue in a rather informal way. Effective negotiating talks are not dependent upon professionally designed methods and step-by-step manuals of instruction. However useful these may be, they may entice us to forget the unpredictable complexity of actual negotiations. Informal, receptive and flexible ways of negotiating should therefore never be frowned upon. Even those who have a great deal of experience (and even book knowledge) of negotiation may do well to keep an open mind when involved in a negotiating event in real life. It does happen that experts, struggling to make something out of an untidy but perhaps fragile process, are surprised by the contributions of members of a family or a neighbourhood.

It can also happen, however, that all the informal discussions and negotiations do not lead to a satisfactory solution of the underlying problem. Then real mediating expertise may be enlisted more formally. But this formality is not one derived from professional accreditation. It is a formality that takes shape within the immediate social context. Its first implication is that mediators are sought within the family or families concerned and/or within the neighbourhood concerned. The second implication is that people are looked for who enjoy social recognition for their experience and integrity. (If these qualities are present in a mediator, the issue of uninvolvedness is usually not regarded as important. A mediator from a particular family or neighbourhood will inevitably be associated with one of the disputing parties.) A third, obvious implication is that more than one mediator must be found. Usually a smaller or larger group is used, which may consist of people selected to help resolve a particular conflict, or of an already existing assembly or council of mediators.

All over Africa elders are respected as trustworthy mediators. Elderly people obviously have more decades of accumulated experience, and usually also a greater treasure of practical wisdom. Traditionally preference was given to men, but nowadays gender equity is becoming more widely accepted.

Depending on traditions, circumstances and personalities, mediators are found in various roles. Apart from the pressurising or manipulating role already referred to, there are various leading roles in which mediators are allowed to make recommendations (like reciprocal offers or package deals), give assessments (of information or of proposals), or convey a suggestion on behalf of a party (who for face-saving reasons refrains from suggesting it themselves). Mediators may fulfil a facilitating role, by clarifying information, promoting clear communication, interpreting standpoints, summarising discussions, emphasising relevant norms or rules, envisaging the situation if an agreement is not reached, or repeating points of agreement already attained. Mediators may even limit themselves to a passive role, as when they are simply there to represent important shared values. Moreover, since the process of mediation does not have to follow a predetermined model, mediators are entitled to change their roles from time to time according to the needs they sense at various times.

This does not mean that mediators may allow their personal preferences to determine their behaviour. It does mean, however, that the social context may at certain times imply shifts in approach or emphasis.

Although the entire process, from discussion through negotiation to mediation, is unprescribed, flexible and dynamic, and although it defies analysis, we may tentatively think in terms of constituent parts. This may give us a stimulating overview of the way in which each contributing part of the conflict resolution talks is related to and influenced by the social context.

When the background and causes of a conflict are explored, the social situation of each individual or party is considered. This may of course be done in an apathetic way or in a prejudiced way, but often it is indeed done quite sympathetically and honestly. The idea is to form an impression of the interests and needs, aspirations and motivations of each party.

In all fairness to conflict resolution methods from abroad, we have to add that the probing of interests and needs is duly emphasised in most methods. There is, however, a subtle difference which may be spotted. According to the perspective of many imported models it is seen as an effort that has to be undertaken. It is usually listed as an important item of the information gathering stage. When social perspectives are taken seriously, however, there may be an already existent sensitivity to interests and needs. From the beginning of the conflict resolution process there may be an automatically present inclination to understand more about the inner motives of the parties.

As the talking proceeds, an openness to feedback or influence from the social surroundings is maintained. This may lead to a modification of perceptions or positions. It is not only the mediators that can be receptive to new input, but also the parties themselves. It is not only the constituencies of the parties whose reactions are acknowledged; the entire social group is regarded as a major constituency whose response is to be respected. After all, the solution that is worked out during the talks will have to be implemented in families or neighbourhoods that form part of the social network in the community.

Another important contribution which the community can make while the talks are in progress, is that of empowerment. It may become clear that a particular party feels insecure and acts unassertively in spite of the fact that they have a just case. At the talks the mediators may play their part to help such a party realise which power they and their just case are indeed wielding. If the mediators' efforts are then also endorsed by the community, it can strongly enhance the party's sense of empowerment and confidence, and increase the self-assertiveness of their behaviour.

As the point of actual decision making is approached, even more attention could be given to considerations of social importance. Ongoing social relations and internal solidarity are crucial elements. Reasonable reciprocity is an option that can be strongly propagated from the social perspective. This too, is a possibility that is well known in models of negotiation and mediation used outside Africa. But there it is usually called by a name taken from the language of bargaining: trade-offs. The way of thinking seems to be more or less as follows: We (the one party) want you (the other party) to lower your demand, and so we offer you something which will hopefully induce you to do what we want. Africa's social approach may change the way of thinking to the following: Having looked at both sides, your community is suggesting that you (the one party) make this concession, and that it would then be fair to expect you (the other party) to respond by a reciprocating concession from your side. Here the overtones are not those of pressurising for own gain, but rather those of fair exchange for public recognition.

As a consequence of the social approach, the method generally preferred is to work towards consensus. This may develop into an extended search, for which much patience is needed. But when the goal has been reached, the reward is real satisfaction. Every new consensual outcome confirms the validity and value of the time-proven tradition of consensus seeking. It gives all who participated the feeling that they have been involved in a thorough and worthwhile process. And it creates confidence that such a jointly developed decision will prove to be effective and long lasting.

When an agreement has eventually been reached, the good news should be shared with the groups and communities concerned. Each particular society may have its appropriate ritual way of affirming such an agreement as a social contract. It could vary from a handshake in public to an elabourate ceremony as required by tradition. This event obviously serves a dual purpose. It spreads the news about the satisfactory conclusion of the conflict resolution process. And it places an additional obligation on the parties to observe the agreement, which has now become public knowledge.

The society can therefore play a very important role when the agreement is implemented. From the beginning of this final stage, members of the families and the neighbourhood can check whether the parties are really doing everything to which they have committed themselves. If a party needs some face-saving, or empowerment, or encouragement, sympathetic members of the community can render their valuable assistance.

The advantages of all this social involvement throughout the conflict resolution process should be obvious. It can lead to a more profound and shared understanding of the conflict as it has arisen in a particular relational and socio-cultural context. It can encourage the acceptance of aims which deliberately include the relational life after the resolving of the conflict. It can make the conflict resolving talks participatory in a fuller sense of the word than just the inclusion of the parties and the mediators. It can promote a sense of belonging, which, in turn, may contribute to the restoring, maintenance and building of relationships.

...

Tuso describes the Gada *system of conflict resolution within the Oromo society in Ethiopia. This system is celebrated as democratic and effective in ensuring sustainable peace among the community.*

TUSO, H 'INDIGENOUS PROCESSES OF CONFLICT RESOLUTION IN OROMO SOCIETY' (2000)

in Zartman IW (ed) *Traditional cures for modern conflicts: African conflict 'medicine'*

Boulder, Colorado: Lynne Rienner Publishers

...

The *Gada* system

The *Gada* system may be the most studied indigenous African institution. The first writer on the *Gada* system on record is a sixteenth-century Abyssinian ecclesiastic by the name of Bahrey. Other travellers, diplomats, and social scientists studied the *Gada* system during the nineteenth and twentieth centuries, many of them considering it uniquely democratic. For example, W Plowden, who travelled in the region in the nineteenth century, stated that among republican systems, *Gada* is superior. Atsime Giorgis, another Abyssinian writer at the end of the nineteenth century, wrote that the *Gada* system unites and mobilises all members of Oromo society into a formidable and invincible force. Paul Baxter, a contemporary British anthropologist, wrote, 'They [Oromos] have especially captured the imagination of travellers and ethnographers because of their ancient, enduring and complex system of age-grading, *Gada*, which, it has been consistently reported, has also served as the basis of a uniquely democratic political system'. Asmarom Legesse, an Eritrean anthropologist who is considered to have written the most definitive interpretation of the *Gada* system, observed:

> The *Gada* system is an institution that appears so exaggerated that it is readily dismissed by laymen and scholars alike as a sociological anomaly. Anomalous though it may lie, it is one of the most astonishing and instructive turns the evolution of human society has taken ... *Gada* seems to be one of the universals that binds the entire nation into a coherent system and gives people a common political basis for understanding each other. It constitutes a shared political idiom.

This, then, is the philosophical vantage point from which we view the character of Oromo democracy. What is astonishing about this cultural tradition is how far the Oromos have gone to ensure that power does not fall into the hands of war chiefs and despots. They achieve this goal by creating a system of checks and balances that is at least as complex as the systems we find in the Western societies.

In the *Gada* system, men are organised along two sets of five categories. The first set is a chronologically based age-grade designation. In this set each male goes through five grades of eight years each where he performs a set of duties and responsibilities prior to moving to the next period. Ideally, a male enters into this generation-grade system on the day he is born and stays in the system through his life, completing the cycle when his active duties are completed at age forty-eight. After that, he retires from active duties but remains an elder statesman who counsels and makes peace within the society. However, Oromo society being a polygamous society, children are born at different parental age periods, which creates major gaps in the age-grade system. The two major purposes in this differentiation in the generation-grade system are to provide the necessary human power for the society all the time and also to prevent sons and fathers from entering into the ruling period at the same time. Each eight year period in the cycle has a name for the generation grade: (1) *Iti Mako* (8-16 years); (2) *Daballe* (16-24 years); (3) *Folle* (24-32 years); (4) *Qondala* (32-40 years); (5) *Luba* (40-48 years).

The second critical component in the *Gada* institution is the *luba* system. The equivalent concept for *luba* in the English language is 'party'. Men are organised into five *luba* (party) sets. The *luba* system is known by other names, such as *misenssa* and *gogsa,* among Oromos. Scholars have used the term 'classes' or 'age-sets'. Thus, each male is born into a party and each party goes through the five periods (generation set system) as described above...Thus *Gada*, as a system, is conceived as a unity of interacting parts. The system organises the social order by dividing all men into groups and providing a blueprint that specifies an arrangement of strategies (grades); the relationships among different grades; rights, rules of behaviour, and the tasks to be performed in each grade; and the process by which groups (parties) move from grade to grade.

The result is a hierarchical system of authority or legitimate power. Authority is transferred to a new generation grade every eight years; authority is held in balance, and corruption and nepotism are prevented through the institution of succession; the party in power for eight years assumes responsibility in military, economics, politics, rituals, and peace and reconciliation; the leadership of the ruling party is chosen through open and fair elections; the system has pluralistic characteristics; the system prohibits the political leadership from amassing wealth while in office; and there is a mechanism to recall officers in case of incompetence or corruption. The nature of the system forces every party to enter new generation grades every eight years when the party acting as *luba* (the ruling party) retires at the end of the forty-year cycle. Thus, for example, sons and fathers cannot be in the same or even successive ruling generation grade.

The *Gada* system of conflict management moves through thirteen identifiable steps on its way to managing and resolving conflict and arriving at *arara* (reconciliation) so that harmonious relations can be restored among conflicting parties, God the Creator, the community, and the surrounding world. These steps are in regard to the most dramatic and emotional of any kind of social conflict, violence leading to loss of life.

As soon as the community learns that there has been violence that has caused the death of an Oromo, male or female, it is shaken by the news and becomes mobilised. The kin (up to the clan level) both of the person who committed the crime and of the dead person want to avoid the escalation of the conflict into a cycle of violence. Whether accidental or intentional, the death of an Oromo is treated by both kin groups with the same level of anxiety and vigilance. Of course, if it is learned early on that the death was accidental tensions are lessened since Oromos are usually willing to look at such accidents as the will of Waaqa and are much more disposed to give the reconciliation process the matter of due course. If, however, the killing is shown to be an intentional act, then the pressure to mobilise the resources for the purpose of revenge would be enormous and, indeed could escalate so much that the conflict could get out of hand.

Thus, the community members, being cognisant of this enormous danger, move with great speed, essentially to achieve three critical goals at this stage: to mobilise the community leadership for immediate intervention; to warn the killer's kin that they should conform to the Oromo traditional law of collective responsibility in the case of death caused by a kinsman, considering every kinsman of the killer to be a party to the killing and therefore liable for revenge by the kin of the victim; and finally to avoid spilling more blood. The Oromo believe that spilling Oromo blood would poison the total environment, risking health to all the communities concerned; in Oromo mythology for example, if a person touches or steps upon spilled blood, even when he or she has no part in the incident, he or she in due course, would develop leprosy or a similar disease.

Thus it becomes important to recruit *jarsa biya* (elders) of the killer's kin groups to assure the kin of the dead person that they are working on the case in compliance with the law *(sera)* and custom *(adda)*, that they will soon begin criminal procedures *(gumma)*, and that they are eager to work earnestly on reconciliation *(arara)*.

In step two of the process, the appropriate *jarsa biya* are selected. The qualification of *jarsa biya* are many, and steps required for the selection of the elders to serve at this level of societal responsibility are rigorous. At the philosophical level, they must have a commitment to the Oromo societal ideology, which encompasses the five major themes of effort, truth, justice, punishment, and reconciliation. The key qualifications for eldership in such matters include: thorough knowledge of both law and custom; intellectual ability to grasp issues and interpret them according to the *sera* and *adda*; skills in managing group dynamics including communication; absolute integrity of character; commitment to the Oromo ideology relative to the cause of truth, justice, and reconciliation; and earned trust from one's peers and the community.

The process of selecting the *jarsa biya* may be initiated at different levels. Usually members of the family of the person who committed the crime approach the elders of their community and ask for assistance. In cases where family leadership does not exist, the elders of the clan or subclan may come forward with the initiatives in selecting the *jarsa biya*. Usually two elders are selected from each side and one person from each representing the *Gada* institution. The persons representing the *Gada* institution physically sit between the elders representing the parties at conflict. The *jarsa biya* meet to develop a common understanding of the crisis at hand and the strategy to take. They use a legal inquiry procedure known as *qorra*, in which they are allowed to ask any question with respect to the law and custom relating to the case at hand, sifting information and establishing basic facts. Once consensus is reached as to the nature of the problem, they send a message to the other party that the kin of the defendant wish to settle the matter in accordance with the *sera* and *adda* and respectfully request to meet with the *jarsa biya* from the other side as soon as possible.

In a case where no one has admitted to the act, if the family of the dead person knows the killer or suspects someone, a member will approach the kin and clan to begin the process of charging the suspected person. In such cases, the process of identifying the *jarsa biya* and developing strategy could be laborious and time-consuming, but once agreements have been reached on the selection of the elders, the next steps are the same.

In step three, the selected elders and the representatives of the *Gada* institution meet by themselves for the first time to exchange ideas and work out procedures and to select *haiyu* (judge) from among themselves. For a person to be selected *haiyu*, one needs to have qualities as a member of the *jarsa biya*, plus a superior ability to use proverbs and metaphors, leadership ability to steer the discussion and keep tempers cool, and a record of success in making peace in the community. Once the *jarsa biya* and the *Gada* representatives meet, they usually go to the clan *(gossa)* of the dead person to ask that the matter be given to the *jarsa biya* and the *Gada* representatives and to give permission for the use of three critical places by the family and clan of the person who committed the crime: residence (that means they do not have to flee from their homes), river, and the market. In the meantime they assist the family in burying the dead and stay with the family during the entire period of mourning, ranging from one to four weeks. These activities and gestures are designed to ensure de-escalation of the conflict by both demonstrating sympathy and exercising surveillance, so that no one would take the matter in one's own hands and seek revenge.

In step four, the *jarsa biya* deliberate on the nature of the conflict, the law that was broken and the customs that have been violated, and the laws and customs that could be applied in resolving the case. Essentially, they begin to move from the stage of diagnosis to that of finding a formula for resolution.

In step five, the elders meet separately with conflicting parties. This is a very critical strategy for the purpose of controlling the tempers of the parties and the process, consistent with the Oromo philosophy of forestalling escalation and maintaining civility. They listen carefully to the concerned parties and make inquiries. If need be, they may break to caucus *(maqqo)* and discuss it privately.

After meeting with the parties, step six is to meet with the witnesses. The presiding elders instruct the witnesses to tell the whole truth and examine the responses point by point as they interrogate the witnesses.

In step seven, the elders then recess again to debate among themselves on the issues that remain unresolved. If there is still uncertainty or if they feel that the defendant is not telling the truth, the elders (with the plaintiff, in accordance with Oromo tradition) will require the entire family, subclan, and clan of the defendant to swear in accordance with the Oromo law and customs that every person in the community has been socialised through family, civic, and religious teachings to tell the truth and do justice, to keep harmony in the society and the environment; they are placed before their social responsibility, failure in which would lead to the loss of blessings from Waaqa. If the family and clan believe that their member has been accused unfairly or he or she is telling the whole truth, they defend him or her. After all, to defend a family and clan member against any unfair treatment and false accusations is part of their moral and social obligation.

Everyone looks forward to the verdict *(murtte)* — step eight — that will produce *arara* between the parties and restoration of peace and harmony among the spirits of the people, the deity, and the ecosystem. To the elders who have accepted the responsibility of peacemaking and to the presiding *haiyu* this is a very critical moment too, for their task is not only to declare their findings but to do so in such a manner as to bring the expected peace and reconciliation. The presiding *haiyu* will cite an Oromo prayer to Waaqa that their efforts will bear fruit and ask that the spirit move the parties to accept the *murtte* and move forward in peace and reconciliation. He then provides a brief summary as to the reasons why they had come together, the work the elders have done and their readiness to declare a *murtte* and facilitate peacemaking and reconciliation between the parties at conflict. Then the elders will begin *qorra* (legal inquiry) into the issues, the laws and customs, investigations, and the process of reaching the *murtte* (verdict).

Once the process of *qorra* is completed, the *haiyu* will begin carefully declaring the *murtte* followed by the appropriate course of action in response to the findings. If, for example, murder was involved, there will be a determination of the blood payment price *(gumma)*. Usually in such a case, the family members of the dead person, with assistance of the kin and clan wise men, will put forward the demands for the *gumma*. However, the guilty party may petition for lenience, and the elders usually support moderation in such matters and may lean toward recommending more symbolic gestures in paying the *gumma* rather than profit making. All of these things are sorted out ahead of time (perhaps in step seven).

In step nine, the *haiyu* representing the elders will proceed and implore the guilty party to accept *balessa* (wrongdoing). In this process, they repeat their findings and remind the party to consider the *sera* and *adda*. The guilty party usually accepts such *murtte* rather readily, as his relatives and wise people from his community will urge him to do.

Once the guilty party accepts his wrongdoing, the elders will turn their attention to the grieved party, in step ten, and implore him to accept the *dhuga* (truth), to forgive, and to be reconciled. Since the aggrieved party has been represented in the composition of the *jarsa biya* by the elders he and his party selected, and since it is in everyone's vital interest to complete *ibis* process and move toward reconciliation, he too usually readily accepts the essence of the *murtte*, including the acceptance of the *dhuga* decided by the elders.

Step eleven is the administration of penalty. In the Oromo traditional system, human life is considered precious, and the penalties *(guma)* for committing a crime against another Oromo are designed to reinforce this social value. They are intended to serve as a deterrent. This is shown by the amount of cattle one is required to pay and the quality of the animals designated as fitting for such purpose. Symbolically, the amount is usually referred to as *kuma toko* (one thousand) cattle; however, in reality, it may be about a hundred. Only cows and horses are acceptable, not other animals such as donkeys, mules, or goals. Cows and horses are the most loved and respected in Oromo society, and one hundred is a sizable number for an average person in that economy. In step eleven, the task is to announce the penalty to the parties in public, and agree on the nature, amount, and time of its payment.

The twelfth step in the long and arduous process of conflict resolution in the Oromo cultural system is a legal as well as a religious service for the conflicting parties and for the entire community. It is aimed at reconciliation between the parties and between the community and the divine, the earth and the entire psychological and spiritual ecology. It is aimed at cleansing the anger and ill feelings from everyone concerned. At the spiritual level, Oromos believe that receiving continued blessings from Waaqa is dependent upon their forgiving, forgetting, and totally reconciling, making sure that family and clan members will not inherit bitterness and animosity as the result of the conflict.

Thus the conflicting parties and members of their respective communities gather for the ceremony of *arara*. Some kind of drink is prepared for the occasion – *bulbulla* (honey mixed with water) or *dadhi* (soured *bulbulla)* or coffee. The participants share the drink as the elders conduct the ceremony. A variant of the blessing offered on such occasions, as captured by Rinnant, from his work among the Gugi Oromos, contains the central themes of blessings delivered at such ceremonies:

> *biyya arrara* (let the country be reconciled)
> *guda arrara* (let the big, senior, powerful be reconciled)
> *dikka arrara* (let the little, junior, weak be reconciled)
> *loni arrara* (let the cattle be reconciled)
> *nu arrara* (let us be reconciled)
> *nu nagaes* (let us be at peace)
> *nu itit* (let us be thick like yogurt)

The last step is bonding. The activities the conflicting parties undertake during the post-reconciliation ceremony are also very critical. For example, if the conflict has involved the loss of human life, family members usually will take further steps to overcome the memory of bitterness and animosity resulting from the conflict. Such actions may involve marriage arrangements or *gudifachaa* (child adoption) between the family members. Another type of activity involves providing lifelong services to a family member whose livelihood has been affected seriously as the consequence of the death of a person in the conflict. For example, if a mother has lost her son, depriving her of the natural help she would normally receive from him, the person and the family responsible for the death will provide lifelong assistance on the farm and other areas of her needs.

The processes discussed thus far are dominated by men. However, Oromos have developed a complex system relating to the role of women in conflict resolution. In the Oromo social system, women are the only group that are protected from physical attack by any party in any conflict. They are sacred humans. Thus, women play important roles as messengers of peace; they organise themselves and physically intervene between the conflicting parties in case of violence; they mobilise the community to respond to the situation of conflict quickly and appropriately; and they serve as a moral voice in times of social turmoil.

...

While traditional methods of conflict resolution are often hailed in literature, their capacity to secure peace could be limited in the modern context by a number of factors, including politicisation, the character of conflict and their localised applicability.

OSAGHAE, EE 'APPLYING TRADITIONAL METHODS TO MODERN CONFLICT: POSSIBILITIES AND LIMITS' (2000)

in Zartman IW (ed) *Traditional cures for modern conflicts: African conflict 'medicine'* Boulder, Colorado: Lynne Rienner Publishers

...

For proponents of contextual conflict management, who seem to have received a great boost from the failure of conventional peacekeeping operations in Somalia and Rwanda, there can be no question about the relevance of traditional practices and the need to incorporate them into mainstream conflict management strategies. An examination of the larger question of the relevance of traditional thought systems and institutions to modern times leads to the conclusion that notwithstanding the phenomenal transformations of African societies and the introduction of new state structures and (peripheral) capitalist formations, traditional thought and institutions provide a necessary backdrop for present political practices and can as such be selectively put to positive use. Making a similar point, the historian Afigbo argues that the relevance of the African past can be assured only when historians succeed in reconstructing a usable and problem-solving-oriented past rather than ferreting out facts and more facts about a glorious Africa of old. That he says is both the poverty and challenge of African historiography. In other words, as much of what is said to be traditional is invented, the 'traditional' can be constructed in such a way as to give prominence to the most expedient and positive aspects, while discarding, if possible, the negative aspects of the past.

It can be argued that traditional means of dealing with conflicts are mainly applicable to, and useful in, resolving simple disputes: matrimonial disputes, intra-family quarrels, land disputes, and the like, which are not as complex or threatening as the conflicts of national and even supranational proportions. This argument underestimates the volatility of so-called simple conflicts that can quickly degenerate to involve most groups in the community because of the organic character of traditional communities. One lesson to be learned from the social fabric approach to conflicts and their management that characterises traditional management in Africa is that simple and larger scale or complex conflicts are actually two sides of the same coin and mutually reinforcing. Consequently, resolution of day-to-day conflicts helps to ensure the stability needed for the prevention or resolution of more serious and expansive ones — in short, resolution of more serious conflicts is impossible without management of less serious conflicts at the lower levels.

A good example of this was the resolution of the crisis in the eastern regional branch of the National Council of Nigerian Citizens, one of the major political parties of colonial and immediate postcolonial Nigeria, that threatened the constitutional order in the country in 1952 and 1953, through recourse to the

Igbo *Igobandu* system, under which the party leaders swore on oath to be loyal to Nnamdi Azikiwe. Besides, experience gained from familiarity with resolving conflicts at lower levels is always found useful at higher levels of engagement, which probably explains the preference of the warlords in Liberia for reconciliatory bodies headed and composed mainly by chiefs and other traditional authorities. But usefulness is a function of ultimate goals-reconciliation versus dominance — which explains the severe attitudes of warlords to local conflict management mechanisms in southern Somalia, as reported by Menkhaus.

Attempts have indeed been made to apply traditional strategies of conflict management to modern conflicts of a more complex nature at national levels with varying degrees of success. Examples include the centrality of the Baganda kingdom to the resolution of political conflicts in Uganda, the statutory involvement of traditional rulers in conflict management bodies at the local, state, and federal levels in Nigeria, and the attempts by the post-apartheid government of South Africa to employ the good offices of the king of Zululand to resolve the violent conflicts in the KwaZulu/Natal Province. One of the most recent of these, which has become the standard reference point, is the role played by clan elders in reconciling warring factions in northern Somalia, as noted by Menkhaus. At several points in the Liberian civil war, traditional rulers were involved in the search for peace along the lines of the famous 'palaver hut' reconciliatory meetings. Although this had limited success, there is no doubt that the intervention of traditional leaders, with all the mythical powers they are assumed to have, made negotiations among the warlords possible.

On the other hand, there seem to be serious and even insurmountable obstacles to the application of traditional strategies to modern conflicts. These limits derive for the most part from the characteristics of conflict management in traditional societies as discussed in the previous section. The first of these is that management strategies were localised and particularistic, and that in spite of the similarities and common assumptions they involved, few, if any, strategies were generalised beyond local boundaries.

The absence of a generalised model of conflict management may indeed be regarded as one of the weaknesses of traditional systems, but this does not prevent us from elabourating on and extending successful models if some of the difficulties discussed below can be overcome. In the alternative, a wholly new and eclectic model, built from composite elements of various relevant models, can be constructed, as is suggested in the concluding section of this paper.

In the postcolonial period, traditional conflict management strategies remain localised, although the exigencies of colonial rule necessitated the generalisation of practices among enlarged ethnic groups. This was how, for example, the Ogboni society, which was originally Oyo, became a Yoruba institution, extending to the Egba, Ekiti, Ibadan, and so on. In effect, the strategies remain located in ethnic groups and this, in the circumstances of intense ethnic rivalry in African states, makes the adoption of one strategy more likely to be seen as a continuation of ethnic hegemony (especially where the strategy adopted comes from the ethnic group of the incumbent head of state). Forster points to the experience of Malawi where President Banda's so-called cultural nationalism was seen by many as an attempt to perpetuate the domination of his Chewa group. In circumstances like this, the adoption of supposedly traditional strategies of conflict management is more likely to worsen and exacerbate, rather than ameliorate, political conflicts.

The relevance and applicability of traditional strategies have been greatly disenabled by the politicisation, corruption, and abuse of traditional structures, especially traditional rulership, which have steadily delegitimised conflict management built around them in the eyes of many, and reduced confidence in their efficacy. Kofele-Kale's finding from his Cameroonian study that most people in urban and rural areas prefer modern judicial approaches – courts, police, and gendarmerie – to customary-traditional approaches in resolving disputes is reflective of this growing tendency. The co-optation of traditional rulers as agents of the state, and their manipulation to serve partisan ends, which dates back to colonial times, not to mention the corruption of modern traditional rulers, have considerably reduced the reverence and respect commanded by this institution and, therefore, the ability of traditional rulers to resolve conflicts.

To take an interesting example, attempts by the African National Congress (ANC) – led government of national unity in South Africa to employ the good offices of the king of Zululand in resolving the violent wars in the KwaZulu Province of the country had very limited success because of fears by the Zulu-based opposition Inkatha Freedom Party (IFP) that the king supported the ANC and was being used by the party. A similar situation exists in Nigeria, where successive governments, but especially military governments that lack grass-roots support, have struggled to keep traditional rulers (labelled as 'fathers of the nation') on their payrolls as mobilisers of support. This has obliterated the perceived neutrality of these rulers, which was a crucial requirement in their traditional conflict resolving roles, in the eyes of opposition groups. Even in cases of land dispute where, being the traditional custodians of land, traditional authorities are the key arbitrators, their neutrality has been compromised by their miscarriage of justice in favour of those offering the highest pay-offs or bribes.

The limit placed by localisation is reinforced by the fact that modern states in Africa, with the diverse groups that compose them, do not have the common moral and customary order on which conflict management is hinged in the traditional society (a similar point is made by Gluckman in his consideration of the possibility of applying Nuer feuding strategy to resolving international conflicts). The experience of Somalia, whose uniethnic situation was for a long time regarded as a recipe for unity, peace, and stability, has demonstrated the whole point about localisation and absence of a moral order: National consensus was difficult precisely because of the interclan differences reinforced, as they were, by religious cleavages. It was even more difficult to find common grounds for reconciling the warlords from diverse groups who were the major actors in the conflicts in Liberia, Sudan, Somalia, Sierra Leone, and so on – the Charles Taylors and Alhaji Kromahs, John Garangs, Farah Aideeds, and Foday Sankohs. This in turn points to another area where traditional conflict management systems had shortcomings, since contests for power were often only resolved through splitting the polity and vanquishing the rivals.

Finally, the expansive nature of modern conflicts also limits the extent to which traditional strategies can be applied. Although most present-day conflicts, like those in traditional society, centre on struggles for power and succession disputes among powerful individuals and groups, the wide range of actors and forces, including external ones, as well as the national and sometimes regional score of the conflicts, render expedient traditional strategies inadequate. This partly explains why the traditional strategies applied in northern Somalia have had only limited success. The same can be said for Liberia, Sierra Leone, Burundi, Rwanda, Uganda, and Angola, where the involvement of peacekeeping forces and other foreign interests has removed the primary responsibility for resolution from the domestic arena.
...

REGIONAL CONFLICT RESOLUTION

Kindiki assesses the capacity of the African Union to protect human rights and maintain international peace and security. He also highlights contradictions that may arise out of the interpretation of this normative framework and the mandate of the UN, and the potential of strong countries within the continent for manipulating the interpretation of normative standards, among others.

KINDIKI, K 'THE NORMATIVE AND INSTITUTIONAL FRAMEWORK OF THE AFRICAN UNION RELATING TO THE PROTECTION OF HUMAN RIGHTS AND THE MAINTENANCE OF INTERNATIONAL PEACE AND SECURITY: A CRITICAL APPRAISAL' (2003)

3 *African Human Rights Law Journal* 97

...
By the middle of the 1990s, threats to peace, security and the preservation of human rights posed by armed conflicts in Africa became a source of concern for African leaders and the broader international community. This concern was reflected by the myriad conferences and summits held by the OAU to discuss the issue of conflicts and the array of treaties, protocols, declarations, and communiqués that emanated from these meetings. It was soon realised that amidst armed conflicts, it would be difficult to achieve the objectives of the 1991 Treaty Establishing the African Economic Community (the Abuja Treaty), which was intended to set the stage for greater economic co-operation amongst African states.

In order to address the challenges posed by armed conflicts, the OAU Mechanism for Conflict Prevention, Management and Resolution was established in 1993. Despite any normative and institutional developments that the regime of the Mechanism may have brought, it has been criticised for the apparent failure to halt the genocide in Rwanda, stop the civil war in Liberia, mitigate the crisis in Burundi or put an end to the conflict in the Democratic Republic of Congo (DRC). The end of the millennium presented an opportunity for re-positioning the OAU in order to set the African continent as a whole on a firm path to development, peace and the respect for human rights. On 8 and 9 September 1999, 44 Heads of State and Government of the OAU met in Sirte, Libya, in an extraordinary session of the OAU Assembly requested by Libyan leader Muammar Gaddafi, to discuss the formation of a 'United States of Africa'. The theme of this summit, 'strengthening OAU capacity to enable it to meet the challenges of the new millennium', was intended to provoke the leaders to seek solutions for the myriad political, economic and social problems confronting the continent.

At this meeting the leaders adopted the 'Sirte Declaration', which called for the establishment of an African Union, the shortening of the implementation periods of the Abuja Treaty, and the speedy establishment of all institutions provided for in the Abuja Treaty, such as the African Central Bank, the African Monetary Union, the African Court of justice and the Pan-African Parliament.

The details regarding the designing of this Union was to be left to the legal experts who were instructed to model it on the European Union, taking into account the Charter of the OAU and the Abuja Treaty. The Declaration further stated that the decision to establish the AU had been reached after 'frank and extensive discussions'. The OAU legal unit then drafted the Constitutive Act of the African Union (the AU Act). The OAU Assembly of Heads of State and Government in Lomé, Togo, on 11 Jury 2000, adopted the Act. All members of the OAU had signed the Act by March 2001, and therefore the OAU Assembly at its 5th extraordinary summit held in Sirte, Libya from 1 to 2 March 2001, declared the establishment of the AU.

The Constitutive Act had to be ratified by two-thirds of the member states of the OAU. After this had been achieved, the AU became legal and political reality a month thereafter (on 26 May 2001), when the Constitutive Act entered into force. The Union was eventually launched in Durban, South Africa, on 10 July 2002.

The AU Act clearly departs from the regime of the OAU Charter in the area of human rights. The importance of human rights was sparingly recognised under the OAU Charter, which only made reference to the United Nations (UN) Charter and to the Universal Declaration of Human Rights (Universal Declaration), but further established through the adoption of the African Charter on Human and Peoples' Rights (African Charter or Charter) in 1981. The OAU 4th extraordinary summit held in Sirte did not specifically address the issue of human rights.

However, the protection of human rights was captured in the Summit's general determination to 'eliminate the scourge of conflicts' in Africa and to 'effectively address the new social, political and economic realities in Africa and the world'. The Summit also pledged 'to play a more active role and continue to be relevant to the needs of our peoples and responsive to the demands of the prevailing circumstances'. The above provisions of the Sirte Declaration was a reaffirmation of the OAU Ministers' Grand Bay Declaration of 16 April 1999, which acknowledged that:

> [O]bservance of human rights is a key tool for promoting collective security, durable peace and sustainable development as enunciated in the Cairo Agenda for Action on relaunching Africa's socio-economic transformation.

The AU Act confirms a growing attachment to the importance of human rights in Africa by providing that it shall be the objective of the AU to 'encourage international co-operation, taking due account of the [UN Charter] and the Universal Declaration of Human Rights'. The Act provides that the AU shall strive to 'promote and protect human and peoples' rights in accordance with the African Charter on Human and Peoples' Rights and other relevant human rights instruments'. The principles of the AU include the 'promotion of gender equality, respect for democratic principles, human rights, the rule of law and good governance' as well as 'respect for the sanctity of human life'.

...

The AU Act contains provisions that are of relevance to humanitarian intervention, consisting of, the use of force by states or states to pre-empt or halt gross human rights violations leading to massive loss of lives, without the consent of the target state. Since humanitarian intervention is a response to human rights atrocities that may amount to breaches of peace and security, this section discusses some of the AU Act provisions, which could be invoked to support, a right of humanitarian intervention under the auspices of the AU.

The Act states that the AU shall 'promote peace, security and stability on the continent'. Furthermore, it is provided that the AU shall function in accordance with the principles of the 'establishment of a common defence policy for the African Continent', the right of member states 'to live in peace and security', and the right of any member state of the AU 'to request intervention from the [AU] in order to restore peace and security'.

A cursory evaluation of the above provisions prompts an impression that they contradict the time-honoured customary international law principle of non-intervention forming part of the AU Act. Article 4(g) enshrines the non-intervention principle, stating that the AU shall function according to the principle of 'non-interference' by any member state in the internal affairs of another. Arguably, this provision completely negates those discussed in the previous paragraph.

However, a closer examination of the wording of article 4(f) reveals otherwise. The AU provision differs fundamentally from its UN Charter 'equivalent' contained in article 2(7) of the UN Charter, which provides, *inter alia,* that:

> Nothing contained in the present Charter shall authorise the [UN] to intervene in matters which are essentially within the domestic jurisdiction of any state.

The UN Charter provision above is addressed to the UN acting as such, and not to the member states. In contrast, article 4(f) of the AU Act is directed at member states, by requiring that no member state should interfere in the 'internal affairs' of another. Thus it is argued that article 4(f) does not have the same effect as article 2(7), because the former provision does not restrain the AU from intervening in the internal affairs of individual states. An additional argument to support the view that the AU provisions permitting intervention do not contradict article 4(f) is that human rights issues are not matters falling within the description of 'internal affairs'.

A provision of the AU Act of prime relevance to this contribution is article 4(h). Importantly, it gives the AU the 'right to intervene in a member state pursuant to a decision of the Assembly in respect of grave circumstances, namely: war crimes, genocide and crimes against humanity'. Article 4(h) is couched in terms of a 'right', meaning that the AU Assembly has the discretion to decide whether or not to intervene. The consent of the target state will not be required. It would have been better if the provision required the AU to intervene as a matter of 'duty' because a sense of obligation to intervene is more likely to move the AU into action. Nevertheless, the provision raises at least two general legal issues, which are discussed below.

First, a question might arise whether or not article 4(h) is in conflict with article 2(4) of the UN Charter, which states that:

> All members [of the UN] shall refrain in their international relations from the threat or use of force against the territorial integrity or political independence of any state, or in any other manner inconsistent with the purposes of the UN.

It may be argued that the above provision precludes any consent that African states have given the AU to intervene in their internal affairs. In such a situation, then article 4(h) would be void for incompatibility with article 2(4), which is regarded as *jus cogens*. Such a view would be strengthened by the fact that the UN Charter provides that obligations of member states under the UN Charter supersede their obligations under any other treaty. Furthermore, the Vienna Convention on the Law of Treaties provides that '[a] treaty is void, if at the time of its conclusion, it conflicts with a peremptory norm of general international law'.

A response to such a concern would be that the means of force prohibited by article 2(4) is that which is 'against the territorial integrity or political independence of states'. Intervention under article 4(h) would not infringe upon the territorial integrity or political independence of the African states that are members of the AU. Had the provision been designed to allow such Interference, the member states may not have agreed to allow the provision in the Act. The provision in article 4(h) presumes prior consent by every member state of the AU to the effect that the Union is allowed to intervene in their respective territories. One recent study adopts this reasoning, and argues as follows:

> What the AU members contracted out of by giving their consent to intervention by AU is the principle of 'non-intervention' ... By ratifying the AU Act, African states must be understood to have agreed that the AU can intervene in their affairs accordingly. In empowering the Union [AU] to that effect under article 4(h), the states must be taken to have conceded a quantum of their legal and political sovereignty to the African Union [AU].

Second, article 4(h) does not clarify who determines when to intervene and by what means. Indeed, the article is quite clear that it is the AU Assembly of Heads of State and Government that will make a decision for intervention. The means of intervention are not stated, but considering that the intervention under this provision will be responding to 'grave circumstances', of which are specified as 'war crimes, genocide and crimes against humanity', one may plausibly presume that the intervention will be by use of armed force. War crimes, genocide and crimes against humanity are most likely to be committed in the context of armed conflicts. Therefore, only proportional use of armed force is likely to address these 'grave circumstances'.

It must be accepted that it is the AU Assembly of Heads of State and Government that decides when to intervene, and that the intervention is likely to involve the use of armed force. Two subsidiary issues arise from this proposition. The first is that the Assembly's power to determine the existence of war crimes, genocide and crimes against humanity may be 'hijacked' by more powerful states within the AU. These states may want to politicise the interpretation of these terms.

Fortunately, these terms have already been defined in the 1998 Rome Statute of the International Criminal Court (ICC). This means that it may be difficult to develop other definitions. Furthermore, a decision to intervene will only require an endorsement of two-thirds of the member states, and no single member of the AU has the power to veto. This will ensure that no single state can control the decision making process in respect of the operation of article 4(h) and the AU Act in general.

The second subsidiary issue arising from the above concern is that the AU Act does not envisage the AU's supervision by the Security Council. Yet, the UN Charter provides that the UN Security Council has 'primary responsibility' concerning the maintenance of international peace and security. Indeed, the UN Security Council in exercising its primary responsibility has the mandate to supervise the AU, which is a regional arrangement or agency within the meaning of article 52 of the UN Charter. Under such supervision, the AU would be bound by article 53 of the UN Charter, which states as follows:

> The Security Council shall, where appropriate, utili[s]e such regional arrangements or agencies for enforcement action under its authority. But no enforcement action shall be taken under regional arrangements or by regional agencies without the authori[s]ation of the Security Council ...

The above provision restrains all activities of regional organisations with regard to the use of force, unless the Security Council has authorised such action. Yet, the AU Act in article 4(h) purports to authorise the AU to intervene without the authority of the Security Council. The AU Act does not anticipate the supervision of the UN Security Council, at least with regard to intervening in AU member states where war crimes, genocide or crimes against humanity are being committed. This may imply that the AU considers that it will not be expedient to wait for UN Security Council authorisation before responding to situations of war crimes, genocide and crimes against humanity.

The omission by the AU Act of the requirement that the Security Council should supervise article 4(h) interventions is arguably intentional. This is because the same year the AU Act was adopted, the OAU Solemn Declaration on Security Stability Development and Co-operation in Africa expressly recognised that the primary responsibility for the maintenance of international peace and security [lies] with the [UN] Security Council [with] the OAU in close co-operation with the [UN] and [sub-regional intergovernmental organisations] remaining the premier organi[s]ation for promoting security, stability, development and co-operation in Africa. In this Declaration, the 'primacy' of the UN Security Council in matters of international peace and security was recognised, although even then, the framers carefully added that the OAU remained the 'premier' organisation for the same purpose when it comes to the OAU's region of competence – Africa.

An approach similar to that of the AU had been taken in the past. The Economic Community of West African States (ECOWAS) intervened in Liberia and in Sierra Leone in 1990 and 1997 respectively, without the authority of the Security Council. In both cases, ECOWAS authorities invoked the doctrine of humanitarian intervention, as well as the provisions of the Protocol on Mutual Assistance and Defence. ECOWAS is likely to continue with this trend under the provisions of the 1999 Mechanism for Conflict Prevention, Management and Resolution. Similarly, NATO's use of force in Kosovo was not authorised by the Security Council.

The reason behind the increasing tendency by regional organisations to acquire power to intervene in member states, to use the words of the AU Act, in 'grave circumstances', arises from the fact that the UN Security Council's bureaucratic procedures cannot guarantee a quick response in cases of gross human rights violations. Furthermore, the Council has either ignored some conflicts or has shown discrepant standards in those conflicts to which it has responded. Weller, for instance, notes that in Liberia, the Council first declined to intervene, then intervened, only after ECOWAS did, with considerably less vigour than it did in the Former Yugoslavia. Thus, it may be argued, that where the UN Security Council refuses to intervene in a crisis of a UN member state, this enables concerned regional arrangements or agencies to undertake whatever actions deemed necessary.

The right conferred upon the AU under article 4(h) can serve to complement the powers of the African Commission under article 58 of the African Charter. Under this article, the Commission may draw to the attention of the Assembly of Heads of State and Government any 'existence of a series of serious or massive violations of human and peoples' rights' that may be revealed by communications before the Commission. The Assembly may then request the Commission to 'make an in-depth study' of these cases and to make findings and recommend specific action.

However, the mandate of the Commission under article 58 is limited to the extent that it can only be exercised with the consent of the state where the violations are reportedly occurring. Under the AU dispensation, article 4(h) will enable the Assembly to intervene, without the consent of the target state, in situations of gross violations of human rights, so long as the violations constitute the 'grave circumstances' specified in the article.

In light of the foregoing discussion, we conclude that the AU Act presents an opportunity for the AU to engage in treaty-based humanitarian intervention without the authority of the UN Security Council or of the target state. The AU Act, unlike the OAU Charter, has clear provisions relating to the protection and promotion of human rights. The AU has taken the right decision in incorporating into the AU framework, the main OAU human rights organs. This not only ensures continuity, but also avoids duplicity and the dissipation of resources.

Article 4(h), which permits intervention to pre-empt or stop war crimes, genocide and crimes against humanity, envisages humanitarian intervention under the auspices of the AU. Moreover, the restriction of the circumstances in which the AU can intervene in such matters, is considered to be of 'the greatest concern to the international community.

Finally, it is likely that the norm of humanitarian intervention may be espoused by further enactments by the AU in the future. This is so because of the fundamental difference between the contents of article 3 and that of article 4 of the AU Act. The provisions of the former article are expressed, as 'objectives' while those of the latter are expressed as 'principles'. Maluwa has stated that 'principles' form the main process by which the OAU embarked on lawmaking. Arguably, this trend is likely to continue under the new dispensation of the AU.

The Protocol Relating to the Establishment of the Peace and Security Council of the AU (the protocol) was adopted at the 1st ordinary session of the AU Heads of State and Government in Durban, South Africa. Ratification by a simple majority of member states is required for its entry into force.

The Protocol seeks to establish an African Peace and Security Council to take over the work of the OAU Mechanism for Conflict Prevention, Management and Resolution, which, as stated earlier, is now part of the institutional structure of the AU.

The Peace and Security Council of the AU shall be composed of 15 member states of the AU elected for a term of two years with due regard to equitable geographical representation, and provided that five of the members shall be elected for a term of three years to ensure continuity. To qualify for election, the prospective member state shall manifest among others commitment to uphold the principles of the Union, including humanitarian intervention.

Such member states should also demonstrate respect for constitutional governance, the rule of law and human rights. If these criteria are followed, it is likely that the humanitarian intervention envisaged in article 4(h) of the AU Act will be realised. Indeed, states constituting the Peace and Security Council are bound to be relatively democratic. These states should not shield those states involved in massive violations of fundamental human rights, as was the case during the existence of the OAU.

Moreover, the provision in the Protocol for decisions to be made by a simple majority if they concern procedural matters and by two-thirds majority if they relate to any other matter, will empower the Council to make decisions, which may be contested by some members. One of the obstacles on the functioning of the 1993 OAU Mechanism, as stated earlier, is the requirement that decisions are to be made by consensus.

The AU Protocol also provides that decisions of the Peace and Security Council shall be guided by the principle of consensus, but in cases where consensus cannot be reached, decisions must conform to the manner described above. Each member of the Peace and Security Council shall have one vote. The Peace and Security Council shall meet at the Addis Ababa Headquarters of the AU at the lever of Permanent Representatives, Ministers or Heads of State and Government.

The Council is required to be so organised to enable it to function continuously. For this purpose, the Council shall, at all times, be represented at the Headquarters of the AU. This provision envisages that most of the decisions of the Council will be made at the level of Permanent Representatives for referral to the Council of Ministers and Heads of State and Government who, according to the Protocol will meet less frequently. With regard to humanitarian intervention, the continuity of the work of the Peace and Security Council is particularly important. The Council may be required to take decisions to intervene to pre-empt mass loss of life or massive violations of human rights on short notice.

The objectives of the Peace and Security Council will include the anticipating and pre-empting of armed conflicts, and preventing massive violations of fundamental human rights. It will also aim at the promotion and encouragement of democratic practices, good governance, the rule of law, human rights, the respect for the sanctity of human life and international humanitarian law.

Among the principles to govern the Peace and Security Council is the principle in article 4(h) of the AU Act, by which the AU may intervene pursuant to a decision of the Assembly of Heads of State and Government, in member states with respect of genocide, war crimes and crimes against humanity. Also, the functions of the Council shall include 'intervention, pursuant to article 4(h) of the [AU Act]'.

In order to enable the Peace and Security Council to perform this and other responsibilities, the Protocol provides for the establishment of the African Standby Force, composed of standby contingents 'for rapid deployment at appropriate notice'. Such standby contingents shall be established by member states of the AU, in terms of 'standard operating procedures' of the AU. It appears from these provisions that the African Standby Force shall be an *ad hoc* force, constituted as need arises. The functions of the African Standby Force shall include 'intervention in member states in respect of grave circumstances in order to restore peace and security, in accordance with article 4(h) [of the AU Act]'.

The Protocol defines the role of the AU Chairperson with regard to conflict prevention and resolution including the maintenance of peace, security and stability on the continent. His role includes bringing to the attention of the AU Peace and Security Council or the Panel of the Wise, any matter that is relevant for the promotion of peace, security and stability in Africa. He may also use his good offices to prevent potential conflicts, resolve actual conflicts and promote peacebuilding and post-conflict reconstruction. The Protocol requires the Chairperson to use the information gathered under the Protocol's 'early warning system' to advise the AU Peace and Security Council on potential conflicts and threats to peace and security in Africa and recommend the best course of action.

The Protocol, once in force, will clarify at least three issues that the AU Act has left open for interpretation. First, as stated earlier, the Act is silent on who determines when the 'grave circumstances' justifying intervention in a state, and by what means is the intervention to be carried out. We argued that the specified 'grave circumstances' of genocide, crimes against humanity and war crimes have already been defined in the Rome Statute of the ICC, and that these definitions may offer guidance. The Protocol supports this view, by providing that the AU Peace and Security Council will have the power to recommend to the AU Assembly of Heads of State and Government, intervention pursuant to article 4(h) of the AU Act in respect of 'war crimes, genocide and crimes against humanity as defined in relevant international conventions and instruments'.

Concerning the means of intervention under article 4(h) of the AU Act, we argued earlier that the use of force is envisaged. This position is supported by the provision of the Protocol requiring the establishment of an African Standby Force with both 'military and civilian contingents' for purposes of 'rapid deployment at appropriate notice'.

Second, we observed in the discussion of article 4(h) of the AU Act that neither the provision nor the rest of the Act clarifies the relationship between the AU and the UN in relation to issues touching on international peace and security. We concluded that the drafters of the Act deliberately left out any definition of this relationship, in order to ensure that the AU can act in emergency cases of the 'grave circumstances' and to attend to massive violations of fundamental rights. The protocol appears to discount this assumption by detailing out how the Peace and Security Council of the AU will work together with the UN Security Council.

In its preamble, the Protocol recognises the 'provisions of the Charter of the [UN] on the role of regional arrangements or agencies in the maintenance of international peace and security, and the need to forge closer co-operation and partnership between the [UN], other international organisations and the [AU], in the promotion and maintenance of international peace, security and stability in Africa'.

Also, the Peace and Security Council of the AU shall be guided by the principles of the AU Act and those of the UN Charter and the Universal Declaration. The AU Council also has power to 'promote and develop a strong partnership for peace and security between the [AU] and the [UN] and its agencies ...'. Furthermore, the AU Peace and Security Council is enjoined by the Protocol to 'co-operate and work closely with the [UN] Security Council', which has the primary responsibility for the maintenance of international peace and security.

The above provisions manifest a sustained effort by the drafters of the Protocol to provide for an African regional mechanism for the maintenance of international peace and security that is subservient to the UN Security Council. Therefore, it may be argued that the Protocol clarifies that the AU will only intervene militarily in member states with the approval and under the, supervision of the UN Security Council. However, it is possible that the drafters of the Protocol were either oblivious of the relevant provisions of the AU Act, or they intended to define the relationship between the AU and the UN Security Council, which the AU Act had omitted.

It is interesting to note that there exists an internal contradiction regarding the provisions of the Protocol on the relationship between the AU Peace and Security Council and the UN Security Council. The Protocol states that the AU 'has the primary responsibility for promoting peace, security and stability in Africa'.

Despite the elaborate provisions by the Protocol recognising the primacy of the UN Security Council in the promotion of international peace and security, that primacy only relates to peace and security in other parts of the world. Within Africa, the Protocol adopts the position taken under the AU Act – that of according the AU the primary role in matters of international peace and security, including the use of force in the maintenance thereof. This argument is supported by the fact that the Protocol does not provide anywhere that the AU Peace and Security Council or the AU Assembly of Heads of State and Government will require the authorisation of the UN Security Council before engaging in humanitarian intervention under article 4(h) of the AU Act.

The third and final issue in respect of the AU Act that the Protocol has clarified relates to the relationship between the Peace and Security Council of the AU and the African Commission on Human and Peoples' Rights. The Protocol provides that the Council 'shall seek close co-operation' with the Commission in all matters relevant to the mandate and objectives of the Council. The Commission is obliged under the Protocol to bring to the attention of the Council 'any information relevant to the objectives and mandate of the [Council]'. These provisions are likely to 'give teeth' to the Commission's mandate under article 58 of the African Charter, by attracting the attention of the OAU (AU) Assembly situations of gross and systematic violations of human rights. Information provided by the Commission under the Protocol may be a basis of a recommendation by the Council to the AU Assembly for humanitarian intervention under article 4(h) of the AU Act.

Finally, the prominent role of eminent personalities that was prominent in the functioning of the AU has also been recognised in the Protocol. A 'Panel of the Wise' is established with the mandate to 'advise the [Peace and Security Council of the AU] and the Chairperson of then [AU] Commission on all issues pertaining to the promotion and maintenance of peace, security and stability in Africa'. The Panel of the Wise is to be composed of 'five highly respected African personalities from various segments of society who have made outstanding contributions to the cause of peace, security and development on the continent'.

The advice on the Panel of the Wise is likely to be headed by the machinery. The personal intervention of the Panel in situations of armed conflicts where massive violations of fundamental human rights are taking place may succeed in reconciling the warring parties, given Africa's respect for elders. The provision for the Panel of the Wise is an important development, as it will ensure that the use of force will only be resorted to if the Panel's mediation, conciliation and other peaceful methods of intervention have failed.

...

In line with the vision captured by the AU normative framework and the vision for peace and security, African leaders, during the launching of the AU Peace and Security Council in 2004, expressed their commitment to the promotion of a stable, secure, peaceful and developed Africa.

STATEMENT OF COMMITMENT TO PEACE AND SECURITY IN AFRICA, ISSUED BY THE HEADS OF STATE AND GOVERNMENT OF MEMBER STATES OF THE PEACE AND SECURITY COUNCIL OF THE AFRICAN UNION (25 MAY 2004)

Also available at http://www.africa-union.org

We, the Heads of State and Government of the member states of the Peace and Security Council (PSC) of the African Union (AU), meeting in Addis Ababa, Ethiopia, on 25 May 2004, for the solemn ceremonial launching of our new Council and having reviewed the state of peace and security on our continent, have adopted the following Statement:

(1) The establishment of the Peace and Security Council of the African Union marks an historic watershed in Africa's progress towards resolving its conflicts and the building of a durable peace and security order. Our meeting today is both a reaffirmation of our commitment to the promotion of a stable, secure, peaceful and developed Africa, as well as a significant step towards realising the ideals enshrined in the Constitutive Act of the Union and the Protocol relating to the Establishment of the Peace and Security Council. It is also a reflection of our desire to assume a greater role in the maintenance of peace and security in Africa.

(2) Over the years, we have signed and ratified several Protocols and Declarations that signalled our collective commitment to peace, as well as the rejection of the use of force in settling disputes. Unfortunately, some of these have not been fully implemented. The continental peace and security architecture that we are putting in place needs to be nurtured and strengthened, to enable our Union to meet the aspirations of our people for sustainable development. To this end, we shall ensure that the authority vested in the Peace and Security Council is fairly and proactively exercised.

(3) We undertake to ensure that we shall at all times move first, in a timely manner, to address conflicts in our continent. We, therefore, realise that this endeavour must be backed by the resources and commitment of our member states, with the full and active support of our peoples and international

Partners. We are determined to deal effectively and objectively with each and every conflict as it arises, using every means at our disposal.

(4) To achieve our objective of creating the conditions for durable peace and development on the African continent, we are determined to address the root causes of such conflicts in a systematic and holistic manner. We are mindful of the fact that to accomplish these goals, we must set for ourselves and achieve ever-higher standards in the areas of human rights, democracy, good governance and conflict prevention, which are a prerequisite for achieving the socio-economic development and integration of our continent.

(5) We recognise that the foundation for peace and security in Africa is intrinsically linked to the concept of human security. Accordingly, we reaffirm our commitment to the promotion of a comprehensive vision of human security.

(6) We shall also move speedily, to implement Africa's Common Security and Defence Policy, and strengthen the common values underpinning peace and security in the continent.

(7) We shall not shrink from decisive actions to overcome the challenges confronting the continent. Henceforth, there will be no conflict on our continent that will be considered to be out of bounds for the African Union. Where grave abuses of human rights, crimes against humanity and genocide occur, the Peace and Security Council must be the first to condemn, and take swift action, consistent with the letter and spirit of the Constitutive Act of the Union and other relevant instruments that we subscribe to.

(8) Our member states should commit themselves to support the African Union Peace Fund in concrete terms, including raising the statutory contribution from the AU regular budget to the Fund.

(9) We are resolved to establish the African Standby Force, and to ensure that sufficient troops and observers are made available for rapid deployment when and where they are required.

(10) As we take stock of the landscape of conflicts and peacemaking initiatives on our continent, we remain gravely concerned at the prevalence of conflicts in different parts of Africa. However, we note that there are encouraging signs of progress in the efforts towards resolving some of these conflicts. We, therefore, urge that the relevant principles from the Constitutive Act of the African Union and the Protocol establishing the PSC, serve as the basis for a continental renewal plan, to tackle conflicts on the continent.

(11) Against the backdrop of these challenges that we are confronted with, we are committed to fostering political dialogue as the essential mechanism for preventing recourse to insurrection and armed struggle. We shall also address ourselves to the other underlying issues that have contributed to: conflict and insecurity, including ethnic and religious extremism; corruption; exclusionary definitions of citizenship; poverty and disease, with special attention on the HIV/AIDS epidemic, which has now become a security

problem on our continent; the illegal exploitation of Africa's renewable and non-renewable natural resources; mercenarism; the illicit proliferation, circulation and trafficking of small arms and light weapons; and the continuing toll exacted by anti-personnel landmines.

(12) We shall also work tirelessly to prevent and combat the phenomenon of terrorism through the effective implementation of the relevant international and AU instruments, including in particular the Algiers Convention of 1999 and the Plan of Action of 2002. We equally undertake to work with the international community combating terrorism.

(13) We shall continue to strengthen our close working relations with the United Nations Security Council, bearing in mind that the UN Security Council has the primary responsibility for the maintenance of global peace and security, and Africa is part of that international community.

(14) We welcome the establishment of the Peace Support Operations Facility by the European Union and look forward to its support for initiatives to be undertaken under the authority of the African Union. We shall continue to rely upon our major partners in the Americas, Asia and Europe, to show solidarity with our efforts in the spirit espoused by NEPAD, the African Union programme that seeks to build a partnership based on indivisibility of peace, security, good political and economic governance.

(15) On the occasion of the solemn launching of our Peace and Security Council, which has coincided with the celebration of the Africa Day, we, the Heads of State and Government of member states of the Council, hereby commit ourselves to the building of an African continent that is not only at peace with itself but is also at peace with the rest of the world.

Moni explores some of the challenges facing the AU in responding to the Darfur crisis, including the lack of capacity and faltering political will among many actors.

MONI, R 'THE UN REPORT ON DARFUR: WHAT ROLE FOR THE AU?' (2005)

Pambazuka News 193

The UN International Commission of Inquiry established by Security Council Resolution 1564 on 18 September 2004 to 'investigate reports of violations of international humanitarian law and human rights law in Darfur by all parties, to determine also whether or not acts of genocide have occurred' completed its work and submitted its findings to the UN Secretary-General on 31 January 2005.

Although the report did not find genocide to have occurred in Darfur, it confirms that serious violations of international human rights law and humanitarian law by all parties have taken place and are continuing. In particular, the Commission found that government forces and militias conducted indiscriminate attacks, including killing of civilians, torture, enforced disappearances, destruction of villages, rape and other forms of sexual violence, pillaging and forced displacement, throughout Darfur.

These acts were conducted on a widespread and systematic basis, and therefore may amount to crimes against humanity. The Commission recommends that the International Criminal Court (ICC) should prosecute those persons allegedly responsible for the most serious crimes as part of the solution to the Darfur crisis.

It is notable that the report sparingly mentions the AU and does not prescribe any role it should play in the punishment of the violators of international human rights law and humanitarian law. The AU on its part has steered clear of the definition game of what is or is not 'genocide'.

When the then US Secretary of State Colin Powell announced on 9 September 2004, that the killing, raping and displacement of black Africans by horse-mounted Arab fighters amounted to genocide, the AU called it a 'big mistake' and criticised Powell for 'undermining the AU'. The AU wiggled out of intervening in Darfur by arguing that it will 'call it genocide' after carrying out a 'full investigation'.

However, it would be wrong to assume that the AU's refusal to acknowledge, despite the teeming evidence in its field reports, that genocide has taken place in Darfur is the decision of one official.

In a communique issued in July, the AU Peace and Security Council (PSC) stated that even though the crisis in Darfur was grave with unacceptable levels of deaths, human suffering, and destruction of homes and infrastructure, the situation could not be defined as 'genocide'.

The AU's highest organ, the Assembly of Heads of State and Government, also reiterated this position during the 6-8 July 2004 Summit, when it noted 'that, even though the humanitarian situation in Darfur is serious, it can not be defined as a genocide'.

Indeed, the UN Commission has concluded that although inhuman acts may have been committed 'with genocidal intent no genocidal policy has been pursued and implemented in Darfur by the Government authorities, directly or through the militias under their control'.

But the AU should not rest on its laurels and feel that it has been exonerated from intervening in Darfur to protect civilians who are being victimised by the Government-supported armed militia groups, the Janjaweed. According to article 4(h) of the Constitutive Act, the AU has 'the right ... to intervene in a Member State pursuant to a decision of the Assembly (of Heads of State and Government) in respect of grave circumstances, namely war crimes, genocide and crimes against humanity'.

If we accept the findings of the UN Commission report that 'war crimes and crimes against humanity' are taking place in Darfur, then the AU should be urged to invoke article 4(h) to intervene in Darfur and protect the civilian population. However, for the following reasons, the AU is incapable of invoking article 4(h) to intervene in Darfur.

Lack of political will

African leaders at the moment have no political will to authorise the AU to intervene in one of its most important member-states. As the Darfur decisions of the July 2004 and January 2005 Summit show, African leaders are not interested in ordering actions that would set precedents. Africa is replete with Darfurs. There are at least half a dozen African states that are currently facing serious political crisis that could lead to civil wars. If the AU intervenes in Darfur, it must prepare to intervene in the near future in Zimbabwe and Nigeria, which have simmering civil conflicts, and in Ivory Coast and Uganda, which are embroiled in seemingly intractable civil wars.

It would be a form of poetic justice for Nigerian President Olusegun Obasanjo, to preside over the AU intervention in Sudan and in 2006 have the same organisation, under the chairmanship of Omar al-Bashir, intervene in Nigeria, assuming the situations in the Delta and Plateau regions are not contained. Likewise, AU leaders, particularly South African president Thabo Mbeki, would find it difficult to authorise AU intervention in Zimbabwe or Uganda to protect civilian populations of those countries.

AU lacks institutional capacity

Assuming that African leaders had the political will to intervene in Darfur pursuant to article 4(h) of the AU Constitutive Act, the AU would still not be able to do so as it does not have the requisite capacity.

As the chaotic deployment of the AU Mission in Sudan (AMIS) has proven, poor logistical planning and lack of trained personnel, funds, and experience in intervening to protect civilians have exposed the AU to be a mere child that has not even learned to walk on its own. It has been more than six months since the AU made the decision to send 3,300 troops to protect its own civilian monitors in Darfur.

So far, it has been unable to deploy half the troops. The haphazard way in which AMIS was conceived, planned, deployed and is being operated has brought back the sad memories of the OAU peacekeeping mission in Chad in early 1980s.

The Sudan factor

Even if African leaders had the political will and the AU had the capacity to intervene in Sudan to protect the civilian population of Darfur, it would still find it difficult to make the decision and marshal regional, continental and international support needed for such an intervention.

Regionally, such an intervention will need the support of the Intergovernmental Authority on Development (IGAD). A decision by IGAD supporting such an intervention will have to be made by the IGAD Assembly of Heads of State and Government, which is chaired by President Yoweri Kaguta Museveni, who will not allow IGAD to make such a decision for reasons pointed out above. Were IGAD to make such a decision it would have to be implemented by the Executive Secretary, Dr Attala Hamad Bashir, who is Sudanese.

Continentally, the AU would have to rely on the expert advice of the African Commission on Human and People's Right (ACHPR) on matters relating to international human rights and violation of the African Charter on Human and People's Rights. The ACHPR would not easily and expeditiously arrive at recommendations on violations of human rights in Sudan as its vice chairman is Yassir SA El Hassan, who is an official of the Sudan Ministry of Justice. The inability of the ACHPR to conduct an investigation of human rights violations in Darfur is now apparent as the resolution it adopted on 4 June 2004 to do so has yet to be implemented.

Were the ACHPR to come up with a report showing that human rights violations were taking place in Darfur and that urgent action was needed to protect civilians, that report would be presented to the PSC, the AU body with the responsibility of deciding on matters of intervention. The PSC has 15 members without veto powers. Sudan is a member of the PSC. However, it is an open secret in Addis Ababa that Sudan has 'veto power' on the PSC through its powerful Permanent Representative, Osman Said, who is the dean of the diplomatic corps and former head of the national intelligence service.

Sudan is also a member of the Bureau of the Assembly of the AU, the leadership body that includes Mali, Senegal, Burundi, Chad, Libya, Saharawi Arab Democratic Republic, Ethiopia, Botswana, Equatorial Guinea and Swaziland. The Bureau decides on important matters of the Assembly including the venue and the agenda.

Originally Sudan was supposed to host the AU Summit in July 2005 but this venue has been changed to Libya. However, Sudan will still host the January 2006 Summit. It is traditional that the country that hosts the AU Summit also assumes the organisation's Chairmanship and it is most likely that Sudan would do so when it host the January 2006 Summit.

Internationally, an intervention in Darfur would have to get the Security Council's stamp of approval, under article VIII of the UN Charter. Sudan has powerful friends, Russia and China, in the Security Council who are most likely to veto such a decision. Russia is the main supplier of arms to the Khartoum government while China has secured lucrative oil deals in Sudan.

It is apparent that the time has come for the role of the AU in Darfur to be evaluated, as the above facts have clearly pointed to one conclusion: It is time the UN Security Council assumed its primary responsibilities of maintaining peace and security in the whole of Sudan. The AU should be thanked for the role it has played so far and be asked to back out now with grace before things get messier.
...

The following report examines the capacity of African institutions on the continental, sub-regional, national and local levels to engage in peacebuilding activities. It recommends, among other things, the urgency of creating both state and non-state capacities to bolster work in conflict prevention, management and resolution.

INTERNATIONAL PEACE ACADEMY *THE INFRASTRUCTURE OF PEACE IN AFRICA: ASSESSING THE PEACEBUILDING CAPACITY OF AFRICAN INSTITUTIONS* (2002)

Full report available at http://www.ipacademy.org/PDF_Reports/FORD.pdf
...

The Economic Community of West African States (ECOWAS)

Conceived as an organisation for promoting economic development, ECOWAS was untested in the 1970s when West Africa experienced relative calm akin to a *Pax West Africana*. Guinea-Bissau's war of liberation ended in 1974, while brief border clashes between Burkina Faso and Mali in 1975 and 1985 were managed through local mediation efforts. However, insecurity began to loom large with the outbreak of the Liberian civil war in December 1989. In July 1990, invoking the Protocol on Mutual Assistance on Defense (1981), Liberian autocrat Samuel Doe requested ECOWAS to send a peacekeeping force to Liberia to end a civil war that had led to mass killings and massive refugee flows. ECOMOG's intervention would profoundly change the security landscape in West Africa.

ECOMOG in Liberia, Sierra Leone and Guinea-Bissau

Liberia and Sierra Leone both endured almost a decade of civil wars that resulted in over 250,000 deaths and over one million refugees. Liberia's civil war lasted from December 1989 to early 1997 and was mainly fought by eight factions. The Sierra Leone war lasted from March 1991 until a cease-fire in July 1999, and was fought between successive civilian and military governments in Freetown, in alliance with civil defense groups including local hunters, the Kamajors, against the RUF. It took 18 peace agreements (14 in Liberia and four in Sierra Leone) to end — at least temporarily — both conflicts. ECOMOG's involvement in Sierra Leone's civil war was inextricably linked to its eight-year peacekeeping effort in Liberia's civil war.

In March 1991, the Revolutionary United Front (RUF) invaded Sierra Leone with the assistance of Charles Taylor's National Patriotic Front of Liberia (NPFL). Several hundred Nigerian, Ghanaian, and Guinean troops were sent to Sierra Leone to defend the government. A second ECOMOG mission was established in Sierra Leone after Nigerian leader, General Sani Abacha, diverted peacekeepers from the successful Liberia mission to Sierra Leone in an attempt to crush a military coup by the Sierra Leonean army in Freetown in May 1997. They were later joined by contingents from Ghana, Guinea and Mali. The military junta invited the RUF to join its administration. Nigerian troops reversed the coup in February 1998 and restored President Ahmed Tejan Kabbah to power. However, the unsuccessful but devastating rebel invasion of Freetown in January 1999 showed that ECOMOG has been unable to eliminate the RUF as a military threat. In both cases, an ill-equipped and poorly funded ECOMOG has been unable to defeat the rebels in guerrilla warfare or prevent violations including rapes, killings, kidnappings and disarming of UN peacekeepers.

ECOMOG launched a third intervention into Guinea-Bissau between December 1998 and June 1999 to end the civil conflict between President João Vieira, backed by Senegalese and Guinean military forces, and his former army chief, General Ansumane Mane. The ECOMOG intervention involving troops from Benin, Gambia, Niger, and Togo, and funded entirely by the French government, failed to achieve its peacekeeping objectives and had to be withdrawn prematurely. The difficulties of peacemaking in Guinea-Bissau can be explained by three main factors. First, Guinea-Bissau's two main protagonists, Vieira and Mane, were unwilling to settle their differences through peaceful means and sought to manipulate the support of external forces. Second, Senegal and Guinea were compromised as neutral peacekeepers and had to be replaced by troops from other West African states with no prior involvement in the fighting. But the size of ECOMOG's contingent – 712 men – was insufficient to protect the capital from attack and to disarm the combatants, a situation exacerbated by its logistical weaknesses. Finally, though external actors like the UN, the World Bank, the EU and several bilateral donors supported some peacebuilding efforts in Guinea-Bissau, continuing instability in the country has made donors reluctant to deliver on most of the pledges made at a conference in Geneva in May 1999.

The ECOWAS security mechanism

The ECOWAS Mechanism for Conflict Prevention, Management Resolution, Peacekeeping and Security was adopted at the ECOWAS summit in Lomé in December 1999. The Mechanism expanded two previous subregional security initiatives: a Protocol on Non-Aggression signed in 1978, and a Protocol Relating to Mutual Assistance on Defense (MAD) in 1981. The first Protocol called on members to resolve their conflicts peacefully through ECOWAS. The second promised mutual assistance for externally instigated or sponsored aggression and called for the creation of an Allied Armed Force of the Community, consisting of standby forces from ECOWAS states. The Mechanism of 1999 was also shaped by ECOMOG's experiences in Liberia, Sierra Leone and Guinea-Bissau. This Mechanism evolved out of the activities of ECOWAS'

Standing Mediation Committee (SMC) established in 1990 following the outbreak of the civil war in Liberia.

The ECOWAS Mechanism of 1999 comprises six distinct bodies, designed to help contain and defuse impending conflicts. The first is the Mediation and Security Council, the main decision-making body on all matters concerning conflict prevention, peacekeeping, security and other areas of operation. It is made up of ten members who are elected to two-year terms. The second important body of the new Mechanism is the Defense and Security Commission, which examines all technical and administrative issues and assesses logistical requirements for peacekeeping operations. The Commission consists of military technocrats and advises the Mediation and Security Council on mandates, terms of reference and the appointment of Force Commanders for military missions. One pressing need of the ECOWAS Secretariat is to appoint more staff to oversee its Mechanism. Until recently, this responsibility fell largely on three overworked Legal Affairs officers. General Cheikh Diarra was appointed Deputy Executive Secretary for Political Affairs, Defense and Security in early 2001 and is in the process of increasing his staff.

The third body of the Mechanism is the Council of Elders, a group of eminent persons mandated to use their good offices in the prevention, management and resolution of conflicts. The Council of Elders is to consist of eminent persons from Africa and outside the continent, including women, traditional, religious, and political leaders appointed on an *ad hoc* basis. Seventeen of its thirty-two members met for the first time in Niamey, Niger, from 2 to 4 July 2001. The fourth body of the mechanism is the Executive Secretariat and particularly the Executive Secretary, who coordinates the activities of the various bodies of the Mechanism and the implementation of its decisions. The fifth body of the new Mechanism is the Early Warning Observation System, which collects and transmits data to the ECOWAS Secretariat on impending signs of conflict. Finally, ECOMOG, a body that will consist of standby forces from member states, is to be the peacekeeping and monitoring arm of the Mechanism. ECOWAS' new Mechanism also calls for improved co-operation among its members in the areas of early warning, conflict prevention, peacekeeping operations, cross-border crime, and the trafficking of small arms and narcotics. Many of these ideas were based on ECOMOG's experiences in Liberia, Sierra Leone, and Guinea-Bissau.

Since it has already undertaken three military missions, it is important to discuss ECOWAS' military arm in more detail. The ECOWAS Mechanism calls for the establishment of a brigade-size standby force, consisting of specially trained and equipped units of national armies, ready for deployment at short notice. The force's main tasks involve observation and monitoring, peacekeeping, humanitarian intervention, enforcement of sanctions and embargoes, preventive deployment, peacebuilding operations, disarmament and demobilisation, and policing activities including anti-smuggling and anti-criminal activities. These were many of the tasks that ECOMOG performed in Liberia and Sierra Leone. The proposed subregional force is expected to embark on periodic training exercises to enhance the cohesion of the troops and the compatibility of equipment. It will undertake exchange programmes in West African military training institutions, as well as external training involving the UN and OAU. Four thousand troops from Benin, Burkina Faso, Chad, Côte d'Ivoire, Niger, Togo and Ghana took part in war games in the Burkinabé town of Kompienga and northern Togo in May 1998, with Nigeria involved in the military planning for these exercises.

The ECOMOG force is mandated to intervene in four cases: first, a situation of internal armed conflict within a member state; second, conflicts between two or more member states; third, internal conflicts that threaten to trigger a humanitarian disaster or pose a serious threat to subregional peace and security, and situations that result from the overthrow or threat to a democratically elected government; and fourth any other situation that the council deems 'appropriate'. While the first two scenarios were included in the ECOWAS Protocol Relating to Mutual Assistance on Defense of 1981, the third scenario was a conscious effort to provide legal cover for future interventions, again, based on the Liberia, Sierra Leone, and Guinea-Bissau experiences. In Liberia and Guinea-Bissau, ECOMOG intervened by arguing that the situation posed a humanitarian disaster and a threat to subregional peace and security. In Sierra Leone, ECOMOG restored a democratically elected government to power after its overthrow by soldiers. The interventions in Liberia and Sierra Leone were controversial and questioned on legal grounds, even by some ECOWAS members.

The ECOMOG interventions in Liberia, Sierra Leone, and Guinea-Bissau exposed the logistical weaknesses of West Africa's armies. For the foreseeable future, such logistical support will have to come from external donors until the subregion develops its own capabilities. The issue of financing is particularly important to the building of ECOMOG's standby force. The ECOWAS security mechanism foresees troop-contributing countries bearing financial costs for the first three months of military operations, before ECOWAS takes over the costs. The initial agreement for the ECOMOG mission in Liberia was for each contingent to fund its own troops for the first month of the mission, after which time the full ECOWAS would assume responsibility for ECOMOG. But Nigeria ended up footing about 90 per cent of the costs (over US$1.2 billion) while francophone countries opposed to ECOMOG were unwilling to contribute to a mission they did not support. France entirely financed the ECOMOG mission to Guinea-Bissau. Under the ECOWAS security mechanism, a Special Peace Fund is to be established to raise revenue. Funding will be raised from member states, corporate bodies, the UN, multinational organisations, the OAU and the rest of the international community.

The three ECOMOG missions demonstrated the importance of securing financial support before embarking on an intervention. Such costs can prove a disincentive to future interventions in a subregion saddled with a crippling debt burden. OAU peacekeepers from Tanzania and Uganda withdrew from ECOMOG's mission in Liberia in 1995 in large part because their financial and logistical needs were not being met. Other ECOWAS states, like Togo, declined to contribute troops to ECOMOG due to the costs of maintaining peacekeepers in Liberia. The Nigerian-led OAU intervention force in Chad between 1979 and 1981 was forced to withdraw largely because it lacked the funding and logistical support to sustain it. All these experiences underscore the significance of financial and logistical support for future subregional efforts at conflict management.

The ECOWAS security mechanism has so far received funding from the AU and several donor governments. The OAU gave ECOWAS $300 000 for its deployments in Sierra Leone and Liberia. The European Union (EU) (2 million Euros), the US Agency for International Development (USAID) ($250 000) and the governments of the United Kingdom, Japan (US$100 000) and Germany have also made contributions in support of the ECOWAS security mechanism. Canada has contributed $300 000 for the establishment of an ECOWAS Child Protection Unit. The government of the Netherlands has also expressed an interest in funding the mechanism.

Beside ECOWAS, the Mano River Union (MRU), comprised of Guinea, Liberia, and Sierra Leone also works to resolve conflict in the region, through the Joint Security Committee (JSC), which was created at the Summit of MRU Head of State in Conakry in April 2000. The JSC Committee was born out of the need to address the deteriorating security situation along the borders of the three MRU states. The JSC consists of a Technical Committee and a Border Security, and Confidence-Building Unit, with a mandate to address and monitor joint security and border issues. One of the first tasks undertaken by the JSC was to investigate the persistent cross-border incursions between Guinea and Liberia. However, since the conclusion of this investigation, the MRU states have not been able to implement the recommendations made by the JSC, as the security situation along the borders between Liberia and Guinea has deteriorated and tensions between the two countries have increased.

A further factor complicating the resolution of the Liberia/Guinea conflict is the fact that members of the JSC are parties to the dispute. More fundamentally, political differences among ECOWAS member states, relating to disagreements over conflict management strategies, continue to test the capacity and resolve of ECOWAS to address conflicts in the subregion. ECOWAS leaders have often not spoken in unison on these issues. Although ECOWAS appeared at first to support a plan by the international community to impose sanctions on Liberia in 2001 in order to deter its support for Sierra Leonean RUF rebels, it later called for a two-month moratorium before such sanctions could be imposed. Following the imposition of sanctions on Liberia by the UN Security Council in May 2001, some ECOWAS leaders have publicly questioned the wisdom of punishing Charles Taylor while seeking his co-operation for the disarmament of RUF rebels in Sierra Leone. We next turn to the role of SADC in managing regional conflicts.

The Southern African Development Community (SADC)

An understanding of the role of the Southern African Development Community in responding to conflicts and crises is impossible without recognising a key feature of security in this subregion: the overwhelming military and financial preponderance of South Africa. SADC's predecessor, the Southern African Development Co-ordination Conference (SADCC), was established in 1980 specifically to counter the economic, military and political dominance of South Africa. While its creation symbolically signaled a shift from defence against apartheid to regional co-operation, the specter of South African economic and military power continues to affect the dynamics within SADC.

SADC set itself an ambitious regional development agenda: working toward creating a free trade area; establishing frameworks to ensure macroeconomic stability; facilitating financial and capital markets; encouraging public-private partnerships (PPPs); and building regional infrastructure. Thus far, this commitment has remained largely rhetorical. While some progress has been made on bilateral (and in rare cases multilateral) co-operation on specific issues (such as aspects of cross-border policing), progress toward regional integration remains minimal. The entire SADC Secretariat currently stands at only 50 persons — this includes professional and support staff. SADC is therefore clearly both understaffed and overstretched. Only about five officers are directly involved in SADC's security work. The organisation envisaged that, after the completion of an ongoing restructuring process, its staff would be increased to 200 people. But this is more a medium- to long-term goal. In the short term, SADC is aiming to increase its staff to 60 people. On the issue of funding, SADC member states, through the SADC Fund and other regional funds, are responsible for the operational costs of its Secretariat. As with other regional organisations in Africa, however, SADC members do not always pay their dues on time or in full, and 80 per cent of SADC funding comes from external donors, largely from the European Union (EU).

The SADC Organ on Politics, Defense and Security

Since its creation in 1996, the SADC Organ on Politics, Defense and Security (OPDS) has not achieved much in terms of promoting collective security in the region. Its strategic vision on how to address the insecurity facing southern Africa is still undefined, and it has been wrecked by divisions among its members. The organ remains captive to the political rivalry between South Africa and Zimbabwe, countries which represented the two opposing conceptions of the functioning of the organ. Zimbabwe felt that incorporating security within the SADC Secretariat in Botswana, rather than leaving it as a specialised task for the chair in Harare, would divert the organisation's attention from its main objective of economic development and integration. In contrast, South Africa argued that the organ should be placed within the structure of the SADC and run by the SADC chair.

These differences have paralysed the operation of the OPDS. At the SADC summit in August 1997, President Nelson Mandela of South Africa, then acting Chairman of the organisation, threatened to resign from the SADC chairmanship if the OPDS was not brought under the central SADC chair. This dispute between Mandela and Zimbabwe's President Robert Mugabe, who had held the chair of the SADC organ since its creation, led the SADC summit to suspend the organ. SADC leaders then appointed a committee composed of a 'troika' of Malawi, Mozambique and Namibia to identify a suitable solution to this problem. The SADC Treaty provides little direction in resolving this problem since it does not contain any details about the nature and functioning of a security organ. Since 1997 SADC has struggled to find a solution to this impasse. Two main proposals emerged: first, to transform the organ into separate committees and work on an *ad hoc* basis to integrate the organ into the SADC framework under a deputy chairperson from one of the troika countries; and second, to operate the organ on the basis of specific protocols signed by member states. The SADC summit held in 2001 finally rotated the chairmanship of the organ from Zimbabwe to Mozambique.

With the paralysis of the organ, SADC's Interstate Defense and Security Committee (IDSC), established in the mid-1980s, often coordinated SADC's security efforts. SADC leaders proposed the establishment of a brigade-level standby force to which member states would contribute with units and Headquarters staff to intervene in regional conflicts. But progress on this issue has remained stalled. SADC states did, however, undertake joint military exercises called 'Operation Blue Crane', funded by EU states. SADC has also undertaken police operations involving Mozambique, South Africa, and Zambia.

The SADC organ needs to be operationalised and strengthened if the organisation is to play an effective role in conflict management. Dealing with security requires addressing three main issues. First, a common vision of security must be nurtured and strengthened within SADC. This can be facilitated through the signing of defence and non-aggression pacts, promoting the protection of human rights, having a moratorium to limit arms smuggling, and creating pacts for environmental protection and the protection of vulnerable groups during conflicts. Second, the region needs to embark on institutional development at both national and subregional levels to implement and monitor the various accords established by SADC. Finally, SADC must set priorities, establish a programme of action in security matters, and draw up a calendar to be ratified by national governments.

South Africa: The giant on the Limpopo

South Africa has the largest, most diversified and advanced economy in the region with a GDP three times that of Nigeria and Egypt. It possesses a modern financial and industrial sector with excellent infrastructure and accounts for some eighty per cent of the region's economic output. Trade flows between it and the rest of Southern Africa are disproportionately in Pretoria's favour at a ratio of four to one. South Africa possesses the fourth largest electricity utility in the world, ESKOM, and accounts for sixty per cent of Africa's electricity generation. Its military is larger and better equipped than that of any of its neighbours, although military sophistication should not be confused with military readiness, as South Africa's intervention in Lesotho in 1998 clearly demonstrated.

The Southern African Customs Union (SACU), which supplies some of its members with almost 50 per cent of their government's revenues, will be undermined by the newly negotiated Free Trade Pact between South Africa and the EU. Notably, Botswana, Lesotho, Namibia and Swaziland will lose 3.5 billion Rand a year. The South Africa/EU pact could also have a fundamental bearing on SADC, forcing states to make substantial adjustments to cope with the new trade regime. Some analysts argue that the likely negative economic spin-offs of the agreement for Southern Africa may make it more difficult to negotiate equitable SACU and SADC economic relations. This situation has generated tension between South Africa and its neighbours, most of whose economies depend overwhelmingly on Pretoria. SADC states are vulnerable to the penetration of South African capital, particularly since its democratic transition between 1990 and 1994.

This economic dominance tends to undermine a spirit of subregional co-operation within SADC, with other states expressing skepticism about Pretoria's professions of not wanting to bully or dominate its neighbours. In the case of relations between South Africa and Zimbabwe, SADC's second largest economy, tensions emanating from the failure of Nelson Mandela's government between 1994 and 1999 to renew an existing bilateral preferential trade agreement contributed to an atmosphere of tension that spilled over into disputes over the chairmanship of SADC. It remains to be seen if the SADC Trade Protocol, establishing an asymmetrical Free Trade Area within the region, can help reverse the economic imbalances feeding such tensions. The resulting tensions between South Africa and its neighbours have complicated the attempt by this subregion to co-operate in managing and resolving conflicts that have affected its member states in places like Angola, DRC and Lesotho. SADC continues to confront problems in its efforts at extending democracy, maintaining peace, and strengthening weak states. In recent times, attempts to address these challenges have tended to highlight divisions and rivalries among SADC members. South Africa has also experienced challenges from regional rivals like Zimbabwe and Angola.

SADC: A house Balkanised?

Southern Africa is a deeply divided subregion, a situation that threatens stability in the SADC subregion. These tensions and threats have forced SADC to prioritise political co-operation and conflict resolution over economic integration. The most striking example is the war in the DRC, following its admission to SADC in 1997, which has polarised SADC. Although SADC states remain theoretically committed to co-operation, their solidarity and cohesion is frayed and may be beyond repair, at least in the short term. The conflict in the DRC has split SADC into at least three groupings.

The first group consists of countries seen as the proponents of democracy in SADC: South Africa, Botswana, and Mozambique. Apart from their democratic credentials, these states are bound by close economic relationships. While this group of states has as its objective the promotion of democracy, respect for human rights and the political settlement of disputes, their pursuit of these goals is inhibited by fear of dominance by South Africa and the failure to build an effective regional coalition. These states declined to support military engagement in the Congo, arguing that only an inclusive political settlement could resolve the conflict, a theme often repeated by Pretoria in its response to African conflicts. However, South Africa and Botswana intervened militarily in Lesotho in 1998, reviving, despite Botswana's participation in the exercise, fears of South Africa's 'giantism' and accusations of 'double standards' from rival SADC camps, given Pretoria's refusal to intervene militarily in Congo.

The second group of countries consists of Zimbabwe, Namibia, and Angola – states that intervened militarily in the DRC to prevent the toppling of Laurent Kabila by Ugandan- and Rwandan-backed rebels in 1998. These three countries seem to be united by what they perceive to be the continuation of South Africa's apartheid policies. This is illustrated by Zimbabwe's claim that after ten years of fighting in Mozambique alongside Frelimo against the apartheid regime, South Africa is reaping the benefits of peace by securing large investments in that country. Mugabe has also attempted to maintain his subregional influence, which he felt was threatened by the emergence of a black-led government in South Africa in 1994. Even after the assassination of Laurent Kabila in 2001, Mugabe embraced Joseph Kabila and continued to exercise significant influence in the DRC.

As further evidence of the balance-of-power politics that continues to play itself out in the southern and central African subregions, Angola has a strong security interest in opposing South Africa's foreign policy. Despite the strong ties between the African National Congress (ANC) and Angola's ruling MPLA, built up during the years of struggle against apartheid, bilateral relations between Pretoria and Luanda since South Africa's 1994 elections have been less cordial than expected. The Movimento Popular de Libertasão de Angola (MPLA) saw the continuation of the supply of arms from South Africa to territory held by União Nacional pela Independencia Total de Angola (UNITA) as a betrayal, and this has been a source of tension between the two governments. Contrary to the widespread belief that Angola's concern in the DRC related exclusively to its security, there are clear indications that economic interests are high on the agenda: Angola, whose troops occupy the oil towns on the DRC's coast, has formed a joint oil-exploration company with the Kinshasa government called Sonangol-Congo. Namibia's involvement in the DRC war is based on its close security and political relationship with Angola and Zimbabwe forged during the struggle for independence in all three countries.

The third group of states in SADC comprises 'neutral' SADC members: Zambia, Tanzania, Mauritius, Seychelles, Lesotho, Swaziland, and Malawi. Mauritius and Seychelles do not feel the direct impact of the conflicts in the subregion. Malawi, Lesotho, and Swaziland are too small militarily, financially, and in terms of human resources to be able to play an influential 'balance-of-power' role in SADC. Zambia and Tanzania share borders with the DRC and are directly affected by the conflicts. Though Zambia was reported to have provided free passage to pro-Kabila rebels, enabling them to attack areas in Southern Congo during the first rebellion that ousted Mobutu in 1997, Lusaka has since refused to take sides in the conflict. Former Zambian leader Frederick Chiluba emerged as a key mediator in the conflict. Three reasons best explain this situation. First, Chiluba was constrained from supporting Kabila, as his domestic political opponents could have linked such support to his perceived Congolese origins. Second, the Chiluba government was keen to maintain Zambia's international prestige built up during Kenneth Kaunda's 27 year leadership. Third, Chiluba recognised that the DRC war would be long, costly and unsustainable. With Angolan president Eduardo Dos Santos accusing Zambia of aiding late UNITA leader Jonas Savimbi in Angola's civil conflict, the relationship between Luanda and Lusaka was another weak link in SADC's security chain.

The interventions by SADC states in the DRC and Lesotho and their non-intervention in Angola have revealed fundamental differences of perception and conduct in the security arena within SADC. Interveners in Congo and Lesotho have claimed that their interventions were legitimised by SADC. But in both cases, there were disputes over SADC legitimisation of the interventions. The two military interventions highlight SADC's weakness as a guarantor of peace and security in the subregion. For many observers, this confirms the fear that SADC's Organ on Politics, Defense and Security can be used as a political tool by subregional leaders to pursue their own narrowly-defined interests.

Several SADC states portrayed the Angolan conflict as a clash between 'good' and 'evil', between an elected MPLA government committed to peace and UNITA, a recalcitrant guerrilla movement. In reality, the conflict was one between two elites, one of which (the MPLA) has a near monopoly on oil, while the other (UNITA) had a seemingly unlimited supply of diamonds. The epicentre of this conflict repeatedly spilled over Angola's borders. SADC's inability to contain or resolve the conflict until Savimbi's death in February 2002 had threatened subregional stability.

Challenges for conflict resolution and peacebuilding

Conflict over water resources in Southern Africa remains a potential source of future conflicts because water is in short supply even as the subregion is experiencing increasing population growth. Already Namibia and Botswana are engaged in serious disputes over shared water sources. South Africa uses some 80 per cent of water consumed in Southern Africa. Pretoria also shares many rivers with neighboring countries, thereby increasing the potential for future conflicts. A further source of conflict – over gemstones – might emerge in SADC. Diamonds cross the Angola-Zambia border with impunity and are, for some informal dealers, a key source of income. Here, and perhaps in other areas of economic activity, efforts at more effective control could lead to conflicts between states and could also involve diamond traders. The security environment in Southern Africa remains fluid, and the DRC conflict remains the greatest challenges confronting SADC and its embryonic security architecture. Joseph Kabila's succession to the leadership of the Kinshasa government following his father's assassination in January 2001 has presented the greatest challenge to the subregion. Although withdrawals of foreign troops from areas in the DRC have begun and UN peacekeepers have been deployed, there remains uncertainty about the commitment of the government in Kinshasa and other parties to implement the Lusaka accord of 1999. Without the backing of Angolan, Zimbabwean and Namibian troops the balance of military power in Congo would shift to the Rwandan-backed faction of the RCD and to the Ugandan-backed faction of Jean Pierre Bemba's Congolese Liberation Front (FCL). The UN report detailing the plundering of the DRC's resources by Rwanda and Uganda, and Ugandan leader Yoweri Museveni's threat to opt out of the Lusaka peace process, further complicated the peace process in the DRC. The FCL appears to have strengthened its position with its reported pact with the *Mai Mai* aimed at policing and pacifying the DRC's Northeastern border with Uganda, Rwanda and Burundi.

Ironically, the improving prospects for peace in the Congo are not a guarantee of regional stability. This is particularly true in the case of the Congo's neighbours, Rwanda and Burundi. If peace breaks out in the Congo, rebels from both countries fighting in the DRC are likely to take their wars back home so that 'any Congolese deal could spell trouble for Congo's smaller neighbours'. This carries the unsettling possibility of destabilising both countries and leading to a regional conflagration. This situation would seem to require a need to link the Lusaka peace process to that of the Central Africa and Great Lakes regions.

An accelerated peace process in the DRC should enable Zimbabwe to undertake an honourable exit from a commitment that has exacerbated that country's economic decline. But it is not clear whether bringing the troops back home would contribute to or detract from Zimbabwe's internal tensions. The genuine land issue in Zimbabwe has been manipulated by the ruling ZANU-PF as a way of remaining in power at all costs. It does appear though that SADC is gradually disengaging from Mugabe's leadership by its decision in 2001 to rotate the chairmanship of the SADC Organ on Politics, Defence and Security and to replace Zimbabwe with Mozambique. Continuing instability in Zimbabwe following controversial elections in March 2002, which saw Mugabe retain power, are a continuing source of concern.

The Economic Community of Central African States (ECCAS)

Recognising the need to co-operate to solve common problems within a wider subregional grouping, the member states of the Central African Customs and Economic Union created in 1981, and of the defunct Economic Community of the Great Lakes States (CEPGL), combined to establish the Economic Community of Central African States in 1983. Conceived as a tool to pursue economic development, promote regional co-operation and establish a Central African Common Market, ECCAS brought together eleven countries: Angola, Burundi, Cameroon, Central African Republic, Chad, Congo, Democratic Republic of Congo, Equatorial Guinea, Gabon, Rwanda, and São Tomé and Principe. In an attempt to address the perennial conflicts in Central Africa, ECCAS leaders decided to create an Early Warning Mechanism in 1996. At a meeting in Libreville in 1997, called to discuss the political crisis in what was then Zaire, ECCAS leaders proposed the idea of an interstate security co-operation mechanism for the prevention and management of conflicts in the subregion. The aim of the mechanism was to establish a legal and institutional framework to promote and strengthen peace and security in Central Africa. Thereafter the *Conseil de Paix et de Securité de l'Afrique Centrale* (COPAX) was established under the auspices of the UN standing committee for Security Questions in Central Africa. COPAX had a dual mandate: to prevent, manage and resolve conflicts in Central Africa; to undertake any necessary action to deal effectively with political conflicts; and to promote, preserve and consolidate peace and security in the subregion.

Over the years, however, technical problems associated with creating ECCAS's structures, coupled with the pursuit of narrow national interests, have blocked the effective operation of the security mechanism. ECCAS members, for instance, do not agree on the relationship between ECCAS, COPAX and its Early Warning Mechanism. Some states argue that since ECCAS is a weak organisation, the security mechanism should be an independent body, while others advocate that the mechanism work within existing institutions. This suggests a general lack of political will among countries in a region afflicted by conflicts. The political and security environment in Central Africa has made it difficult for ECCAS to become institutionalised as a regional organisation. States in the subregion have responded to this failure by seeking membership in alternative subregional organisations. For instance, the DRC is a member of SADC, while Burundi and Rwanda have applied to join the East African Community. Any revitalisation of ECCAS would have to resolve how to deal successfully with multiple memberships of regional organisations, a phenomenon that is not peculiar to this subregion.

The Common Market for Eastern and Southern Africa (COMESA)

Established in 1994, the Common Market for Eastern and Southern Africa was the successor organisation to the Preferential Trade Area for Eastern and Southern Africa. COMESA is currently Africa's largest intergovernmental organisation, with twenty members: Angola, Burundi, Comoros, DRC, Djibouti, Egypt, Eritrea, Ethiopia, Kenya, Madagascar, Malawi, Mauritius, Namibia, Rwanda, Seychelles, Sudan, Swaziland, Uganda, Zambia, and Zimbabwe. COMESA seeks to create a fully integrated and competitive region where goods, services, capital and people move freely. But the organisation has increasingly acknowledged the importance of peace and security as critical components in regional integration. COMESA is currently developing a peace and security policy to enhance its overall objectives. At its fourth summit in August 1999, COMESA decided to deal with the many devastating conflicts among its member states without compromising its agenda of economic development and subregional integration or duplicating the work of other organisations.

The COMESA summit in 2000 linked the issue of sustainable development to peace and security. This meeting discussed the resources needed to address the causes of conflicts, and sought to draw lessons from other subregional organisations in Africa engaged in various aspects of conflict management. Before designing their strategy, COMESA leaders requested its secretariat to develop a co-ordination mechanism with the OAU and Africa's subregional organisations and to recommend a division of labour and responsibilities between different subregional institutions in order to avoid duplication of tasks. COMESA leaders insisted during its 2000 summit that other stake holders, including NGOs, civil society, the business community, and parliamentarians, be involved in the development of a viable security policy in East and Southern Africa. This initiative led to the first COMESA Workshop on 'The Role of the Private Sector, the NGOs and the Civil Society in the Promotion of Peace and Security in the COMESA Subregion'. Recommendations from this workshop form an integral part of the COMESA policy on peace and security.

In order to execute its policy, COMESA developed a three-tier structure consisting firstly of the Bureau, made up of Heads of State and Government, as the supreme policy organ responsible for peace and security issues. The second body, the Bureau of Ministers of Foreign Affairs on Peace and Security, meets once a year to consider ways of promoting peace and security in the COMESA region. Under the rules and procedure of the Authority, the Bureau of Ministers is to carry out the function of conflict prevention and resolution. It performs these tasks taking into account the need to consult the Central

Organ of the OAU/AU Mechanism for Conflict Prevention, Management and Resolution and other African subregional organisations. COMESA' s Council of Ministers is its second highest policy organ and makes policy decisions on its programmes and activities, including monitoring and reviewing its financial and administrative management. The third body, the Committee of Officials on Peace and Security, comprising high-level officials of regional Ministries of Foreign Affairs, meets regularly to ensure the effective discharge of COMESA's security responsibilities.

The COMESA secretariat initiates actions, convenes meetings and utilises information from non-governmental sources in its security work. The secretariat undertakes research and studies as a basis for implementing the decisions adopted by its policy organs. COMESA's Secretary-General, assisted by two Assistant Secretaries-General, directs its security operations. The Office of the Secretary-General includes the Legal and Institutional Affairs Division, a Strategic Planning and Research Section, a Public Relations Unit, and an Audit Section. A consultant has been hired to undertake the COMESA Peace and Security Study with the assistance of a legal adviser. As the policy on peace and security is fairly new and still awaiting further input from other actors such as parliamentarians, there is no staff in the COMESA secretariat responsible solely for peace and security issues. A major challenge for COMESA is to begin to operationalise its peace and security policy. It will need urgently to increase its staff to achieve this goal. The organisation's security mechanism is still very much a work in progress.

The Intergovernmental Authority on Development (IGAD)

The Intergovernmental Authority on Drought and Desertification (IGADD), comprising Djibouti, Ethiopia, Kenya, Somalia, Sudan and Uganda, was established in 1986. Eritrea joined after its independence in 1993. Initially IGADD was established to act as an early-warning mechanism for alerting the international community of impending humanitarian emergencies and to coordinate resources in responding to crises on the Horn of Africa. Co-operation was thus confined to issues of drought, desertification and food security. IGADD avoided addressing issues related to military security, then conceived as a prerogative of individual states and, therefore, as falling outside the arena of collective action. However, as insecurity continued to curtail economic, social and political developments, IGADD member states started to confront these problems collectively. Out of these efforts emerged a decision to begin to transform the security architecture in the subregion. In March 1996, subregional leaders signed an agreement transforming IGADD into the Intergovernmental Authority on Development (IGAD). The organisation's mandate was expanded to include conflict management, prevention and resolution. Under the new agreement, IGAD prioritised the pursuit of peace and security, and had as its principal aim the maintenance of peace, security and stability on the Horn of Africa. Specifically, the agreement provided for: the creation of a subregional mechanism for the prevention, management and resolution of inter- and intrastate conflicts through dialogue; and collective action to preserve peace, security and stability, defined as an essential prerequisite for economic development and social progress. The agreement proposed dealing with conflicts by eliminating threats to security; called for the establishment of a mechanism for consultation and co-operation for the pacific settlement of disputes; and agreed to deal with disputes among member states within the subregion before referring them to other regional or international organisations. Demonstrating unprecedented political commitment, IGAD states pledged themselves to resolving outstanding security problems and conflicts, and to preserving subregional stability.

In seeking security and peace, IGAD pursued a dualtrack approach. To deal with conflicts likely to polarise the organisation, IGAD often creates semiautonomous *ad hoc* mechanisms, outside of its Secretariat, which are then mandated to deal with a particular issue. The secretariat on the Sudan Peace Process, based in Nairobi, is one such mechanism. The process that led to the restoration of a transitional government in Somalia in 1999 was another such mechanism. IGAD's second peacemaking track revolves around its secretariat in Djibouti, which addresses issues on which its members have forged a consensus, such as the establishment of a Conflict Early Warning and Response Mechanism (CEWARN) (discussed below), a campaign against small arms, and a diverse range of humanitarian issues.

The Sudan peace process

In 1993, IGAD leaders established a Standing Committee of Foreign Ministers of Eritrea, Ethiopia, Kenya and Uganda to draw up an agenda and programme of work for a negotiated peace settlement in Sudan. The following year, Kenya was mandated to chair this committee and led the drafting of the Declaration of Principles (DOP), adopted by the parties as a basis for negotiations. However, the effective working of this committee was stalled by disputes over the question of the separation of state and religion and the right to self-determination of the South. This stalemate continued until 1997 when IGAD convened an extraordinary summit to revive the peace process. This meeting led to several positive developments, four of which are particularly significant. First, the IGAD Partners Forum (IPF), composed of Norway, the United States, Canada and the EU, agreed to fund the peace process. Second, the parties to the conflict committed themselves to the self-determination of the South within an (unspecified) interim period, supervised by international observers. Third, both sides agreed to facilitate the free and unimpeded flow of humanitarian assistance to areas affected by famine. Fourth, it was agreed that the boundaries of southern Sudan would be set at those existing on 1 January 1956. However, the parties in Sudan disagreed over the interpretation of the Declaration of Principles, stalling the implementation of the peace accord.

To ensure continued engagement with the parties to the conflict, IGAD leaders established a secretariat for the Sudan peace process, otherwise referred to as the Nairobi Secretariat, in 1999. Seeking to engage at both political and technical levels, the secretariat created two committees: a political committee that seeks to reach a political settlement, and a transitional committee to deal with interim arrangements prior to the exercise of self-determination by southern Sudan.

In spite of these initial steps, the ability of the Nairobi Secretariat to resolve the Sudan conflict is limited by several constraints. Among the greatest challenges is the lack of expertise within the committees to interpret the technical details of areas of agreement and points of difference in the Declaration of Principles. Particularly problematic are issues related to: the relationship between the state and religion; the delineation of borders; self-administration; and the sharing of wealth and power. For instance, in the first meeting that explored the question of wealth-sharing, agreement was reached about an equitable distribution of resources between North and South Sudan. However, this plan was never fully elaborated and led to two contradictory interpretations by both sides. The position of the Sudan Peoples Liberation Army/Movement (SPLA/M) is that there should be a halt to the drilling of oil. The government of Sudan, which refuses to cease oil drilling, prefers to share the proceeds from oil exploration with the SPLA, an offer the latter rejects. Any further negotiations will require assisting the parties to reach a common interpretation and understanding of this issue.

The Nairobi secretariat receives limited support from Djibouti and relies on third-party support, in particular the IGAD Partners Forum. However, resources have been insufficient, averaging $1 million between 1999 and 2000. This lack of funding has greatly limited the secretariat's activities. Although the IGAD Partners Forum reiterated its support for the Sudan peace process in June 2000 (Oslo) and March 2001 (Rome), it failed until April 2002 to provide substantial funds to the process. Responding to this constraint, IGAD leaders have agreed to allow the secretariat to undertake its own fundraising.

In addition to being cash-strapped, the Nairobi secretariat has to contend with an inflexible structure in using its available funds. IPF funds are earmarked for costs related to facilitating meetings and cannot be used for any activities. These funds cannot pay for resource persons, consultations, and gathering of information, all necessary for IGAD's preparatory work. Nor can such funds be used for diplomacy or for negotiations before and after meetings. This type of funding limits the operations of the secretariat which, owing to its limited capacity, must depend on contracted resource persons. Furthermore, this situation denies the secretariat the flexibility it needs to take advantage of opportunities in the Sudan peace process. The short-term disbursement of funds, in periods of between three to six months, further accentuates the effects of limited resources.

Institutionally, the Nairobi secretariat lacks structures to support negotiations. It comprises three core staff: the special envoy and two rapporteurs. While IGAD ambassadors in Nairobi and advisers from the countries designated to guide the peace process also support the core staff, their input is small. Further, co-ordination is poor between the IGAD secretariat in Djibouti and the Nairobi secretariat. IGAD procedures require that the Special Envoy report to IGAD Foreign Affairs ministers, who then report to the IGAD Council and Summit, leaving the secretariat out of the chain of command. The disbursement of funds for the Nairobi Secretariat also comes through Djibouti, creating major tensions between the two institutions.

The secretariat needs to have funds for core expenditure, in particular to pay the salaries of its main staff. In June 2001, staff had not received salaries for five months and their morale was very low. Resources are also required to enable the Special Envoy to travel and mobilise support for the peace process. Currently, the Secretariat is in need of experts to advise on borders, on models of governance such as federalism or confederacy, and on the sharing of resources. Such a pool of experts would make it possible for the secretariat to put together a variety of consultants who can, at short notice, undertake studies and in-depth analyses of issues.

Seeking peace and reconciliation in Somalia

Following the failed international effort to restore peace to Somalia in the early 1990s, responsibility for ending the Somali civil war increasingly came to rest on subregional actors. Compared to the Sudan peace process, the Somali process was fluid and less structured. However, this process did reveal the potential of state and civil society actors playing complementary peacebuilding roles. Between 1991 and 1998, a dozen failed attempts were made to restore peace to Somalia. Finally, in October 1998, in co-operation with the IGAD Forum Partners Liaison Group, IGAD member states created a Standing Committee on the Somali peace process, chaired by Ethiopia. Based on the format of the Sudan peace process, this committee was mandated to organise a peace process in Somalia by providing a consultative forum for negotiations aimed at reconciliation and restoration of a government in Somalia.

The ensuing process involved initial consultations among state and intergovernmental actors, namely IGAD, the Arab League, the OAU and the UN, as well as a broad spectrum of Somalis including clan leaders, Muslim clerics, warlords and members of civil society. From March through to May 2000, a series of consultations with Somali intellectuals, professionals, former politicians and representatives from the business community was organised in Djibouti by IGAD. The last of these meetings involved 200 Somali traditional leaders and 100 women delegates. The Somali National Peace Conference took place on 4 June 2000, in Arta, Djibouti. This meeting identified arms control, disarmament of militias, restoration of looted property, and determining the status of Mogadishu as priority issues. Special committees were created to address each issue. By the time the national peace conference ended on 13 August 2000, a Transitional National Assembly (TNA), composed of 245 members, had been established. A week later, members of the TNA elected Mr. Abdul-Kassim Salat Hassan as president of Somalia. After his inauguration in Djibouti, Salat moved his government to Mogadishu. Shortly thereafter, a new legislative assembly and a cabinet were formally established. The government continues to face serious difficulties, including the challenging of its authority by warlords controlling different areas in Mogadishu and the non-participation of representatives from Somaliland and Puntland. Despite these problems, Somalia was readmitted to IGAD during its November 2000 summit.

The IGAD Conflict Early Warning and Response Mechanism (CEWARN)

The IGAD secretariat's work in the peace and security field is located in two divisions, namely the Conflict Prevention, Management and Resolution (CPMR) division and the Humanitarian Affairs division. Four critical projects have emerged within the CPMR since 1996. The first, focusing on the strengthening of capacity within the IGAD secretariat and of key actors within member states, is funded by the EU and the government of Sweden. The second project deals with demobilisation and post-conflict reconstruction, including the control of illicit trafficking in small arms and light weapons. Conducted in partnership with Saferworld, this activity is funded by the UK's Department for International Development (DFID) to the tune of 300 000 pounds sterling. The third project seeks to promote a culture of peace and tolerance on the Horn of Africa. The fourth, and by far the most developed project, is the development of IGAD's Conflict Early Warning and Response Mechanism, which requires closer scrutiny.

Keen to address crises before they erupt into full-blown conflicts, IGAD Heads of State mandated the secretariat in Djibouti to establish a Conflict Early Warning and Response Mechanism in 1998. Following this decision, the secretariat contracted the Forum on Early Warning and Early Response (FEWER) as its partner in March 2000 to establish the mechanism. This process led to three CEWARN workshops. The first, held in July 2000, drew participants from a wide range of state and nonstate actors and discussed conceptual issues related to developing the early warning system. A decision was reached to contract consultants from all IGAD states to reflect on the recommendations from the workshop. The consultants were mandated to: identify national systems of early warning and conflict management; assess their strengths and weaknesses; and examine the possibility of linking such systems to similar mechanisms at the subregional, regional, and international levels.

The findings from the country-based studies were discussed at the second CEWARN workshop held in September 2000. Among the significant outputs of this meeting was the identification of four entry focus areas for IGAD's early warning work: pastoral communities and cattle rustling; small arms and environmental security; peace processes; and civil society. The meeting agreed to locate national early warning systems in each country's Ministry of Foreign Affairs. An examination of the agreement establishing IGAD revealed two principal problems: First, the treaty does not link CEWARN to other regional and early warning systems; and second, there is no clear decision making process within both the IGAD secretariat and the CEWARN mechanism itself. The September 2000 meeting recommended engaging a team of legal experts to examine and draw lessons from other early warning mechanisms, and to inform IGAD governments about the legal and institutional issues related to the establishment of CEWARN. The meeting also recommended the drafting of a Declaration of General Principles on the establishment of CEWARN and a protocol on early warning.

The third IGAD workshop on this issue was held in October 2000 and discussed both the Draft Declaration of Principles as well as the Draft Protocol on CEWARN. The meeting established a Bureau to facilitate the adoption of the

CEWARN programme and a Draft Declaration and Protocol on CEWARN. The proposed CEWARN protocol was discussed by IGAD's Council of Ministers and signed at its summit in January 2002. Still in its infancy, the IGAD early warning system faces two critical challenges: shaky political will and lack of technical capacity. Given that a CEWARN system will be based on the availability of information, some of which is sensitive, there is no provision for dealing with a state that is unwilling to facilitate the collection of relevant information. The chances of the mechanism succeeding depend almost entirely on the political co-operation of member states. Aside from the issue of political co-operation, IGAD's early warning system also lacks much of the infrastuctural support and technical capacity needed to collect and analyse relevant information and disseminate such information to its members. The CEWARN process has been funded by the US and German governments to the amount of $700 000.

The East African Community (EAC)

In November 1999, the Heads of State of Kenya, Uganda and Tanzania signed the treaty that reestablished the East African Community, which entered into force in July 2000. The three East African countries have a long history of regional co-operation dating back to the colonial period. Most significant among these organisations was the East African Community, which collapsed in 1977. The new treaty of 2000 was driven largely by the economic imperative to 'improve the standard of living of the population by facilitating an adequate and economically, socially and ecologically sustainable development process ... that allows an optimal utilisation of the available resources'. But the EAC also recognised that security and political stability are a prerequisite for sustainable development. Co-operation was partly conceived by EAC leaders as a strategy for conflict prevention. In their view, regional integration is a vehicle for regional peace. The ultimate aim of EAC co-operation is the establishment of a political federation to ensure 'a peaceful neighborhood'. Underpinning the EAC treaty is the notion that economic prosperity and regional integration will have the multiplier effect of reducing the possibility of conflict and enhancing security. Hence, a number of provisions in the treaty cast the EAC as an instrument of regional peace and security.

Security co-operation in the EAC

A Memorandum of Understanding on Common Defence and Security issues was drafted by EAC leaders in April 1998. At the time, it was thought that this memorandum could develop into a military pact. However, citing constraints relating to command structures and procedural irregularities, the Heads of State suggested that defense matters were best left for the last phase of co-operation. Nonetheless the EAC secretariat in Arusha, Tanzania has engaged in a range of confidence-building measures in the security sectors of its three members. While the Heads of State were reluctant to undertake common defense initiatives, they allowed the creation of a Defence Liaison unit within the secretariat, manned by three military defense attachés from each country. In 2000, EAC leaders signed a Memorandum of Understanding on Interstate Security, calling for the establishment of border committees between countries that experience cross-border clashes. EAC leaders have also called for harmonising policies on the treatment of refugees.

The EAC secretariat has facilitated regular visits by military personnel and has undertaken joint military training and exercises between its members. Together, these activities have introduced minimal elements of common procedure among armies with different histories. For instance, a series of joint natural fires training sessions organised in 1999, 2000 and 2001 enhanced the sharing of experiences and generated case studies to guide responses to disasters and to improve civil-military relations. The Defence College in Karen, Kenya, which trains senior officers from a number of countries in East, Central and Southern Africa, has introduced peacekeeping into its curriculum. For students from EAC countries, such training is useful for common operations and creates the possibility of the subregion contributing a regional force for future peacekeeping operations.

Operationalising a preventive model

The EAC secretariat is confining itself to facilitating meetings, selecting experts, and hosting deliberations between technical personnel from the three EAC countries on issues of mutual security concern. This method has two major advantages: first, it does not overwork the lean secretariat allowing to develop, design and implement its programmes; second, it ensures that ownership of the process remains with partner states. Networking between the EAC and other subregional organisations in Africa has been limited and has so far been confined largely to economic matters. In conflict-related issues, the EAC is attempting to learn from more experienced organisations such as ECOWAS and SADC. In March 2001, EAC officials visited Abuja to consult with their ECOWAS counterparts. The EAC secretariat has had more frequent exchanges of views with IGAD on a range of common security issues. The two organisations have produced a draft joint protocol on Small Arms and Light Weapons (SALW).

The EAC's emphasis on conflict prevention means that it can concentrate on a diplomatic approach to conflicts and avoid becoming embroiled in military conflicts. This is as much out of choice as necessity: the EAC, in any case, lacks the mechanism for dealing with armed conflicts. The organisation, however, provides an opportunity for NGOs to seek observer status in order to enhance their participation in its work. The challenge for the EAC's preventive model of conflict management is how to change negative state attitudes toward NGOs, some of which have the potential to complement government efforts in the area of conflict prevention. This task will require establishing a division of labour between the EAC secretariat, partner states and other actors. The EAC treaty provides for partnerships with civil society and observer status for NGOs interested in working with the secretariat. The EAC could also establish an NGO liaison office to mediate the relationship between governments and civil society. Currently, the EAC public relations office is expected to coordinate NGO-related activities. But this office is clearly too overburdened to perform this task effectively. There is also limited networking between the EAC's information unit and the defense liaison unit. Furthermore, there is an urgent need to strengthen the EAC's outreach programme, possibly through the hiring of an information officer who focuses solely on NGO activities, collects information on conflict management, and disseminates such information to member states and officials.

Having assessed the seven main regional and subregional organisations engaged in conflict management in Africa, we will now turn our attention to assessing the security capacity of semiformal organisations in Africa.

...

INTERNATIONAL CONFLICT RESOLUTION

Turning to the role of international conflict resolution mechanisms, the following extract by former UN Secretary-General Boutros Boutros Ghali outlines the various activities encompassed in preventive diplomacy, peacemaking, peacekeeping and post-conflict peacebuilding.

GHALI, BB *AN AGENDA FOR PEACE: PREVENTATIVE DIPLOMACY, PEACEMAKING AND PEACEKEEPING* (1992)

Full report available at http://www.un.org

...

Definitions

(20) The terms preventive diplomacy, peacemaking and peacekeeping are integrally related and as used in this report are defined as follows:

Preventive diplomacy is action to prevent disputes from arising between parties, to prevent existing disputes from escalating into conflicts and to limit the spread of the latter when they occur.

Peacemaking is action to bring hostile parties to agreement, essentially through such peaceful means as those foreseen in Chapter VI of the Charter of the United Nations.

Peacekeeping is the deployment of a United Nations presence in the field, hitherto with the consent of all the parties concerned, normally involving United Nations military and/or police personnel and frequently civilians as well. Peacekeeping is a technique that expands the possibilities for both the prevention of conflict and the making of peace.

(21) The present report in addition will address the critically related concept of post-conflict peacebuilding action to identify and support structures which will tend to strengthen and solidify peace in order to avoid a relapse into conflict. Preventive diplomacy seeks to resolve disputes before violence breaks out; peacemaking and peacekeeping are required to halt conflicts and

preserve peace once it is attained. If successful, they strengthen the opportunity for post-conflict peacebuilding, which can prevent the recurrence of violence among nations and peoples.

(22) These four areas for action, taken together, and carried out with the backing of all Members, offer a coherent contribution towards securing peace in the spirit of the Charter. The United Nations has extensive experience not only in these fields, but in the wider realm of work for peace in which these four fields are set. Initiatives on decolonisation, on the environment and sustainable development, on population, on the eradication of disease, on disarmament and on the growth of international law – these and many others have contributed immeasurably to the foundations for a peaceful world. The world has often been rent by conflict and plagued by massive human suffering and deprivation. Yet it would have been far more so without the continuing efforts of the United Nations. This wide experience must be taken into account in assessing the potential of the United Nations in maintaining international security not only in its traditional sense, but in the new dimensions presented by the era ahead.

Preventive diplomacy

(23) The most desirable and efficient employment of diplomacy is to ease tensions before they result in conflict – or, if conflict breaks out, to act swiftly to contain it and resolve its underlying causes. Preventive diplomacy may be performed by the Secretary-General personally or through senior staff or specialised agencies and programmes, by the Security Council or the General Assembly, and by regional organisations in co-operation with the United Nations. Preventive diplomacy requires measures to create confidence; it needs early warning based on information gathering and informal or formal fact-finding; it may also involve preventive deployment and, in some situations, demilitarised zones.

Measures to build confidence

(24) Mutual confidence and good faith are essential to reducing the likelihood of conflict between States. Many such measures are available to Governments that have the will to employ them. Systematic exchange of military missions, formation of regional or subregional risk reduction centres, arrangements for the free flow of information, including the monitoring of regional arms agreements, are examples. I ask all regional organisations to consider what further confidence-building measures might be applied in their areas and to inform the United Nations of the results. I will undertake periodic consultations on confidence-building measures with parties to potential, current or past disputes and with regional organisations, offering such advisory assistance as the Secretariat can provide.

Fact-finding

(25) Preventive steps must be based upon timely and accurate knowledge of the facts. Beyond this, an understanding of developments and global trends, based on sound analysis, is required. And the willingness to take appropriate preventive action is essential. Given the economic and social roots of many

potential conflicts, the information needed by the United Nations now must encompass economic and social trends as well as political developments that may lead to dangerous tensions.

(a) An increased resort to fact-finding is needed, in accordance with the Charter, initiated either by the Secretary-General, to enable him to meet his responsibilities under the Charter, including article 99, or by the Security Council or the General Assembly. Various forms may be employed selectively as the situation requires. A request by a State for the sending of a United Nations fact-finding mission to its territory should be considered without undue delay.

(b) Contacts with the Governments of member states can provide the Secretary-General with detailed information on issues of concern. I ask that all member states be ready to provide the information needed for effective preventive diplomacy. I will supplement my own contacts by regularly sending senior officials on missions for consultations in capitals or other locations. Such contacts are essential to gain insight into a situation and to assess its potential ramifications.

(c) Formal fact-finding can be mandated by the Security Council or by the General Assembly, either of which may elect to send a mission under its immediate authority or may invite the Secretary-General to take the necessary steps, including the designation of a special envoy. In addition to collecting information on which a decision for further action can be taken, such a mission can in some instances help to defuse a dispute by its presence, indicating to the parties that the Organization, and in particular the Security Council, is actively seized of the matter as a present or potential threat to international security.

(d) In exceptional circumstances the Council may meet away from Headquarters as the Charter provides, in order not only to inform itself directly, but also to bring the authority of the Organization to bear on a given situation.

Early warning

(26) In recent years the United Nations system has been developing a valuable network of early warning systems concerning environmental threats, the risk of nuclear accident, natural disasters, mass movements of populations, the threat of famine and the spread of disease. There is a need, however, to strengthen arrangements in such a manner that information from these sources can be synthesised with political indicators to assess whether a threat to peace exists and to analyse what action might be taken by the United Nations to alleviate it. This is a process that will continue to require the close co-operation of the various specialised agencies and functional offices of the United Nations. The analyses and recommendations for preventive action that emerge will be made available by me, as appropriate, to the Security Council and other United Nations organs. I recommend in addition that the Security Council invite a reinvigorated and restructured Economic and Social Council to provide reports, in accordance with article 65 of the Charter, on those economic and social developments that may, unless mitigated, threaten international peace and security.

(27) Regional arrangements and organisations have an important role in early warning. I ask regional organisations that have not yet sought observer status

at the United Nations to do so and to be linked, through appropriate arrangements, with the security mechanisms of this Organization.

Preventive deployment

(28) United Nations operations in areas of crisis have generally been established after conflict has occurred. The time has come to plan for circumstances warranting preventive deployment, which could take place in a variety of instances and ways. For example, in conditions of national crisis there could be preventive deployment at the request of the Government or all parties concerned, or with their consent; in inter-State disputes such deployment could take place when two countries feel that a United Nations presence on both sides of their border can discourage hostilities; furthermore, preventive deployment could take place when a country feels threatened and requests the deployment of an appropriate United Nations presence along its side of the border alone. In each situation, the mandate and composition of the United Nations presence would need to be carefully devised and be clear to all.

(29) In conditions of crisis within a country, when the Government requests or all parties consent, preventive deployment could help in a number of ways to alleviate suffering and to limit or control violence. Humanitarian assistance, impartially provided, could be of critical importance; assistance in maintaining security, whether through military, police or civilian personnel, could save lives and develop conditions of safety in which negotiations can be held; the United Nations could also help in conciliation efforts if this should be the wish of the parties. In certain circumstances, the United Nations may well need to draw upon the specialised skills and resources of various parts of the United Nations system; such operations may also on occasion require the participation of non-governmental organisations.

(30) In these situations of internal crisis the United Nations will need to respect the sovereignty of the State; to do otherwise would not be in accordance with the understanding of member states in accepting the principles of the Charter. The Organization must remain mindful of the carefully negotiated balance of the guiding principles annexed to General Assembly Resolution 46/182 of 19 December 1991. Those guidelines stressed, *inter alia*, that humanitarian assistance must be provided in accordance with the principles of humanity, neutrality and impartiality; that the sovereignty, territorial integrity and national unity of States must be fully respected in accordance with the Charter of the United Nations; and that, in this context, humanitarian assistance should be provided with the consent of the affected country and, in principle, on the basis of an appeal by that country. The guidelines also stressed the responsibility of States to take care of the victims of emergencies occurring on their territory and the need for access to those requiring humanitarian assistance. In the light of these guidelines, a Government's request for United Nations involvement, or consent to it, would not be an infringement of that State's sovereignty or be contrary to article 2, paragraph 7, of the Charter which refers to matters essentially within the domestic jurisdiction of any State.

(31) In inter-State disputes, when both parties agree, I recommend that if the Security Council concludes that the likelihood of hostilities between neighbouring countries could be removed by the preventive deployment of a United Nations presence on the territory of each State, such action should be taken. The nature of the tasks to be performed would determine the composition of the United Nations presence.

(32) In cases where one nation fears a cross-border attack, if the Security Council concludes that a United Nations presence on one side of the border, with the consent only of the requesting country, would serve to deter conflict, I recommend that preventive deployment take place. Here again, the specific nature of the situation would determine the mandate and the personnel required to fulfil it.

Demilitarised zones

(33) In the past, demilitarised zones have been established by agreement of the parties at the conclusion of a conflict. In addition to the deployment of United Nations personnel in such zones as part of peacekeeping operations, consideration should now be given to the usefulness of such zones as a form of preventive deployment, on both sides of a border, with the agreement of the two parties, as a means of separating potential belligerents, or on one side of the line, at the request of one party, for the purpose of removing any pretext for attack. Demilitarised zones would serve as symbols of the international community's concern that conflict be prevented.

Peacemaking

(34) Between the tasks of seeking to prevent conflict and keeping the peace lies the responsibility to try to bring hostile parties to agreement by peaceful means. Chapter VI of the Charter sets forth a comprehensive list of such means for the resolution of conflict. These have been amplified in various declarations adopted by the General Assembly, including the Manila Declaration of 1982 on the Peaceful Settlement of International Disputes and the 1988 Declaration on the Prevention and Removal of Disputes and Situations Which May Threaten International Peace and Security and on the Role of the United Nations in this Field. They have also been the subject of various resolutions of the General Assembly, including Resolution 44/21 of 15 November 1989 on enhancing international peace, security and international co-operation in all its aspects in accordance with the Charter of the United Nations. The United Nations has had wide experience in the application of these peaceful means. If conflicts have gone unresolved, it is not because techniques for peaceful settlement were unknown or inadequate. The fault lies first in the lack of political will of parties to seek a solution to their differences through such means as are suggested in Chapter VI of the Charter, and second, in the lack of leverage at the disposal of a third party if this is the procedure chosen. The indifference of the international community to a problem, or the marginalisation of it, can also thwart the possibilities of solution. We must look primarily to these areas if we hope to enhance the capacity of the Organization for achieving peaceful settlements.

(35) The present determination in the Security Council to resolve international disputes in the manner foreseen in the Charter has opened the way for a more active Council role. With greater unity has come leverage and persuasive power to lead hostile parties towards negotiations. I urge the Council to take full advantage of the provisions of the Charter under which it may recommend appropriate procedures or methods for dispute settlement and, if all the parties to a dispute so request, make recommendations to the parties for a pacific settlement of the dispute.

(36) The General Assembly, like the Security Council and the Secretary-General, also has an important role assigned to it under the Charter for the maintenance of international peace and security. As a universal forum, its capacity to consider and recommend appropriate action must be recognised. To that end it is essential to promote its utilisation by all member states so as to bring greater influence to bear in pre-empting or containing situations which are likely to threaten international peace and security.

(37) Mediation and negotiation can be undertaken by an individual designated by the Security Council, by the General Assembly or by the Secretary-General. There is a long history of the utilisation by the United Nations of distinguished statesmen to facilitate the processes of peace. They can bring a personal prestige that, in addition to their experience, can encourage the parties to enter serious negotiations. There is a wide willingness to serve in this capacity, from which I shall continue to benefit as the need arises. Frequently it is the Secretary-General himself who undertakes the task. While the mediator's effectiveness is enhanced by strong and evident support from the Council, the General Assembly and the relevant member states acting in their national capacity, the good offices of the Secretary-General may at times be employed most effectively when conducted independently of the deliberative bodies. Close and continuous consultation between the Secretary-General and the Security Council is, however, essential to ensure full awareness of how the Council's influence can best be applied and to develop a common strategy for the peaceful settlement of specific disputes.

The World Court

(38) The docket of the International Court of Justice has grown fuller but it remains an under-used resource for the peaceful adjudication of disputes. Greater reliance on the Court would be an important contribution to United Nations peacemaking. In this connection, I call attention to the power of the Security Council under articles 36 and 37 of the Charter to recommend to member states the submission of a dispute to the International Court of Justice, arbitration or other dispute-settlement mechanisms. I recommend that the Secretary-General be authorised, pursuant to article 96, paragraph 2, of the Charter, to take advantage of the advisory competence of the Court and that other United Nations organs that already enjoy such authorisation turn to the Court more frequently for advisory opinions.

(39) I recommend the following steps to reinforce the role of the International Court of Justice:

(a) All member states should accept the general jurisdiction of the International Court under article 36 of its Statute, without any reservation, before the end of the United Nations Decade of International Law in the year 2000. In instances where domestic structures prevent this, States should agree bilaterally or multilaterally to a comprehensive list of matters they are willing to submit to the Court and should withdraw their reservations to its jurisdiction in the dispute settlement clauses of multilateral treaties;
(b) When submission of a dispute to the full Court is not practical, the Chambers jurisdiction should be used;
(c) States should support the Trust Fund established to assist countries unable to afford the cost involved in bringing a dispute to the Court, and such countries should take full advantage of the Fund in order to resolve their disputes.

Amelioration through assistance

(40) Peacemaking is at times facilitated by international action to ameliorate circumstances that have contributed to the dispute or conflict. If, for instance, assistance to displaced persons within a society is essential to a solution, then the United Nations should be able to draw upon the resources of all agencies and programmes concerned. At present, there is no adequate mechanism in the United Nations through which the Security Council, the General Assembly or the Secretary-General can mobilise the resources needed for such positive leverage and engage the collective efforts of the United Nations system for the peaceful resolution of a conflict. I have raised this concept in the Administrative Committee on Co-ordination, which brings together the executive heads of United Nations agencies and programmes; we are exploring methods by which the inter-agency system can improve its contribution to the peaceful resolution of disputes.

Sanctions and special economic problems

(41) In circumstances when peacemaking requires the imposition of sanctions under article 41 of the Charter, it is important that States confronted with special economic problems not only have the right to consult the Security Council regarding such problems, as article 50 provides, but also have a realistic possibility of having their difficulties addressed. I recommend that the Security Council devise a set of measures involving the financial institutions and other components of the United Nations system that can be put in place to insulate States from such difficulties. Such measures would be a matter of equity and a means of encouraging States to co-operate with decisions of the Council.

Use of military force

(42) It is the essence of the concept of collective security as contained in the Charter that if peaceful means fail, the measures provided in Chapter VII should be used, on the decision of the Security Council, to maintain or restore international peace and security in the face of a 'threat to the peace, breach of the peace, or act of aggression'. The Security Council has not so far made use of the most coercive of these measures – the action by military force foreseen in article 42. In the situation between Iraq and Kuwait, the Council chose to authorise member states to take measures on its behalf. The

Charter, however, provides a detailed approach which now merits the attention of all member states.

(43) Under article 42 of the Charter, the Security Council has the authority to take military action to maintain or restore international peace and security. While such action should only be taken when all peaceful means have failed, the option of taking it is essential to the credibility of the United Nations as a guarantor of international security. This will require bringing into being, through negotiations, the special agreements foreseen in article 43 of the Charter, whereby member states undertake to make armed forces, assistance and facilities available to the Security Council for the purposes stated in article 42, not only on an *ad hoc* basis but on a permanent basis. Under the political circumstances that now exist for the first time since the Charter was adopted, the long-standing obstacles to the conclusion of such special agreements should no longer prevail. The ready availability of armed forces on call could serve, in itself, as a means of deterring breaches of the peace since a potential aggressor would know that the Council had at its disposal a means of response. Forces under article 43 may perhaps never be sufficiently large or well enough equipped to deal with a threat from a major army equipped with sophisticated weapons. They would be useful, however, in meeting any threat posed by a military force of a lesser order. I recommend that the Security Council initiate negotiations in accordance with article 43, supported by the Military Staff Committee, which may be augmented if necessary by others in accordance with article 47, paragraph 2, of the Charter. It is my view that the role of the Military Staff Committee should be seen in the context of chapter VII, and not that of the planning or conduct of peacekeeping operations.

Peace-enforcement units

(44) The mission of forces under article 43 would be to respond to outright aggression, imminent or actual. Such forces are not likely to be available for some time to come. Cease-fires have often been agreed to but not complied with, and the United Nations has sometimes been called upon to send forces to restore and maintain the cease-fire. This task can on occasion exceed the mission of peacekeeping forces and the expectations of peacekeeping force contributors. I recommend that the Council consider the utilisation of peace-enforcement units in clearly defined circumstances and with their terms of reference specified in advance. Such units from member states would be available on call and would consist of troops that have volunteered for such service. They would have to be more heavily armed than peacekeeping forces and would need to undergo extensive preparatory training within their national forces. Deployment and operation of such forces would be under the authorisation of the Security Council and would, as in the case of peacekeeping forces, be under the command of the Secretary-General. I consider such peace-enforcement units to be warranted as a provisional measure under article 40 of the Charter. Such peace-enforcement units should not be confused with the forces that may eventually be constituted under article 43 to deal with acts of aggression or with the military personnel which Governments may agree to keep on stand-by for possible contribution to peacekeeping operations.

(45) Just as diplomacy will continue across the span of all the activities dealt with in the present report, so there may not be a dividing line between peacemaking and peacekeeping. Peacemaking is often a prelude to peacekeeping – just as the deployment of a United Nations presence in the field may expand possibilities for the prevention of conflict, facilitate the work of peacemaking and in many cases serve as a prerequisite for peacebuilding.

Peacekeeping

(46) Peacekeeping can rightly be called the invention of the United Nations. It has brought a degree of stability to numerous areas of tension around the world.

Increasing demands

(47) Thirteen peacekeeping operations were established between the years 1945 and 1987; 13 others since then. An estimated 528 000 military, police and civilian personnel had served under the flag of the United Nations until January 1992. Over 800 of them from 43 countries have died in the service of the Organization. The costs of these operations have aggregated some $8.3 billion till 1992. The unpaid arrears towards them stand at over $800 million, which represents a debt owed by the Organization to the troop-contributing countries. Peacekeeping operations approved at present are estimated to cost close to $3 billion in the current 12-month period, while patterns of payment are unacceptably slow. Against this, global defence expenditures at the end of the last decade had approached $1 trillion a year, or $2 million per minute.

(48) The contrast between the costs of United Nations peacekeeping and the costs of the alternative, war – between the demands of the Organization and the means provided to meet them – would be farcical were the consequences not so damaging to global stability and to the credibility of the Organization. At a time when nations and peoples increasingly are looking to the United Nations for assistance in keeping the peace – and holding it responsible when this cannot be so – fundamental decisions must be taken to enhance the capacity of the Organization in this innovative and productive exercise of its function. I am conscious that the present volume and unpredictability of peacekeeping assessments poses real problems for some member states. For this reason, I strongly support proposals in some member states for their peacekeeping contributions to be financed from defence, rather than foreign affairs, budgets and I recommend such action to others. I urge the General Assembly to encourage this approach.

(49) The demands on the United Nations for peacekeeping, and peacebuilding, operations will in the coming years continue to challenge the capacity, the political and financial will and the creativity of the Secretariat and member states. Like the Security Council, I welcome the increase and broadening of the tasks of peacekeeping operations.

New departures in peacekeeping

(50) The nature of peacekeeping operations has evolved rapidly in recent years. The established principles and practices of peacekeeping have responded flexibly to new demands of recent years, and the basic conditions for success remain unchanged: a clear and practicable mandate; the co-operation of the parties in implementing that mandate; the continuing support of the Security Council; the readiness of member states to contribute the military, police and civilian personnel, including specialists, required; effective United Nations command at Headquarters and in the field; and adequate financial and logistic support. As the international climate has changed and peacekeeping operations are increasingly fielded to help implement settlements that have been negotiated by peacemakers, a new array of demands and problems has emerged regarding logistics, equipment, personnel and finance, all of which could be corrected if member states so wished and were ready to make the necessary resources available.

Personnel

(51) Member states are keen to participate in peacekeeping operations. Military observers and infantry are invariably available in the required numbers, but logistic units present a greater problem, as few armies can afford to spare such units for an extended period. member states were requested in 1990 to state what military personnel they were in principle prepared to make available; few replied. I reiterate the request to all member states to reply frankly and promptly. Stand-by arrangements should be confirmed, as appropriate, through exchanges of letters between the Secretariat and member states concerning the kind and number of skilled personnel they will be prepared to offer the United Nations as the needs of new operations arise.

(52) Increasingly, peacekeeping requires that civilian political officers, human rights monitors, electoral officials, refugee and humanitarian aid specialists and police play as central a role as the military. Police personnel have proved increasingly difficult to obtain in the numbers required. I recommend that arrangements be reviewed and improved for training peacekeeping personnel – civilian, police, or military – using the varied capabilities of Member State Governments, of non-governmental organisations and the facilities of the Secretariat. As efforts go forward to include additional States as contributors, some States with considerable potential should focus on language training for police contingents which may serve with the Organization. As for the United Nations itself, special personnel procedures, including incentives, should be instituted to permit the rapid transfer of Secretariat staff members to service with peacekeeping operations. The strength and capability of military staff serving in the Secretariat should be augmented to meet new and heavier requirements.

Logistics

(53) Not all Governments can provide their battalions with the equipment they need for service abroad. While some equipment is provided by troop-contributing countries, a great deal has to come from the United Nations,

including equipment to fill gaps in under-equipped national units. The United Nations has no standing stock of such equipment. Orders must be placed with manufacturers, which creates a number of difficulties. A pre-positioned stock of basic peacekeeping equipment should be established, so that at least some vehicles, communications equipment, generators, etc, would be immediately available at the start of an operation. Alternatively, Governments should commit themselves to keeping certain equipment, specified by the Secretary-General, on stand-by for immediate sale, loan or donation to the United Nations when required.

(54) Member states in a position to do so should make air- and sea-lift capacity available to the United Nations free of cost or at lower than commercial rates, as was the practice until recently.

Post-conflict peacebuilding

(55) Peacemaking and peacekeeping operations, to be truly successful, must come to include comprehensive efforts to identify and support structures which will tend to consolidate peace and advance a sense of confidence and well-being among people. Through agreements ending civil strife, these may include disarming the previously warring parties and the restoration of order, the custody and possible destruction of weapons, repatriating refugees, advisory and training support for security personnel, monitoring elections, advancing efforts to protect human rights, reforming or strengthening governmental institutions and promoting formal and informal processes of political participation.

(56) In the aftermath of international war, post-conflict peacebuilding may take the form of concrete cooperative projects which link two or more countries in a mutually beneficial undertaking that can not only contribute to economic and social development but also enhance the confidence that is so fundamental to peace. I have in mind, for example, projects that bring States together to develop agriculture, improve transportation or utilise resources such as water or electricity that they need to share, or joint programmes through which barriers between nations are brought down by means of freer travel, cultural exchanges and mutually beneficial youth and educational projects. Reducing hostile perceptions through educational exchanges and curriculum reform may be essential to forestall a re-emergence of cultural and national tensions which could spark renewed hostilities.

(57) In surveying the range of efforts for peace, the concept of peacebuilding as the construction of a new environment should be viewed as the counterpart of preventive diplomacy, which seeks to avoid the breakdown of peaceful conditions. When conflict breaks out, mutually reinforcing efforts at peacemaking and peacekeeping come into play. Once these have achieved their objectives, only sustained, cooperative work to deal with underlying economic, social, cultural and humanitarian problems can place an achieved peace on a durable foundation. Preventive diplomacy is to avoid a crisis; post-conflict peacebuilding is to prevent a recurrence.

(58) Increasingly it is evident that peacebuilding after civil or international strife must address the serious problem of land mines, many tens of millions

of which remain scattered in present or former combat zones. De-mining should be emphasised in the terms of reference of peacekeeping operations and is crucially important in the restoration of activity when peacebuilding is under way: Agriculture cannot be revived without de-mining and the restoration of transport may require the laying of hard surface roads to prevent re-mining. In such instances, the link becomes evident between peacekeeping and peacebuilding. Just as demilitarised zones may serve the cause of preventive diplomacy and preventive deployment to avoid conflict, so may demilitarisation assist in keeping the peace or in post-conflict peacebuilding, as a measure for heightening the sense of security and encouraging the parties to turn their energies to the work of peaceful restoration of their societies.

(59) There is a new requirement for technical assistance which the United Nations has an obligation to develop and provide when requested: support for the transformation of deficient national structures and capabilities, and for the strengthening of new democratic institutions. The authority of the United Nations system to act in this field would rest on the consensus that social peace is as important as strategic or political peace. There is an obvious connection between democratic practices – such as the rule of law and transparency in decision-making – and the achievement of true peace and security in any new and stable political order. These elements of good governance need to be promoted at all levels of international and national political communities.

...

While recognising the dilemma posed by humanitarian intervention, Annan underscores the role and moral duty of the United Nations Security Council to act on behalf of the international community, particularly in situations where mass murder and other crimes against humanity occur.

ANNAN, K *WE THE PEOPLES: THE ROLE OF THE UNITED NATIONS IN THE 21st CENTURY* (2000)

Full report available at www.un.org

...

Addressing the dilemma of intervention

In my address to the General Assembly last September, I called on member states to unite in the pursuit of more effective policies to stop organised mass murder and egregious violations of human rights. Although I emphasised that intervention embraced a wide continuum of responses, from diplomacy to armed action, it was the latter option that generated most controversy in the debate that followed.

Some critics were concerned that the concept of 'humanitarian intervention' could become a cover for gratuitous interference in the internal affairs of sovereign states. Others felt that it might encourage secessionist movements deliberately to provoke governments into committing gross violations of human rights in order to trigger external interventions that would aid their cause. Still others noted that there is little consistency in the practice of intervention, owing to its inherent difficulties and costs as well as perceived national interests – except that weak states are far more likely to be subjected to it than strong ones.

I recognise both the force and the importance of these arguments. I also accept that the principles of sovereignty and non-interference offer vital protection to small and weak states. But to the critics I would pose this question: if humanitarian intervention is, indeed, an unacceptable assault on sovereignty, how should we respond to a Rwanda, to a Srebrenica – to gross and systematic violations of human rights that offend every precept of our common humanity?

We confront a real dilemma. Few would disagree that both the defence of humanity and the defence of sovereignty are principles that must be supported. Alas, that does not tell us which principle should prevail when they are in conflict.

Humanitarian intervention is a sensitive issue, fraught with political difficulty and not susceptible to easy answers. But surely no legal principle – not even sovereignty – can ever shield crimes against humanity. Where such crimes occur and peaceful attempts to halt them have been exhausted, the Security Council has a moral duty to act on behalf of the international community. The fact that we cannot protect people everywhere is no reason for doing nothing when we can. Armed intervention must always remain the option of last resort, but in the face of mass murder it is an option that cannot be relinquished.

...

The UN has the responsibility to protect the world from war. Central to this responsibility is the prevention of conflict. However, in the event that this fails, the UN has the duty to intervene as a means of protection, particularly of civilians. The following excerpt from the International Commission on Intervention and State Sovereignty outlines the principles, as well as thresholds to determine such intervention.

THE RESPONSIBILITY TO PROTECT (2001)

Report of the International Commission on Intervention and State Sovereignty

Full report available at http://www.iciss.ca/report-en.asp

...

The responsibility to protect: Core principles

(1) Basic principles

A. State sovereignty implies responsibility, and the primary responsibility for the protection of its people lies with the state itself;
B. Where a population is suffering serious harm, as a result of internal war, insurgency, repression or state failure, and the state in question is unwilling or unable to halt or avert it, the principle of non-intervention yields to the international responsibility to protect.

(2) Foundations

The foundations of the responsibility to protect, as a guiding principle for the international community of states, lie in:
A. Obligations inherent in the concept of sovereignty;
B. The responsibility of the Security Council, under article 24 of the UN Charter, for the maintenance of international peace and security;
C. Specific legal obligations under human rights and human protection declarations, covenants and treaties, international humanitarian law and national law;
D. The developing practice of states, regional organisations and the Security Council itself.

(3) Elements

The responsibility to protect embraces three specific responsibilities:
A. The responsibility to prevent: To address both the root causes and direct causes of internal conflict and other man-made crises putting populations at risk;
B. The responsibility to react: To respond to situations of compelling human need with appropriate measures, which may include coercive measures like sanctions and international prosecution, and in extreme cases military intervention;
C. The responsibility to rebuild: To provide, particularly after a military intervention, full assistance with recovery, reconstruction and reconciliation, addressing the causes of the harm the intervention was designed to halt or avert.

(4) Priorities

A. Prevention is the single most important dimension of the responsibility to protect: Prevention options should always be exhausted before intervention is contemplated, and more commitment and resources must be devoted to it;
B. The exercise of the responsibility to both prevent and react should always involve less intrusive and coercive measures being considered before more coercive and intrusive ones are applied.

Principles for military intervention

(1) The just cause threshold

Military intervention for human protection purposes is an exceptional and extraordinary measure. To be warranted, there must be serious and irreparable harm occurring to human beings, or imminently likely to occur, of the following kind:
A. Large scale loss of life, actual or apprehended, with genocidal intent or not, which is the product either of deliberate state action, or state neglect or inability to act, or a failed state situation; or
B. Large scale 'ethnic cleansing', actual or apprehended, whether carried out by killing, forced expulsion, acts of terror or rape.

(2) The precautionary principles

A. Right intention: The primary purpose of the intervention, whatever other motives intervening states may have, must be to halt or avert human suffering. Right intention is better assured with multilateral operations, clearly supported by regional opinion and the victims concerned;
B. Last resort: Military intervention can only be justified when every non-military option for the prevention or peaceful resolution of the crisis has been explored, with reasonable grounds for believing lesser measures would not have succeeded;
C. Proportional means: The scale, duration and intensity of the planned military intervention should be the minimum necessary to secure the defined human protection objective;
D. Reasonable prospects: There must be a reasonable chance of success in halting or averting the suffering which has justified the intervention, with the consequences of action not likely to be worse than the consequences of inaction.

(3) Right authority

A. There is no better or more appropriate body than the United Nations Security Council to authorise military intervention for human protection purposes. The task is not to find alternatives to the Security Council as a source of authority, but to make the Security Council work better than it has;
B. Security Council authorisation should in all cases be sought prior to any military intervention action being carried out. Those calling for an intervention should formally request such authorisation, or have the Council raise the matter on its own initiative, or have the Secretary-General raise it under article 99 of the UN Charter;
C. The Security Council should deal promptly with any request for authority to intervene where there are allegations of large scale loss of human life or ethnic cleansing. It should in this context seek adequate verification of facts or conditions on the ground that might support a military intervention;
D. The Permanent Five members of the Security Council should agree not to apply their veto power, in matters where their vital state interests are not involved, to obstruct the passage of resolutions authorising military intervention for human protection purposes for which there is otherwise majority support;

E. If the Security Council rejects a proposal or fails to deal with it in a reasonable time, alternative options are:

(i) consideration of the matter by the General Assembly in Emergency Special Session under the 'Uniting for Peace' procedure; and

(ii) action within area of jurisdiction by regional or sub-regional organisations under Chapter VIII of the Charter, subject to their seeking subsequent authorisation from the Security Council.

F. The Security Council should take into account in all its deliberations that, if it fails to discharge its responsibility to protect in conscience-shocking situations crying out for action, concerned states may not rule out other means to meet the gravity and urgency of that situation – and that the stature and credibility of the United Nations may suffer thereby.

(4) Operational principles

A. Clear objectives; clear and unambiguous mandate at all times; and resources to match;

B. Common military approach among involved partners; unity of command; clear and unequivocal communications and chain of command;

C. Acceptance of limitations, incrementalism and gradualism in the application of force, the objective being protection of a population, not defeat of a state;

D. Rules of engagement which fit the operational concept; are precise; reflect the principle of proportionality; and involve total adherence to international humanitarian law;

E. Acceptance that force protection cannot become the principal objective;

F. Maximum possible co-ordination with humanitarian organisations.

...

2.1 Millions of human beings remain at the mercy of civil wars, insurgencies, state repression and state collapse. This is a stark and undeniable reality, and it is at the heart of all the issues with which this Commission has been wrestling. What is at stake here is not making the world safe for big powers, or trampling over the sovereign rights of small ones, but delivering practical protection for ordinary people, at risk of their lives, because their states are unwilling or unable to protect them.

2.2 But all this is easier said than done. There have been as many failures as successes, perhaps more, in the international protective record in recent years. There are continuing fears about a 'right to intervene' being formally acknowledged. If intervention for human protection purposes is to be accepted, including the possibility of military action, it remains imperative that the international community develop consistent, credible and enforceable standards to guide state and intergovernmental practice. The experience and aftermath of Somalia, Rwanda, Srebrenica and Kosovo, as well as interventions and non-interventions in a number of other places, have provided a clear indication that the tools, devices and thinking of international relations need now to be comprehensively reassessed, in order to meet the foreseeable needs of the 21st century.

2.3 Any new approach to intervention on human protection grounds needs to meet at least four basic objectives:

- to establish clearer rules, procedures and criteria for determining whether, when and how to intervene;
- to establish the legitimacy of military intervention when necessary and after all other approaches have failed;
- to ensure that military intervention, when it occurs, is carried out only for the purposes proposed, is effective, and is undertaken with proper concern to minimise the human costs and institutional damage that will result; and
- to help eliminate, where possible, the causes of conflict while enhancing the prospects for durable and sustainable peace.

We spell out in detail how these objectives might be met. But there is a significant preliminary issue which must first be addressed. It is important that language — and the concepts which lie behind particular choices of words — do not become a barrier to dealing with the real issues involved. Just as the Commission found that the expression 'humanitarian intervention' did not help to carry the debate forward, so too do we believe that the language of past debates arguing for or against a 'right to intervene' by one state on the territory of another state is outdated and unhelpful. We prefer to talk not of a 'right to intervene' but of a 'responsibility to protect'....

In spite of these international standards and principles, the application of humanitarian intervention has been inconsistent with Africa carrying a majority of the 'forgotten tragedies'. In the words of Louis, the respectability of humanitarian intervention is being called in question by the current approaches that mainly serve the interests of the major powers.

LOUIS, PA 'INCONSISTENCY AND THE TRAGEDY OF AFRICA'S NEGLECT' (2001)

Carnegie Council on Ethics and International Affairs *Human Rights Dialogue: Human Rights in Times of Conflict: Humanitarian Intervention* Series 2, Number 5

The concept of humanitarian intervention is based on the alleviation of human rights violations. Recent actions in Sierra Leone and Kosovo, however, suggest that the practice of humanitarian intervention has less to do with stopping abuses than with furthering the interests of the intervening powers and their advocates. As a member of both the United Nations observer mission in Sierra Leone and the interim administration in Kosovo, I was able to witness the contrasting approaches to humanitarian intervention in those two arenas of conflict.

Nigeria, the West African powerhouse, spent considerable human and financial resources to help neutralise a murderous rebellion in Sierra Leone that has caused untold violations of human rights and international humanitarian law. The Nigerian model of humanitarian intervention was marked by a robust use of force to compel the rebels to accept the legitimacy of the elected government. As a regional power with its own human rights problems and a lethargic economy, however, Nigeria needed the assistance of the international community. Since the United States, Britain, and the other permanent members of the UN Security Council had no interests worth pursuing in a poor African country, the international community paid little attention to the plight of the people of Sierra Leone. The largely ill-equipped – if determined – Nigerians and a few hundred Ghanaians, Guineans, and Malians were left to their own meager resources to stanch a humanitarian crisis of unimaginable proportions.

The eventual establishment of a UN peacekeeping force in Sierra Leone following the Lomé Agreement of July 1999 has not changed matters much. Sierra Leoneans have yet to reap the fruits of that intervention; certainly it lacked the robustness of the purported humanitarian intervention in Kosovo. There, from March through June 1999, scarcely two million residents benefited from a horrifying bombing campaign of Yugoslavia, which involved million-dollar missiles and other high-tech weaponry. In the aftermath of the bombing, 40 000 NATO troops deployed in Kosovo have provided protection and other assistance. At the peak of the crisis, NGOs and UN agencies showered the Kosovar refugees with cellular telephones, bottled water, cigarettes, and other amenities. Humanitarian workers and other Western experts crowded the television screens to register their incredulity and outrage that this could happen in Europe on the eve of the twenty-first century.

Meanwhile, the plight of African refugees, who often fled the same kind of ethnic violence as the Kosovar Albanians, faded from the world's consciousness as these refugees tried to survive on the crumbs left over from the Kosovo operation. The United Nations had to scramble to find 13 500 troops and the funds to support the operation in Sierra Leone, a country with nearly six million inhabitants. The US Committee for Refugees estimated that international agencies and NGOs spent 11 cents per Sierra Leonean refugee versus $1.50 per Kosovar refugee. Though I did see destroyed villages in Kosovo, I saw nothing like the wide expanses of burned towns (including Freetown, the capital), amputee camps, droves of sex slaves, and child soldiers that continue to flourish in Sierra Leone. Thus, the concentration of resources devoted to Kosovo and the multiplicity of the actors involved seems excessive when contrasted to the Band-Aid applied to Sierra Leone. This point is not lost on those Sierra Leoneans who are aware of the situation in Kosovo. Even Mary Robinson, the UN High Commissioner for Human Rights, implied at the start of her three-day visit to Sierra Leone in June 1999 that there were disparities in treatment. She acknowledged that there had been more suffering, more loss of life, and more human rights violations in Sierra Leone than in Kosovo.

At the NGO level as well, the attention given to the two populations was shockingly disparate. While working in Sierra Leone as a human rights officer for the UN observer mission, I met a representative of a major international human rights organisation, a US citizen who said that formerly she had been a journalist. Her chief task consisted of monitoring the human rights situation and writing reports. My conversations with her revealed that she possessed little credible experience in Africa and virtually no human rights experience. In Kosovo, by contrast, I met seasoned workers who came to alleviate the plight of the suffering Kosovars. I believe this reinforces the appearance that international NGOs send people to Africa who are seeking only to find themselves and to establish a reputation.

Judging by the disparity between operations in Sierra Leone and Kosovo, not to mention the criminal failure of the international community, under US leadership, to act in Rwanda, humanitarian intervention remains tinged with racialism and the assertion of power to further imperialist aims. Sierra Leone represents a shameful example of disregarding the plight of long-suffering black Africans; Kosovo, on the other hand, appears as a shining and dangerous example of a power foreign to a region, NATO, seeking to find a *raison d'être* in the post-Cold War era. NATO demonstrated its might, lest its imagined adversaries fail to appreciate the 'new world order'.

Reasonable people can disagree about the proper criteria for humanitarian intervention. But if genocide in Rwanda and the horrors of Sierra Leone do not qualify for attention from those countries with the capacity to provide the necessary assistance, then the notion of humanitarian intervention has no validity. Those who doubt the truth of my assertions should re-examine just what is so special about the nature of suffering in Kosovo versus that of African countries in even deeper turmoil. What justifies continuing the huge expenditure of resources on the province of a sovereign nation? One need not be an apologist for Serbia's erstwhile leaders to be puzzled by the difference in treatment — nor need one be naïve about the vagaries of international politics.

The international human rights movement must overcome its biases and argue for even a semblance of consistency. By their current practice of treating different regions of the world unequally, international NGOs and Western governments are effectively subverting the principles of human rights and humanitarianism, which have gained a measure of respectability in the aftermath of the European wars of the last century. That respectability is being called into question by the current approaches to humanitarian intervention, which serve mainly the interests of major powers. Unfortunately, humanitarian intervention has very little to do, in practice, with respect for human rights.

The reluctance of the international community to act in a robust manner was illustrated earlier in the case of the Rwandan genocide as it is set out here by the Commander of the UN Peacekeeping Mission in Rwanda, General Dallaire.

FOREWORD BY LIEUTENANT-GENERAL ROMEO DALLAIRE IN FEIL, S *PREVENTING GENOCIDE: HOW THE EARLY USE OF FORCE MIGHT HAVE SUCCEEDED IN RWANDA* (1998)

A Report to the Carnegie Commission On Preventing Deadly Conflict
Full report available at http://www.wilsoncentre.org/subsites/ccpdc/pubs/rwanda/rwanda.htm

The experience in Rwanda was a watershed for the international community, the United Nations, the contributors to the United Nations Assistance Mission for Rwanda, and, least of all, myself. However, no one noticed that it was a watershed at the time. It was seen as too difficult and not of sufficient interest and value to prevent the outbreak of violence, and once violence had broken out, it still was not of sufficient interest to warrant the expense of resources and risk of more casualties to stop the violence from spreading. While others remained focused on the world's other crises, the people of Rwanda were forgotten. It was not really until the international community noticed tens of thousands of refugees in eastern Zaire, with thousands dying daily of cholera, that they felt truly compelled to act. This three-month delay cost the lives of hundreds of thousands of innocent Rwandans, and countless scars and disfigurements for those who lived through the horrors. Like the crisis at the time, the need for a response mechanism and the consequences of not looking for solutions are guaranteeing the recurrence of other humanitarian catastrophes now and into the future.

Is this a lesson that we need to have taught to us a second time? Do we, the members of the international community, really require that more innocent women and children be slaughtered by the thousands to cause a change in our priorities and level of concern? When the sanctity of human rights can be so blatantly violated and remain tolerated by the international community, there is a problem of such seriousness that words alone cannot explain. I remain mystified that human life, the security of non-combatants, and the prevention of such horrors as the genocide in Rwanda are, sadly, not sufficient to act as a catalyst for a swift and determined response from the international community.

I often ponder the possible solutions to the many problems that the international community and the UN faced in the spring and summer of 1994, and am convinced that it is imperative that these solutions be found quickly. It would be immoral if not outright criminal to allow another tragedy to occur by failing in our collective responsibility to humanity at large. The ingredients and recipes for solutions currently exist but remain in want of a sponsor, a leader with moral determination to bring together the political, the humanitarian, and the security structures and disciplines in synergistic applications of innovative thought to this requirement to respond to human dignity rather than national self-interest.

It behooves us to take the horrible lessons of the Rwandan debacle and prevent future genocide by formalising a pragmatic and cohesive multidisciplinary prevention capability. The killings could have been prevented if there had been the international will to accept the costs of doing so even after the politically difficult losses of peacekeeping in Somalia and the *ad hoc* confusion of April 1994. We need to use our processes to achieve the aim of assisting humanity, as opposed to preserving our processes at the expense of humanity. The coalition of like-minded free nations, with well-developed doctrines respecting human rights, should form the nucleus of a rapid reaction capability for the United Nations to bolster its ability to keep the peace. The looming threat of overwhelming international retribution is still required to keep in check some of the impulses of hate-filled elements. We, as the international community, must be prepared to come to the aid of humanity in a swift yet effective manner. What remains lacking, what is absent, is the will to implement such solutions. We must all strive toward this goal or continue to repress the collective guilt and wash our hands that have been stained with the blood of so many innocent victims of power-hungry and ruthless extremists.

...

Permissions

All chapters in this book were first published in HRPJA, by Pretoria University Law Press (PULP) by Christof Heyns & Karen Stefiszyn; hereby published with permission under the Creative Commons Attribution License or equivalent. Every chapter published in this book has been scrutinized by our experts. Their significance has been extensively debated. The topics covered herein carry significant information for a comprehensive understanding. They may even be implemented as practical applications or may be referred to as a beginning point for further studies.

We would like to thank the editorial team for lending their expertise to make the book truly unique. They have played a crucial role in the development of this book. Without their invaluable contributions this book wouldn't have been possible. They have made vital efforts to compile up to date information on the varied aspects of this subject to make this book a valuable addition to the collection of many professionals and students.

This book was conceptualized with the vision of imparting up-to-date and integrated information in this field. To ensure the same, a matchless editorial board was set up. Every individual on the board went through rigorous rounds of assessment to prove their worth. After which they invested a large part of their time researching and compiling the most relevant data for our readers.

The editorial board has been involved in producing this book since its inception. They have spent rigorous hours researching and exploring the diverse topics which have resulted in the successful publishing of this book. They have passed on their knowledge of decades through this book. To expedite this challenging task, the publisher supported the team at every step. A small team of assistant editors was also appointed to further simplify the editing procedure and attain best results for the readers.

Apart from the editorial board, the designing team has also invested a significant amount of their time in understanding the subject and creating the most relevant covers. They scrutinized every image to scout for the most suitable representation of the subject and create an appropriate cover for the book.

The publishing team has been an ardent support to the editorial, designing and production team. Their endless efforts to recruit the best for this project, has resulted in the accomplishment of this book. They are a veteran in the field of academics and their pool of knowledge is as vast as their experience in printing. Their expertise and guidance has proved useful at every step. Their uncompromising quality standards have made this book an exceptional effort. Their encouragement from time to time has been an inspiration for everyone.

The publisher and the editorial board hope that this book will prove to be a valuable piece of knowledge for students, practitioners and scholars across the globe.

Index

www.ingramcontent.com/pod-product-compliance
Lightning Source LLC
LaVergne TN
LVHW051046220926
848485LV00001BA/29